Music at the Threshold from
the Sacred to the Dangerous

Music at the Threshold from the Sacred to the Dangerous

SEAN WILLIAMS

OXFORD
UNIVERSITY PRESS

Oxford University Press is a department of the University of Oxford.
It furthers the University's objective of excellence in research, scholarship,
and education by publishing worldwide. Oxford is a registered trade mark of
Oxford University Press in the UK and in certain other countries.

Published in the United States of America by Oxford University Press
198 Madison Avenue, New York, NY 10016, United States of America.

CIP data is on file at the Library of Congress

ISBN 9780197761731 (pbk.)
ISBN 9780197761724 (hbk.)

DOI: 10.1093/9780197761762.001.0001

Paperback printed by Marquis Book Printing, Canada
Hardback printed by Lightning Source, Inc., United States of America

The manufacturer's authorized representative in the EU for product safety is
Oxford University Press España S.A. of Parque Empresarial San Fernando de Henares,
Avenida de Castilla, 2 – 28830 Madrid (www.oup.es/en or product.safety@oup.com).
OUP España S.A. also acts as importer into Spain of products made by the manufacturer.

Contents

Figures

Preface

This is a book about the in-between, and how music helps to facilitate moments of transition, ritual, longing, transgression, communication, and more. Perhaps one of the most interesting aspects of studying and teaching about the in-between—*liminality* in academic circles—has been the startled, repeated acknowledgment of its power and importance by my students and colleagues *outside* of ethnomusicology. "Wait, I've never heard of this concept before!" "What did you call it?" And so I begin with a short story.

This book had its inception many years ago on the small island of Bali in Indonesia, where I had brought my parents on their short visit during my doctoral fieldwork in West Java in the 1980s. We were in a Hindu temple, witnessing a nighttime ritual performance of a story about good and evil, in which a male performer, dressed as a very pregnant woman, was sitting on the ground, rocking back and forth and groaning as if in the throes of birth. Behind the performer stood the Hindu character of Rangda—locally conflated with the Indian goddess Durga—hovering with extended nails, bulging eyes, and ferocious teeth. As the Balinese gamelan music increased in intensity and volume, Rangda came closer and closer to the person in labor. Rangda then stole the "child." It was only later that I watched the Margaret Mead documentary film, *Trance and Dance in Bali* (filmed between 1937 and 1939 in the southern Balinese village of Pagutan); a version of *this very moment* appears at the beginning of the film.

It is always the case that dropping into a centuries-old story such as this one, without its deep cultural context, gives one just a passing window on an idea. As a widow figure in chaos and flux, Rangda embodies the instability of attempts to balance good and evil, and the constant motion between chaos and stability (Weiss 2017: 75). The person embodying the spirit of Rangda is a Hindu priest; one must have a great deal of spiritual power to resist Rangda's intense chaotic draw (Bandem and DeBoer 1995: 110). The larger issue, though, is the performance of instability—the in-between—in a way that is sacred, alluring, and dangerous. And music often serves a facilitating function for that moment of instability.

From my own perspective, I recognized that it was the very *centrality* of ambiguity, chaos, and transformation enacted and supported by music in that Balinese temple, and that the moments of birth and death are among the most powerful transformations any of us can experience. I held that thought over the next few decades as I wrote and taught about transformation. My own doctoral dissertation discusses the ways in which urban musicians in West Java play music on boat-shaped zithers to transport listeners back in time to the rural past. Without the music, there is no journey. Without the ritualized journey, there is no chance for safe, regulated, life-changing growth. One has to go away in order to come back transformed, and reading between the lines is where the truth lies.

The use of the performing arts to facilitate all the great life-cycle rituals—birth, puberty, graduation, marriage, retirement, hospice, death, and funerals—has a long history. It is not just the *moment* of these great transitions that is important, however; it is the staged representation of them and the energy of transformation that also captures something of human imagination and its underlying forces. Yet it is more than the act of ritual or the occurrence of sound that has captured my imagination. It is the sense of the ambiguity of borders and boundaries—places and moments of tremendous change—that offer compelling examples worth studying. Susan Thomas writes, in relation to the COVID/post-COVID moment in the early 2020s, that "sonic interstitiality and the musical delineation and transgression of borders is part of the current zeitgeist in particularly highly-charged ways" (Thomas 2020: xi). The availability of sound (both live and mediated) and the fact that those of us who could retreat from COVID by staying home were connected to the world almost exclusively through phones and laptops marked a sea-change in our encounters with others. So many of us encountered new musical materials by ourselves, rather than in the company of friends or thousands of concert-goers, that the ability of sound to bridge social, cultural, and national gaps has become more obvious than ever.

Because it is important to state my positionality before the reader enters this work, I follow in the footsteps of two of my respected colleagues in ethnomusicology. In *Hungry Listening: Resonant Theory for Indigenous Sound Studies*, Dylan Robinson asks readers to " . . . consider the relationships you have with particular voices—how your positionality guides the way you listen to musical subjectivity" (2020: 1). In Jessica Bissett Perea's *Sound Relations: Native Ways of Doing Music History in Alaska*, she asks readers "to consider the existence of multiple simultaneous truths, a density of truths, all of which are culturally constructed, performed, and in some cases politicized and policed" (2021: 6). The importance and centrality of multiple, simultaneous relationships and truths guide my own work. In following this lead, my goal is to move beyond the ideas of enforced and restrictive definitions (along with "it's normal to me because I am white, cisgender female, able, married," etc.), and closer to the subversion of some of my own training with this work.

In developing this book, I have relied on my own direct fieldwork experience in some cases, as well as on the work of others in a partial meta-ethnography; I attempt to make the case for exploring larger hidden patterns surrounding the liminal, whether geographical, spiritual, musical, or otherwise. I am a white American cisgender married woman in my mid-60s, and have been an ethnomusicologist working in music, anthropology, folklore, and area studies my whole adult life. Most of my heritage is Welsh (paternal) and Swiss (maternal), and I attended American public schools from kindergarten (1964) through the PhD (1990). I taught at a public college for thirty-five years before retiring in 2026. I play a bunch of instruments (not all of them well), and I have studied a bunch of languages (not all of them well). In addition to spending large portions of my life on the west coast of North America, I have also lived in parts of Asia and Europe and traveled to many places. I have spent more than thirty years as the member of a Brazilian samba drumming group in the United States. I have been performing and teaching music and musical instruments of many kinds since the 1970s. In graduate school, I also studied with visiting artists from India, Africa, Central America, Southeast Asia, and elsewhere. None of this makes me an expert, specifically, but those experiences combined with research, reading, listening, and communicating across national, musical, and linguistic boundaries instilled in me the *need* to develop this book of ideas.

Acknowledgments

A Hawaiian proverb applies to this section: *A'ohe hana nui ka alu'ia* ("No task is too big when done together"). I begin each chapter in this book with a quote or proverb to allow the wisdom of others to guide me, and us, with my gratitude. I would like to thank my teaching colleagues Sarah Williams and Laurie Meeker, with whom I taught a year-long class titled "Intimate Nature: Communication Older than Words" in 2002–2003. We explored issues of communication across cultures, across media, and across epistemologies. The class, and our faculty seminars, opened my eyes to the possibilities of enhanced critical understanding of the human experience by using the lens of the in-between.

Most summers for the past two decades I have led a workshop titled "Write That Book!" for my faculty and staff colleagues at Evergreen. We discuss our projects, move our writing forward, and celebrate our successes together. My colleagues deserve my thanks for listening to my ideas about the in-between, doing some critical reading of chapter sections, and focusing attention on ideas relevant to *their* fields, not just the interdisciplinary field of ethnomusicology. My students, who explore, discuss, and write about liminality in connection to whatever course I am currently teaching, deserve my gratitude for their continuing sense of wonder and their willingness to explore, no matter what their background is. I have received summer salary support grants from Evergreen, and in the early years of 2009, 2012, 2016, and 2021, I progressed slowly through my preliminary research and writing stages for this book, even as I worked on other books. That support has meant so much to me. And if it weren't for my long-awaited COVID-era sabbatical in 2021, this book might still be festering in my brain and disturbing my sleep with all its implications.

I count on certain friends to focus my attention. In ethnomusicology, Tomie Hahn and I have cajoled, harangued, cheered, and danced each other through various intellectual and creative minefields. This book would look quite different without her support and exceptional ability to ride through brainstorming sessions with me. I will always be grateful for our enduring friendship and our off-center sense of humor. Similarly, Jeffrey Summit meets each year with Tomie and me to go over the past year, think about personal and professional issues, discuss writing, and think deeply and compassionately about how we represent the people with whom we work as ethnomusicologists and as human beings. My dear friend Sonia Seeman, from the first day of graduate school in 1982 to the present, has been an inspiration and an ally. Kyra Gaunt freed me from my writing anxieties by encouraging me to be experimental and playful as I drafted out the chapters; I took her brilliant advice, and the words poured out as if I were panning for gold. I continue to be grateful to the four of them for their friendship and support.

My writing accountability buddies from my 2021 sabbatical—Ed Wolf, Zoe Sherinian, Betsy Pingree, Margaret Sarkissian, Marysol Quevedo, Kyra Gaunt, Sonia Seeman, Amanda Daly Berman, Nicol Hammond, Tes Slominski, Judith-Kate Friedman, and others, including the good people on the Ethnomusicology Writing Group page of Facebook—have helped me to maintain my focus over the years. My brothers in Sundanese music studies include Andrew Weintraub, Henry Spiller, Wim Van Zanten, Randy Baier, Simon Cook, and Robert Wessing. Resonating in my head are the many lessons, publications, lectures, conversations, notes, and other communications from my long-ago professors and/or continuing mentors Ter Ellingson, Christopher Waterman, Lorraine Sakata, Laurel Sercombe, Daniel Neuman, and Robert Garfias (ethnomusicology) at the University of Washington; Alan Dundes, John Niles, Daniel Melia, and Breandán Ó hÉithir (folklore, ballads, and the Irish language) at UC Berkeley; Euis Komariah, Apung Wiraatmadja, Rukruk Rukmana, and Tatang Sobari (tembang Sunda) in West Java, Indonesia; and Joe Heaney, Lillis Ó Laoire, Gearóidín Breathnach, and Liam Mac Con Iomaire (sean-nós singing) in Ireland.

Over several years I have requested my friends and colleagues to read specific segments of chapters, particularly for places where I have not done in-person fieldwork. I offer my deep gratitude to Leticia Nieto, Frank Gunderson, Michelle Kisliuk, Tom Solomon, Henry Stobart, Jonathan Ritter, Keola Donaghy, Stephen Fox, Sarah Morelli, Patricia Krafcik, Richard Miller, Jeffrey Callen, Holly Wissler, Pauline Yu, Johnny Farraj, and Kabby Mitchell. My dear teaching colleagues Bradley Proctor, Devon Damonte, Pauline Yu, Sarah Williams, Ulrike Krotscheck, Stacy Davis, and Drew Buchman have kindly supported my compulsion to teach our students about this subject for the past several years. But the truth is that I have felt like a junior scholar in the field for decades, absorbing the wisdom of so many friends and colleagues that the experience of writing this book has felt more like attending and adding to a years-long conference rather than creating a book.

Several sections of chapters appear elsewhere in print, reflecting my long-term interest in this subject. I directly included unaltered sections of my article titled "Sonic Liminalities of Faith in Sundanese Vocal Music" (Williams 2018: 43–59) in Chapter 3 with the kind permission of editor Jeffers Englehart and the Creative Commons License. I have paraphrased a section of a chapter published in an edited volume in Chapter 5; titled "Music as the Food of Longing in Ireland and Irish America," my chapter originally appeared in *A Symphony of Flavors: Food and Music in Concert* (Williams 2015: 46–64). The paraphrased section is published with the permission of editor Edmundo Murray and Cambridge Scholars Publishing. I extend my sincere gratitude to the editors and publishers involved in getting my work out in the first place.

My family has brought me so much joy and support. My husband David Nelson continues to be an outstanding supporter of my ideas and my work. As a science and math teacher, he brings new ideas from well outside my areas of expertise, and as an educated layperson he helps me to clarify my ideas for readers outside of academia. I have been delighted by his presence in my life since the day we met, ten years before our first actual date! My daughter, Morgan Black, began regularly asking whether I was on my way to deliver one of my "Miss Liminality" lectures by the time she was ten years old. Her down-to-earth sense of humor, her sparkling intelligence, and her high tolerance for hearing her mother talk about liminality for the entirety of her childhood and young adulthood earns her my Most Patient Offspring Award. Her spouse Leo Walczyk, in making my daughter Morgan so happy, has made me a *very* proud mother-in-law. My brother Guy Williams—a historian and language geek—carefully and generously critiqued several chapters, and yet we still get along! His wonderful husband Antonio Navas-Rufino has belonged to our family since the 1980s, and I love the two of them. Gloria Hatch has been my best friend since we first met working as maids in a summer lodge that hired only music majors for every position at Glacier National Park in 1978. Our travels together over multiple decades, our long conversations, our singing and playing sessions, and our mutual impatience with the slow pace of social justice in the United States have been a constant connection for us.

At Oxford University Press I want to acknowledge Suzanne Ryan-Melamed, who first read over an early proposal for this book many years ago and made very helpful recommendations. She has since moved on from

Oxford, but she still holds a warm place in my heart for her help on my previous books and ideas. Editor Lauralee Yeary has waited patiently through the time of my first book prospectus all the way through the editing of the project; she found reviewers and encouraged and supported me through each step. I cannot thank her enough for all that she has done and continues to do on behalf of ethnomusicology and of me personally. Alexandra Rouch, the editorial manager at Oxford, was ultimately responsible for bringing the book from my laptop into your hands. Zara Cannon-Mohammed (project editor at Oxford) and Elakkia Bharathi (project manager at Newgen, a production partner of Oxford), took care of the book's details and sent out updates and queries throughout the final stages. Clare Hoffman designed the beautiful cover using the liminal photograph by Indonesian photographer Rahmad Himawan, who captured a volcano (portal to the center of the Earth) at dawn (neither night nor day) with a rice field (neither fully land nor water). All of these people—my friends, colleagues, and family members; my many teachers in the field; and the people at Oxford University press—are the reason I was able to write this book that is in your hands.

This bright airy office in which I write, and the Evergreen State College that houses it, are on the land of the Medicine Creek Treaty Tribes, including the Squaxin Island, Steilacoom, Nisqually, T'Peeksin, Sa-heh-wamish, Stehchass, S'Homamish, and Puyallup Tribes, who are its historical custodians and to whom I pay my respects. Note that the Smithsonian Magazine calls out the Medicine Creek Treaty, which enabled settlers to "buy" Indigenous land for pennies per acre, as the treaty that "set the stage for Standing Rock" *because* it codified the right to hunt and fish in the tribes' "usual and accustomed grounds and stations" (Ault 2017). And because land acknowledgments can too easily lose their meaning without action, I will contribute a portion of any royalties from the publication of this book to the House of Welcome (Figure A.1) at The Evergreen State College, in support of Native arts and cultural activities at the college's Indigenous Arts Campus.

In many ways, doing a meta-ethnography such as this one requires me to treat all the sources I've read and all the musicians and scholars I've connected with as part of a broad, fascinating seminar group, some members of which have passed on, but whose influences are felt daily. Considering my work on this book as simply joining a seminar of scholar/musicians has helped me to genuinely enjoy the process. Any errors and misunderstandings contained in this text are my own, of course, and I thank you for reading it.

Sean Williams

Figure A.1 House of Welcome logo, Evergreen State College, Olympia, Washington.

About the Author

Sean Williams has taught ethnomusicology, Irish Studies, and Asian Studies at The Evergreen State College in Olympia, Washington, since 1991, retiring from full-time teaching in 2026. Her degrees include a BA in classical guitar performance (University of California at Berkeley), an MA in ethnomusicology with a focus on Irish *sean-nós* singing (University of Washington), and a PhD in ethnomusicology with a focus on *tembang Sunda*, the sung poetry of West Java, Indonesia (University of Washington). She plays with grammar (Captain Grammar Pants is her alter ego on Facebook), enhances her skills by playing geography games daily, and has sung in composer Eric Whitacre's Virtual Choir since 2012 (and in real life at Carnegie Hall in 2022 and Lincoln Center in 2025). In addition to her many articles, her monographs and edited volumes include *The Sound of the Ancestral Ship: Highland Music of West Java* (Oxford, 2001); *The Ethnomusicologists' Cookbook*, vols. 1 and 2 (Routledge, 2006 and 2016); *The Garland Encyclopedia of World Music, Southeast Asia* and *The Handbook of Southeast Asian Music* with Terry E. Miller (Routledge, 1998 and 2008); *Bright Star of the West: Joe Heaney, Irish Song Man* with Lillis Ó Laoire (Oxford, 2011); *English Grammar: 100 Tragically Common Mistakes (and How to Correct Them)* (Zephyros Press, 2019); *Irish Traditional Music*, 1st and 2nd editions (Routledge, 2010 and 2020); and *Musics of the World* (Oxford, 2022).

A Note on Musical Transcription

The only musical notation that I provide in this book is Western staff notation. Is that a problem? Frankly, it is. I struggle with the fact that just a fraction of the world's people can read music notation; that limits my transcriptions' accessibility to just a few readers. Furthermore, most of the world's musical traditions do not fit in the limited twelve tones afforded by staff notation. I have considered other systems, such as cipher notation, and discarded them. Please, please, if notation interests you, I urge you to explore Jon Silpayamanant's fascinating WordPress site that features his Timeline of Music Notation (https://silpayamanant.wordpress.com/timeline-of-music-notation/). It decenters Western staff notation and points to a much longer, deeper history of how people have tracked music by visual means. If you cannot read Western staff notation—or even if you can!—the best practice is to simply look up the examples online and listen to them rather than struggling through the notation. I have kept the transcriptions in, but with misgivings.

1

Poised at the Edge

Nothing is as difficult to see as the obvious. (Bronisław Malinowski, Poland)

At the edge of entering a new book (or building, or country), I want to feel welcome. Readers might hesitate before that first page: will it be interesting? Is it safe to trust the author's interests? That hovering moment—at the threshold—can make a person feel almost giddy with excitement, or perhaps even wary. Please know that I welcome you, poised at the edge here with me as we work together toward understanding the central points of transformation in our lives, and how music helps to facilitate those transformations in particular ways. Whereas many books in ethnomusicology lean on the idea of genre + place + issue, this book has as its focus a specific theoretical issue, supported by examples and commonalities from many different places. We'll start with a single word: *liminality*. This chapter—along with the book— explores its meaning, contexts, and connections with the performing arts.

Liminality describes the state of being at the threshold, the place in-between, or the permeable boundary. The Javanese musician, scholar, and writer Sumarsam notes that "What happens in the liminal phase, the in-between, or a time between times can be characterized by ambiguity, indefiniteness, and blurred conventions within which exploration, creativity, and change can occur" (Sumarsam 2024: 205). Liminality can be a place of both transgression and transformation; it can include such wide-ranging elements as times of day, living creatures, physical locations, states of being, and ways of understanding the world. It is often connected to sound when human beings are involved. This book takes the reader into the in-between territory of ambiguity and change, and it reveals what some people already know instinctively: that those powerful in-between places—the points of transformation in human lives—are facilitated and made manageable through the performing arts, especially music.

Music at the Threshold from the Sacred to the Dangerous. Sean Williams, Oxford University Press. © Oxford University Press 2026. DOI: 10.1093/9780197761762.003.0001

The linguistic connection of the word liminality to contemporary knowledge is in the word's Latin root, *limen*; threshold. Some English speakers have encountered the word *subliminal* ("below the threshold"). Subliminal advertising works to convince people to make a purchase without their awareness that such convincing is taking place; it is below one's threshold of perception. The moment of perceivability, then, is the threshold.[1] The word limen/liminal has some counterparts in other languages, and they carry with those words so much of the cultural weight that liminality has in English; however, noting the existence of the concept in other languages is not a matter of exact equivalences, but rather of acknowledgment. Not everyone uses a specific word to indicate this specific meaning.

This book does more than explore a single meaning of the in-between; it draws upon music to parse the ways in which people and their many expressive cultures can navigate the sometimes-joyful, sometimes-perilous moments of transformation. The chapters of this book contain many examples and case studies of the in-between and its connection to sound across the world. As a partial meta-ethnography, it draws from different wisdom traditions and musical genres to focus attention, again and again, on *how* and *why* liminality is so prevalent across so many cultures, and so connected to local identities. The examples are thematically organized across the chapters, and each one features a larger issue or point—such as longing, eroticism, access, and more—that centralizes the liminal experience one way or another. In that respect, as jarring as it might initially seem to find the thirteenth-century composer Pérotin—of bilingual motet fame—discussed in the same chapter as kabuki theater or the twenty-first-century trip hop artist Lil Nas X, the larger issue in that chapter is *transgression*. Working through each significant issue with the assistance and clarity offered by the examples will bring the focus back to liminal experiences of, in, and through music.

The following example illustrates a number of liminal concepts. In Japan, the liminal blend of—and respect accorded to—its two primary religions (Shintōism and Buddhism) can be seen in many places. In this image from the Shintō shrine on the island of Itsukushima (in Hiroshima Prefecture), the musicians are performing for a wedding ceremony—a major transitional life-cycle event (Figure 1.1). The island itself is believed to be the home of *bodhisattvas*, enlightened beings in Buddhism, while the shrine itself is dedicated to three Shintō goddesses of storms and the sea. The shrine is located on the shore, neither fully on land nor fully in the water; in fact, the buildings

Figure 1.1 Gagaku musicians at the Itsukushima Shintō shrine, Hiroshima Prefecture, Japan

hover over the water at high tide. The musicians are performing *gagaku*, a court genre initially introduced to Japan through Chinese Buddhism, but which features Shintō religious music. Most of the instruments are wind instruments, which connect to the liminal act of breathing. The musicians, positioned underneath an open framework, are neither indoors nor outdoors. In the background to the left is Itsukushima's famous *torii* gate, a 54-foot-tall Shintō structure (with Shingon Buddhist features) which serves as the threshold between the mundane and the sacred. One can walk out to it during low tide, but in high tide it appears to float on the water.

In the Heian period (eighth to tenth century), Japanese architecture had as its focus the connection between humans and the natural world; the shrine exemplifies that liminal connection by being on water. Part of the shrine features a stage and seating area for performances of *noh*, Japan's oldest extant form of theater. Noh draws from both Buddhism and Shintōism. One of noh's important elements is that there is little separation between the audience and the actors, so the audience members join the experience. A bridge (*hashigakari*, upstage right) connects the spirit world with the mundane, and is the means by which the actors enter and leave the main stage. The heavily forested area nearby connects to nearby Misenyama, the island's sacred mountain. Lastly, although the island itself is largely rural, the urban milieu of the mainland is visible in the distance. The many connections between Buddhism and Shintōism in Japan will be detailed further in Chapter 3, but the centrality of liminality in a single setting is not limited to Japan.

Renato Rosaldo wrote about transitional zones as worthy sites of creativity in his book *Culture and Truth: The Remaking of Social Analysis*; he argued against the idea of culture as static and monolithic, and encouraged many of the forward-thinking ideas that ethnomusicologists and those of our sibling disciplines of anthropology and folklore have largely adopted. If we move forward with that—culture as active and changing—in mind, we can imagine something other than a bland inert status for liminal places, objects, people, times, and more.

> Our everyday lives are crisscrossed by border zones, pockets, and eruptions of all kinds. [. . .] Along with "our" supposedly transparent cultural selves, such borderlands should be regarded not as analytically empty transitional zones but as sites of creative cultural production that require investigation. (Rosaldo 1989: 207–208)

Without even realizing it, many people operate along the threshold throughout their lives, whether it is at a moment of graduation, or adolescence, or a specific event that causes a transformation. Humans are, in fact, *drawn* to such moments, as in the following historical example that still occurs in a few places. But are they obvious? Not necessarily. In the following example, I draw from an aspect of Northwestern European folklore that was once quite common among people of certain classes and regions: a kiss under the mistletoe.

In parts of Europe (less so in North America), during the time of the winter solstice (December 21), especially from the eighteenth through the twentieth centuries, a person might be invited to a holiday party. Note that the winter solstice is the moment when—in the Northern Hemisphere— the night is longest and the earth is poised to begin its southward-turning journey. Twilight hovers just between day and night; it is no longer day and it is not yet night. Standing in the threshold—the doorway—to welcome a guest would place the host neither fully inside nor fully outside the home.

As guests arrive, they are no longer in their temporary home (such as a car or other mode of transportation), but not yet in the party; they stand at the threshold to exchange their usual words of greeting and welcome with the host. Music is always part of the sense of welcome offered to the guests;

usually it plays in the background. The words spoken at the threshold are deliberately non-specific to the conditions of either guest or host; they simply serve the purpose of setting up the transition of the guest into the home of the host. What happens as a part of this greeting could happen only in a doorway at the winter solstice time, and only in the presence of mistletoe, a native European plant that grows through its parasitic relationship to a tree. The guest and the host kiss, which is a moment that breaks the social barrier between two people. If, because of their orientation, they wouldn't actually kiss a person of either the opposite sex or of the same sex, they might embrace instead. As soon as the guest crosses the threshold, an alcoholic drink is usually on offer.

Mistletoe—with the interesting etymology of *missel* (droppings) and *tan* (twig) from Proto-Germanic—remains green in the winter, and its berries ripen in December in the Northern Hemisphere. The "droppings" refer to where the plant grows: in bird droppings on tree branches after the birds have swallowed the berries. As a plant that attaches itself to other trees, it hovers between earth and sky. "Birdlime," a sticky substance once used to trap birds, is made by grinding mistletoe berries. The plant features in several European mythologies as a weapon that may have killed the Norse god Balder, as part of the celebration of the Ionian festival Kronia (in honor of Kronos, when rules were suspended), and as a symbol of fertility among some mainland European Celts because it ripened in winter. It came to the Americas from Victorian England, which used it as part of the suspension-of-rules holiday that the solstice encouraged, but its customs did not necessarily last.[2]

The liminal date (solstice), time (twilight), location (doorway), plant (mistletoe), people (host and guest in interaction), act (kiss), and physical state (potential for drunkenness) all create a sacred, alluring, and dangerous context (as will be discussed later in the chapter). For that single moment in the doorway under the mistletoe, the laws of marriage or intimate relationships are suspended in that protected space. No one in that particular historical context would have thought twice about whether it was appropriate or worrisome to kiss someone else's partner. The same action, taken two steps in either direction—back out of the house or further into the house—would break all the rules of propriety; the kiss would suddenly take on a dramatically different set of meanings, and the protected space of the threshold would evaporate.[3]

Let us briefly examine the liminal moment of twilight (German, "half-light" or, in Middle High German, "between-light"). The French idiom for it is *entre chien et loup*—between dog and wolf. If the light is so dim that one cannot distinguish a dog from a wolf, one also has few ways of distinguishing one person from another, or good from bad; colors are reduced to gray. One's hearing is sharpened and attention is focused, but the neither-here-nor-there sense is quite strong. In Hindi, the word *sandhīprakāś* refers to the elision of light with darkness; there are special *rāgas* in Indian music indicated for dawn and dusk (*sandhīprakāś rāg-s*). Unlike the Spanish word *umbra*, which refers to the exclusion of light and the presence of shadow, the implication here is the sense of being *between* darkness and light. Similarly, the term "twilight sleep" can be thought of as slightly conscious sleep; one is between asleep and awake. The power of this ambiguous moment is built into some languages, and the language can serve as a reminder that anything might happen in that special place of in-between.

Because the mistletoe example is specific to a particular subset of people in Western cultures, it is not applicable anywhere else. Indeed, liminal experiences (birth, death, sex, dreaming, and so much more) may well be central to human experiences across the globe, but the local manifestation of them is quite specific. The people of each place, with all its influences, mixtures, historical upheavals, and assertions of identity, understand their own liminal practices. For that reason, this book draws from multiple places and times to posit the idea that the liminal is central to the human experience, and that very centrality rejects the idea that the margin is truly a place of otherness: *whose otherness?*

None of This Is New

Prophets and artists tend to be liminal and marginal people, "edgemen." (Turner 1969: 128)

For many people interested in studies of liminality, most contemporary Western roads lead to Arnold van Gennep (1873–1957), a groundbreaking scholar in discussing the subject, and Victor Turner (1920–1983), who carried the ideas of van Gennep forward through his work in ritual and theater. But the concept and manifestations of liminality itself date from long before van Gennep and Turner noticed their existence and theorized about it. If the transitory state between death and the next incarnation is any indication—as in the *bardo* of Tibetan Buddhism or the *antarabhāva* of Hinduism—then an intermediate state has long been essential to the act of human transcendence. The bardo or "between place" may be understood among Tibetan Buddhists as appearing in six different situations: between birth and death; when humans dream; during meditation; the moment between being alive and being dead; and the point of "karmic becoming" or being between one's death and the next existence (Sherab and Dongyal 2000: 3–4).[4] The fifth-century Buddhist monk and philosopher Vasubandhu said—in the Sanskrit text and early source for Mahāyāna Buddhism, the *Abhidharmakośa-bhāsya*—that "intermediate existence, which inserts itself between existence at death and existence at birth, not having arrived at the location where it should go, cannot be said to be born" (Pruden 1988, v.3: 383).

In many areas of the world, local populations have engaged the assistance not only of spiritual intermediaries and large and small ritual acts in connecting with ancestors and others, but of the land itself serving as a connective feature. The Sámi of northern Scandinavia, for example, have valued and marked meeting points with each other and with the spirit world through the creation of rock art and the development of a deep sense of sacred geography since the Ice Age (Mulk and Bayliss-Smith 2007: 110). Chapter 2 engages these ideas much more directly, but it is important to point out that the threshold is at the height and center of spiritual activity and focus, along with the people and places that inhabit it. To place such people and places at the edges—the margins—is to ignore their centrality, and it runs the risk of silencing their agency.

The word "liminal" appeared in Arnold van Gennep's writing through his work on ritual in small-scale groups. In his *Rites of Passage*, he described a three-step process of the norm, the ambiguous or transitional, and the transformed and reincorporated (van Gennep 2019 [original 1909]). His highlighting of rites of passage or moments of transformation was *not* a "discovery," but simply a recognition and naming of what people do in many parts of the world. Victor Turner's *The Ritual Process: Structure and Anti-Structure* posited the idea that rituals help to mediate one's status in transition (Turner 1969: 107).[5] Scholars since Turner (including his wife, Edith Turner, and his sometime-collaborator, Richard Schechner) have continued to expand on the basic idea of the liminal as a transitional place. To quote James Seale-Collazo, "[Liminality] refers to a particular category of social situation in which structural constraints upon individuals are loosened or released and hierarchies blurred or held in abeyance" (Seale-Collazo

2012: 181). Although liminality can be quite commonplace (such as waiting for a bus) or extraordinary (such as participating in a life-cycle ritual), it does not necessarily have to be transitional. For example, a biracial person will *never* transition through a temporary state of race. In fact, the idea that the liminal—transitory, hybrid, ambiguous—runs in opposition to some notion of purity is contrary to reality. Furthermore, some musicians, by virtue of their social location, can be considered to be "institutionally liminal" (Brown 2007: 20).

The importance of liminality, in Victor and Edith Turner's work, was connected with the sense of *communitas*. Communitas refers to the idea that the members of a community share a liminal experience in common, and that experience is often related to some kind of rite of passage. Through that shared experience, individuals become simultaneously closer and more equal as their distinctions in status become less important. When people share a transitional event or liminal point in life, the intensity of their connection is heightened. A basic version of this experience is common to many Americans: graduation is when students experience the rite of passage of crossing a stage to receive a diploma in front of witnesses.[6]

Communitas can appear among, for example, Central European immigrants who gather at the same tavern in the American Midwest, night after night, to drink beer and listen to (or sing) the songs of home; this type of experience is discussed in greater detail in Chapter 5. Communitas can represent a temporary suspension of status differences, as one might see at a festival or concert where the shared interest in the music supersedes what any one person does for a living outside that moment. Students who travel on study abroad adventures together—regardless of their home country— can share a life-changing experience because of being completely—though temporarily—removed from their normal lives. A military base is a perpetual location of the liminal, with people continually coming and going and the site being simultaneously a home for all, but a home for no one. Experiences such as these, in which all participants experience liminality together, can build an enduring sense of communitas.

In critical pedagogy—the attempt to advance awareness of social injustice and to enable those in education to enhance diversity, equity, and inclusion through action—the agents of change can use concepts and practices of liminality specifically to disrupt and interrogate existing binary ideas: all vs. nothing, rational vs. emotional, mind vs. body, and more. Vidya Shah and Jody Luna describe "turning to cultural and conceptual tools to forefront the liminal or third spaces in-between such binaries, or the contested and contingent and excessive and shadow spaces alongside them, that can allow for even deeper engagement in and with critical pedagogy" (Shah and Luna 2019: 12). Specifically, fighting the hegemony of the binary—and awakening an awareness of the in-between—is one way to reject the systemic -isms that stand in the way of our collective solidarity and common humanity.[7] In basic terms, rather than either/or, it's both/and—and even more in between. While mind and body may well be part of a binary, envisioning a continuum opens the door to more creative approaches and deeper understanding.

It is no coincidence that liminality permeates historical events through the changes brought by shifts in power, colonization, joining and separating of nations, wars, and the appearance and disappearance of no-man's lands. In Lynn Hooker's article on the Romani musicians in the Hungarian folk revival, she points to "the potential not just for social challenges and inversions, but also for spontaneity and creativity" at these liminal points (Hooker 2007: 59). In other words, a liminal moment does not have to refer exclusively to political upheaval. It can refer to a festival rife with joyful, chaotic celebration. Linguistic imperialism through the imposition of a colonial language, for example—such as English over Gaelic, Mandarin over Tibetan, Arabic over Berber, or Spanish over Quechua—forces an initial hybridization and boundary-making structures that can ultimately lead to the erasure not just of local languages (see Chapter 7), but of local song repertoires and entire epistemologies. The reclamation of any language in both speech and song can be a powerful signifier of one's race, class, gender, and status; to experience one's home language wielded as just one more weapon against colonization has a ripple effect of consequences. The issue of resistance to linguistic hegemony appears in Chapter 7 as part of a larger discussion of power and identity.

Sacred, Alluring, and Dangerous

Three adjectival elements—sacred, alluring, and dangerous—characterize in-between beings, places, and times, and reflect the overall organization of this book. That the solstice time of year is sacred is an idea that goes way back; the ancient standing stones and megalithic stone circles of Neolithic Western Europe (4,000–2,000 BCE) are aligned to the solstices and equinoxes. Gathering in the dead of winter to be in a warm place with friends, and to have a drink and enjoy a kiss under mistletoe, is definitely alluring. And yet, the in-between can be dangerous. Going out at twilight is taking a risk. Drinking is taking a risk. Kissing one's host or host's spouse at the doorway is taking a risk. Because those "holiday parties" see an increase in auto accidents (and the first two weeks of January each year see the highest number of Americans filing for divorce!), late December in Europe and North America is fraught with challenges to the collective health and happiness of the people.

The kiss under the mistletoe is just one example, however, and drawn only from its roots in Northwestern Europe, but there is so much more. Each of the major categories that involve the in-between could fill a book on its own, and some do. Liminal places include marshes, crossroads, shores, borders, volcanoes, caves, doors, windows, fords, and springs. Liminal people include teens, biracial people, LGBTQ+ people, bilingual (or multilingual) people, immigrants, spiritual intermediaries, and mythological creatures such as shapeshifters.[8] Liminal times include the equinoxes, solstices, twilight, dawn, and seasonal changes. Liminal animals include seals, whales, crabs, frogs, turtles, birds, butterflies, and salmon. Liminal plants include seaweed, reeds, a large variety of marsh plants, and mistletoe. Liminal conditions include illness, menstruation, wounds, drunkenness, graduation, childbirth, death, sex, and kissing. Note that these moments are *not* generally outside the norm, nor are they considered part of "the Other"; in many places, they *are* the norm, and remain central to the most essential aspects of being human—or belonging to the natural world.

Many of these elements are highlighted, celebrated, or rendered as important through the medium of the performing arts: sound, music, movement, touch, gesture, acting, and so many other cues. For example, the story in the Preface to this book notes that Balinese temple festivals can include the performance of simulated childbirth in the sacred grounds of the temple; attending the birthing character is a demon who illustrates through movement that this sacred moment is dangerous. As another example, Brazilian samba performance draws from African, Portuguese, and Indigenous elements with a combination of drumming, singing, costuming, and dancing with precarious dance steps along the *axis mundi*—balancing, yet neither on one side nor the other. Of course, Balinese temple performances and Brazilian samba dancing are more complicated than this very basic description, but the larger point of their liminality is present nonetheless. It is that exact balancing act, whether physical, performative, emotional, or metaphysical, that creates the possibility for energetic transformation and deep creativity.

In Japan, springtime brings with it a special experience of celebrating the ephemeral—the liminal—with *ohanami*, "flower viewing." Families and friends gather at parks and at the grounds of temples and shrines with picnics, alcoholic drinks, and singing along with karaoke machines or musical instruments to celebrate the transient nature of life (Moriuchi and Basil 2019). Cherry blossoms are so glorious but so brief in their ephemeral perfection (lasting on the tree for just a couple of weeks); they drop from the trees like snow and pile up in fragrant pink drifts. This custom of *ohanami* dates to the eighth century CE in Japan, and today one can watch the evening weather report to see icons of cherry blossoms marching northward on a map of Japan, indicating how soon one can plan one's own ode to the liminal. Again, this activity—acknowledging the transience of life through witnessing falling cherry blossoms with song and *sake* drinking—is central to what it means to be Japanese.[9]

In that the performing arts can serve to highlight or even transform human experiences of the sacred, the alluring, and the dangerous, focusing attention on the means by which these actions take place is a crucial aspect of this book. While the primary focus of the author is on music, it is worth noting that dance and theater engage and enact liminality both onstage and offstage as well. As dancers make transformations into characters, or even perform in non-narrative dance, their bodies engage the spectators' own even when the spectators are sitting still. Theater brings people into the lives of others, melding seamlessly and placing the audience between themselves and the story, neither here nor there.

In my early exploration of the power of the in-between in connection with the performing arts, I kept encountering the three points of sacred, alluring, and dangerous through the works of Turner, van Gennep, and others; the musical connections to those words appeared repeatedly in my own research as well. As for the sacred, on visits to Asia—specifically, while in Indonesia and Japan (long term) and visiting South Korea, Hong Kong, and Singapore (short term)—it was clear that the major faith traditions there included a sense of reverence for the physical thresholds: the crossroad, the bridge, the cave, the shore, the rim of a volcano, and elsewhere. Offerings appeared each day at such places; people spoke of going there to meditate or pray or ask for blessings. The second idea was noting the allure of the in-between: the ways in which sex and drunkenness, the recognition of difference through literature and film (including the "fish out of water" trope), and the access to ways of understanding through knowing other languages seemed to catch fire in people's imaginations. The third idea was about danger and its connection to transgression, risk-taking, and the possibility of transformation by stepping beyond the boundaries of what is societally acceptable. These three terms—sacred, alluring, and dangerous—kept appearing in my studies until I recognized that they were inextricably tied to liminality, and needed to form the backbone of this book.

Sacred

The English word *sacred* goes all the way back to its Proto-Indo-European root form *sak-*, meaning "to sanctify" or render worthy of respect. It connects to other words such as religion, with its various contested etymologies including membership within a community, a mode of worship, a connection between humans and the divine, and others. The life force of the sacred extends to many belief systems, and in a key continuity, the words and concepts each embrace *all* things, including inanimate objects. Whether it is the concept of *prāṇa* in the Sanskrit textual anthology *Chandogya Upanishad* of the sixth century BCE, the discussion of *qi* in fragments of fourth-century BCE Chinese bamboo and silk texts, or *mana* across Polynesia, a heightened awareness of these local connections to a larger life force has the potential for transformation.

The Latin word *spirare* has given us not only "breathe" but also the Latin word *spiritus*, which means both "breath" and "spirit." So to inspire is to breathe in, and to expire is to breathe out. To transpire and to perspire are to breathe across or breathe through, while to respire is to breathe again. A *spiracle* is a breathing hole used by dolphins and whales, two of the great liminal animals of the ocean. Try connecting these ideas with the general idea of "spirit" too; it is an interesting thought experiment. Conspire, as you might imagine, is to breathe together. This concept will return as a point of focus in Chapter 3.

The sacred nature of certain events, objects, places, and creatures is varied and fascinating. Referred to as "doorways to another world" (Carr-Gomm 2009: 6), sacred places are sacred because they *inspire*—they make people breathe in—creating awe, inviting pilgrimage, and invoking artistic responses. Sacred people and sacred animals are seen as links to another world as well. They see what humans cannot see and know what humans cannot know. Birds, for example—featured in Chapter 2—have access to what is "out there" through their capabilities of flight, long-distance vision, and assumption of messenger status to the divine. The fact that they sing, as humans do, gives them extra power. Objects imbued with power—such as certain musical instruments, weapons, vessels, icons, and other items—often achieve that power through the act of blessing or consecration done by human intermediaries. In each case, the sacred element functions as a liminal conduit to something more powerful than the average human possesses.

In many cultures, that which is sacred can carry the societal expectation of special behaviors, special sounds, and special ways of thinking. Many religious communities, for example, use chant and words as a way to create access to the divine because of the links between the voice and the spirit. Bells, rattles, and drums all function as key conductive sounds, time markers, and items imbued with their own sacred powers and connective systems. Going on a pilgrimage is an important way to make a connection with others, to experience living history, and to stand in communion with the divine. When engaging the sacred at a liminal site, event, time, or other experience, one finds that greater attention needs to be paid as a behavior that attends the sacred moment. But so many seemingly normal and liminal things can be sacred—having sex, exploring a cave, crossing a boundary, breathing, dreaming, drinking—that it is the very act of *paying attention to its liminality*—some would call that mindfulness—that offers a kind of personal revelatory transformation of the spirit. Marching straight through an entrance into a temple (synagogue, mosque, church, shrine) without thinking about the shift from public to private or from secular space to divine space is the antithesis of mindfulness.

Alluring

Pinpointing the exact elements that draw someone's attention can be challenging, especially because each person and each culture has culturally bound needs and interests.[10] The initial usage of the word "allure" has to do with the kind of bait used to draw a hawk back to its handler; the implication is that the hawk has a mind and a will of its own, but it has its own reasons to be drawn to the lure. Humans have free will and the ability to make choices, but they tend to be pulled inexorably toward liminal experiences. For many people, the liminal *is* the alluring. Visiting the shore, the volcano, or the stone portal tomb; spotting birds, seals, or whales in the natural world; drinking, listening to music, sitting on a front porch (neither inside nor outside) and connecting with others—all of these are liminal to somebody, and all of them are alluring one way or another.

Music is obviously alluring to many people; they are drawn to it for various reasons: to pass the time, to dance, to listen closely, to connect with others, to create a sonic background, and so on. There is a cultural connectedness to that allure in its dependence on a listener's context, upbringing, position in the community, and much more. For example, in listening to popular music in the United States, there is often a particular moment—the "hook"—in a single track that is deliberately employed to capture one's attention (Bechtold et al. 2023: 353–372). The anticipation builds up as the special musical moment approaches, and then it zips past in real time and is gone. However, such a concept is not universal, because the way humans approach music is not universal.[11]

Some musical genres build on the idea of the ephemeral *as* the alluring point. In another publication (Williams 2022: 408), I wrote about the piece "Sagari Ha" ("Falling Leaf"), played on the Japanese *shakuhachi* (bamboo flute). One of the main aesthetic features of the shakuhachi is its evocation of the ephemeral—through the breathing of the performer, the fact that the music moves through time, and the continually shifting tones and tone colors. Through the exquisite exploration of timbre (tone color), both the player and—if there is one—the listener can be kept in a perpetual state of enchantment by following each new shift in timbre, from rough to breathy to pure to decaying. The title of the piece (the image of a single leaf detaching from a tree, which happens at autumn during the change of seasons), and the continually shifting timbre, serves to remind the listener that the moment a leaf detaches from a tree is ephemeral—just like life. It commands your *attention* and is alluring to those who value ephemerality.

The strong emotions evoked by music—whether the experience is inside the mind and body of a person alone or in a community setting—have been studied and discussed for centuries. In East Asia, music historically reflected the order of the universe through the choice of instrument types and sonic arrangement, and has been used to support entertainment, ritual, propaganda, and so much more (Mingyue 1985: 42); see the following section "Ambiguity and Authenticity." In the West, the ancient Greek myth of Orpheus included the idea that Orpheus could hold sway not only over wild animals but the streams, rocks, trees, and more. Popular images of Orpheus show him playing the lyre surrounded by calm wild animals—both predator and prey. Neuroscientist and music producer Daniel J. Levitin notes that people are drawn to the sounds that their peers listen to, and that music is "a vehicle for social bonding and societal cohesion" (Levitin 2006: 232). It may seem like a simple concept—everybody likes music—but it runs deeper than surface-level likes and dislikes.

Dangerous

Some humans struggle with ambiguity; it can disrupt their sense of what is normal and right, and focuses attention on certain gray areas that they might prefer to be left unexamined. Sometimes people in the United States publicly express "concerns" about migrants, adolescents, biracial people, seasonal workers, and others. Unfortunately, a person's lived experience in the United States teaches such "ambiguous" people that being straightforward—or simply responding in a way that the interlocutor doesn't understand—can lead to misunderstandings and/or violence. But also, why the emphasis on the binary response (bad vs. good)? The anthropologist Robert Wessing—whose work on power and communities in West Java served as an inspiration to my own musical work there—connects ambiguity to the potential loss of power.

> Liminal spaces are seen as dangerous precisely because they are points of transfer where the power is neither fully in one container nor in another. These therefore are points of danger where power may escape and being uncontrolled may pose a threat to the community or state. (Wessing 1993: 8)

That perceived loss of power has led to extreme measures. In medieval Europe, for example, the ability of local villagers and farmers to fall into ecstatic dance led to the banning of dancing in church and its censuring outside of church (Ehrenreich 2006: 91); this issue will appear again in Chapter 6. If they could reach spiritual ecstasy through movement, what need had they of a church to which they had to pay tithes? In 1950s North America, the white appropriation of Black popular music (Maultsby 2017: 47; Morrison 2024), and the apparent uncontrolled enthusiasm of teenagers (of various races) listening to it, dancing to it, and playing it, inspired racism-fueled rage, threats, denouncement, and punishment from parents, clergy, and politicians.

In Indonesia at the same time, that same rock 'n' roll imported from the West led to its banning by then-President Sukarno. He had already asked them to avoid the "cultural imperialism" of music from the West in 1959, and later famously described rock 'n' roll as sounding like "ngak-ngik-ngok" (Yampolsky 1989: 2). Heavy metal musicians have experienced a severe backlash in many places because it is "oppositional and frequently critical of the cultural and political status quo of its nation of origin" (Mayer and Timberlake 2014: 37). In certain parts of the Muslim world, some religious and political leaders have actively tried to suppress instrumental musics of various kinds because of the music's (or the musicians') perceived threat to social control (Levine 2009: 564).

Many aspects of liminality can be seen as dangerous. Drunkenness is dangerous, standing at the shore with your back turned to the waves is dangerous, and having unprotected sex is dangerous. Each one is liminal: neither sick nor well, neither on dry land nor in the ocean, and breaking the boundary between two people. Standing in the middle of a crossroads singing the blues could lead to your being hit by a truck, or perhaps being approached by the Devil with an offer you can't refuse.[12] Listening as a young woman lures you into water with her beauty and her song could lead to your drowning. Anyone who is transgender, non-binary, two-spirit, or obviously outside the cis-heteronormative spectrum knows exactly how dangerous it is to simply try to be oneself and to live in a society that is threatened by difference. For a number of American teenagers, having access to specific kinds of music can mean the difference between thriving in that ambiguous status as neither child nor adult, or merely surviving the volatile vicissitudes of social jockeying for position. Mediating that danger occurs on many different levels, from creating art to performing pieces that engage that liminal danger. Safety is always relative.

Liminality is something one needs to view through an interdisciplinary lens. Though each of these examples barely scratches the surface of liminality's depth and breadth, humans connect with it whether they are even aware of its importance. From a biologist working on the permeability of cells to the historian thinking about transitions in power; from the geographer outlining where the entertainment district meets the industrial district to the farmer noting the moment the seedlings break through the soil;

from the fisherman at the edge between above-water and below-water to the painter blending colors, shadows, and light; people engage with aspects of liminality regardless of their work, hobbies, and passions. In exploring all of these different fields at this level, one could easily begin to make inferences about one's own positionality as an immigrant, a healthcare specialist, a pilot, an attorney, a teenager, a physicist, a baker, a dancer, and more. *Humans* connect to liminality in a variety of ways. In a sense, then, it isn't just what people do; it is who they are. The manifestation of how people use liminality is determined in large part by where they come from and what they do.

Ambiguity and Authenticity Through Displacement

Musical instruments and musicians have always moved around the world. In some cases, they found a home where they continued to perform the sounds, timbres, and musical pieces that they had in their previous homes. In other cases, the instruments were redesigned for local use and fell in with local tunings and melodies. From the Chinese *pipa* that came from Persia along the Silk Road to the West African banjo-type instrument of many names that traveled to North America on ships with enslaved people, musical instrument migration has been the norm, not the exception. In the award-winning 1998 feature film *The Red Violin*, the plot traces the journey of a single violin over several centuries from Italy to Austria to England to China to Montreal. The filmmakers could have added India, Argentina, Tunisia, and Indonesia, all of which have rich, long-standing violin traditions. Whether through colonial or immigrant importation, individual travelers, or the adaptability of musical instruments across ever-shifting borders over centuries, it should be no surprise to find free-reed instruments, for example, as an accordion in a Nigerian *jùjú* band, accompanying *conjunto* verses in San Antonio, playing for crowds of set dancers in Ireland's County Clare, or as a harmonium adding a drone and single melody line in North Indian *rāga* performance.

Melodies themselves can undergo liminal transformation. While many who listen to popular music might be accustomed to songs and their accompaniment staying within the boundaries of major or minor, it is not just the norm but *expected* that a shift in mode adds to the musical richness of an experience.[13] In Figure 1.2, the first line of the Irish emigration song "The Green Fields of Canada" starts out in Mixolydian mode and then shifts into Aeolian mode on the second syllable of the word "farewell." It shifts back into

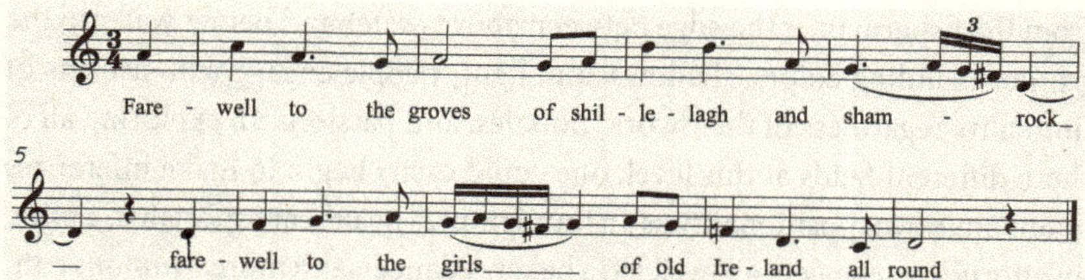

Figure 1.2 "The Green Fields of Canada"

Mixolydian mode right away on the word "girls" and then returns to Aeolian on the first syllable of "Ireland." Every genre of music in the world draws from a specific palette of notes, and many of them shift modes to add musical interest, accomplish a compositional purpose, and create a change in affect. This type of shift occurs in Persian, Arabic, Japanese, and a number of other musics of the world.

In the 1980s, a group of music executives developed the term "world beat" to describe popular music that utilizes instruments, rhythms, or other features from outside of Western Europe. Usually comprising a group fronted by a major (white male) pop or rock musician (e.g., Paul Simon, Sting, Peter Gabriel, David Byrne, etc.), the genre was a marketing success. Louise Meintjes's article about Paul Simon's album *Graceland*, for example, points out that the album signifies collaboration, but the sense of collaboration varies depending on who is listening, whether one values social or musical collaboration, and what is politically embedded in the sound (Meintjes 1990: 38). Such questions are essential in exploring the links between commerce and musical collaboration. However, long before there was "world beat," there were the liminal ensembles that included samba in Brazil, marabi in South Africa, brass bands in India, and various ensembles in the Tang Dynasty of China (618–907 CE), which imported musicians from all over Asia.

The Chinese emperor Xuanzong (685–762 CE) was a gifted musician who valued and facilitated the importation of music and musicians from India, Turkmenistan, Uzbekistan, Korea, and other places. Many of these musicians were sent as tribute from the regions that China had conquered, and the internationalism and bureaucratic entanglements of the Tang Dynasty court system are remarkable even from a twenty-first-century perspective (Xiaodun and Xiaohui 2004: 50–64). To import and export musicians and their instruments wholesale reveals a great deal about both power and imperialism in connection to music at that time and place. The different categories of music in the bureaucracy required a new category of *huyue*—foreign music—to take its place alongside court music—*yayue*—and common music—*suyue*—to distinguish the array of new musical instruments and stylistic influences of the time. The fact that the Chinese already had an official place for music from outside its region by the seventh century CE makes the compositional innovations of nineteenth- and twentieth-century Europe seem not just late to the party, but less remarkable.

Beyond popular music, Western art music has a long history of weaving in local and seemingly exotic sounds from "the folk," whether that takes place in Russia (the Mighty Five: Rimsky-Korsakov, Mussorgsky, Balakirev, Cui, and Borodin); Spain (Albéniz, Rodrigo, de Falla); or Scandinavia (Grieg, Nielsen, Sibelius). Building melodies from very local traditional music was seen as a way to (literally) build nations during the current of Romantic Nationalism that swept Europe and Russia in the eighteenth and nineteenth centuries. Johann von Herder (1744–1803), an eighteenth-century German philosopher, viewed the collection and celebration of folklore as the best way to connect to local authenticities (Bendix 1997: 16). Using and/or appropriating musical materials (without necessarily the musicians themselves) is one way to do that.

In Dylan Robinson's *Hungry Listening: Resonant Theory for Indigenous Sound Studies*, he deftly notes the fact that very often the ways that Indigenous musics and musicians have connected to Western art music has been in such a way that they serve as resources (yet again!) that supplement and reinforce the primacy of art music "without disrupting the norms of concert music performance or ontologies of music making" (Robinson 2020: 8). This gleaning of musical materials (and human resources) from outside the musical power structure to satisfy listeners from *within* that power structure is both long-lived and toxic; it is clearly not limited to American popular music. Instead, it is worth stepping away from the immediacy of sound for a minute to explore the overwhelming power imbalances that characterize a great deal of performative music-making on the one hand but diminish in the face of participatory music-making on the other.

Living with ambiguity is not easy. As mentioned earlier, people who lean toward the perceived mainstream or binary can feel threatened by another person's liminality. The American popular music star Michael Jackson—whose reclusive ambiguity was played up in performance so that he seemed neither Black nor white, male nor female, adult nor child, gay nor straight, or other markers—was in some ways publicly regarded as an increasingly confusing curiosity for decades rather than as a more generic pop star. His multiplatinum song, "Black or White," which was awarded *Billboard Magazine*'s first "No. 1 World Single," was released on his *Dangerous* (!) album in 1991. The music video features a segment in which people of different races and genders morph from one to the next, and incorporated elements of dance from half a dozen places in the world (India, Russia, etc.). Because he had been a star from his early childhood, he grew up in the public eye, becoming increasingly ambiguous and reclusive. And that is the challenge in dealing with the liminal: people might recognize ambiguity, but they don't necessarily like it, so they tend to dismiss it or downplay it as inauthentic or somehow worrisome.

The notion of authenticity as a fixed value is often casually presented as the polar opposite of ambiguity. How can something be authentic if it is ambiguous? Liz Przybylski writes—about Indigenous hip hop—that "Authenticity can be understood as a socially agreed upon quality by which a person or group demonstrates veracity to some valued entity, such as a place or experience" (Przybylski 2018: 493). The very nature of ambiguity is that it *cannot* be socially agreed upon; it is fluid and requires a heightened sensitivity toward change rather than complacency in the knowledge of its stability. Authenticity, as a point of philosophy, requires consistency between actions and beliefs; it might also be thought of as being true to oneself. But when one lives a completely disrupted or disruptive existence—as in the lives of colonized people, immigrants, adolescents, refugees, or spiritual intermediaries—that authenticity has to be fluid in order to keep pace with the changing nature of the self and of one's potentially unstable context. The number of academic works that link these two with such promising claims about "the ambiguity of authenticity" (Benjamin 2018) and "the authenticity of ambiguity" (Skurski 1994) is significant.

This work on the ways in which musicians and musical materials readily cross borders and connect with their own unique kind of authentic ambiguity is a way to highlight what will appear in the following chapters: references to music and desire, music and access, music and hybrid faiths, music and migration, music and transgression, and more. Know that in some cases, the migration of musical materials may not represent collaboration so much as extraction and exploitation. For all the times in this book that a reader might think "but what about X from musical genre (or region or country) Y?" there may well be other moments when one has known this about music all along;

one's impulse to use something one knows to fit into the existing categories in this volume may work seamlessly.

Grids and Deep Maps

Each of us operates our lives along a series of culturally bound grids—metaphors for various structures—that inform the ways in which we think and behave. In a chapter titled "The Grid: A Life Principle," Pedro de Alcantara writes that "The Grid is the structure underpinning any system—a relatively rigid framework [that may be] visible or invisible, audible or inaudible, tangible or intangible. The Grid is organized and predictable, but the energies that oppose it are fluid and unpredictable" (de Alcantara 2011: 38). He uses grids from poetry to illustrate his points: haiku, sonnet, and so on. In this study of music and the in-between, one way in which we can focus our attention is through observing the interplay between the forces that oppose the grids within which we all work and the grids themselves. De Alcantara offers as examples an electrical network (grid) in connection with a power source (energy); a capillary system (grid) with blood (energy); and a chess set (grid) with players (energy), with the energy driving the system that harnesses it (2011: 37–39). For our purposes, it is one thing to have a grid that outlines the right way to play a twelve-bar blues pattern; it is another to put a living, breathing musician with a guitar in dialogue with that pattern. The pattern is the grid (like an electrical network), and the musician is the engaging force (like a surge of power through the network). It is the grid that offers access to the power source, and the connection between the two is the liminal point.

We all recognize that there are certain "right ways" of using eating implements, listening to live music, greeting your potential future in-laws, approaching a strange dog, or caring for a plant. What we don't usually consider is how each one is deeply tied to our cultural orientation. When you listen to live music regardless of the genre, your behavior will likely mirror that of the people around you. A concert at a symphony hall featuring the music of Mozart and Brahms sets up a system of thoughts and behaviors that differ strongly from the thoughts and behaviors that arise at a concert featuring Cuban salsa, British punk, American bluegrass, Japanese bamboo flute, or Brazilian samba. Is there dancing involved? Are people eating food or drinking alcohol? Are they singing along? Are they chatting with each other? Do they appear detached from the music and only pay close attention to each other? Each genre of music has its own grid of what to do and how to do it. And you know this, almost instinctively; otherwise, you might try to mosh at the symphony or dance salsa at a bluegrass festival. Readers: don't do this.

Musicians know their own grids, too. In addition to knowing the twelve-bar blues pattern (and, for that matter, the eight- and sixteen-bar blues), a competent jazz musician can connect with big band standards, bossa nova, cool jazz, bebop, fusion, and more. A Japanese *shamisen* (plucked banjo-type lute) player—even without being able to play each of these genres—understands the instrument's varying styles in *minyō* (folk music), *bunraku* (puppet theater) accompaniment, *nagauta* (kabuki theater) music, *kouta* (short song, associated with geisha) accompaniment, and *sankyoku* (ensemble with shamisen, *koto*, and *kokyū*—two-stringed bowed lute) participation. Shamisen notation appears as a grid. A *riqq* (small frame drum with jingles) player in the Arab world can use the instrument for any number of situations, knowing that the instrument functions as the "beating heart" of the ensemble (Farraj and Abu Shumays 2019: 53). Players build a repertoire of genres associated with the vocal or instrumental tradition with which they are associated, and move accordingly through each tune or song because of their recognition of the authority of the grid, and their own liminal connection to that grid.

Because each of us has multiple internalized metaphorical grids, we generally live our days and lives with confidence and competence. Chances are excellent that—musician or not—you are easily capable of doing the following tasks without asking for directions: preparing and eating your breakfast, brushing your teeth, reading a recipe, getting yourself to and from work, getting dressed, or meeting the friend of a friend for the first time. Each one of these activities is very specific to *you*: where you were raised, who raised you, how you obtained your education, and how you have come into adulthood.

But now think about what it means to step outside the normal boundaries of the grid. Let's look at each of those activities again, but with examples of a different set of behaviors: eating the kind of breakfast that someone in another country would enjoy, brushing teeth without a toothbrush, preparing a dish that you've never tried before, taking a new route to work, getting dressed in a different order, or meeting someone new with no prior connection. These are liminal moments of ambiguity and uncertainty. In each case, you pay far closer attention to what you're doing. There will be results, but they may well be different from whatever you expected when you followed your normal grid to the letter. Because you are veering away from the grid you know and follow, your experiences will be different for you, and your ambiguity may result in discomfort, surprises, and possibly new pleasures. It won't feel right, because although it is still a grid, it isn't *your* grid.

What is it about using an alternative grid that makes it liminal? Imagine speaking another language—see Chapter 7—and learning how it can shape the way you think. Imagine wearing different clothes and seeing what that does to the way your body acts and reacts; your body language will necessarily change. Imagine, after spending your whole life eating with a fork in your left hand—as in most of Europe—and discovering that all eating must be done with the right hand only. Imagine singing every song you know with a wide vibrato because of a belief that the vibrato is the only right way to sing, only to learn that some genres of music and some places in the world have no place for it. These grids are culturally bound, and as soon as people are invited from the known into a place of ambiguity or liminality to explore a different grid, all kinds of transformations can happen. By paying close attention to those differences, creative potential and growth are possible.

The natural world has its own set of grids; as I write this, the cicadas in the eastern United States are in the middle of their seventeen-year cycle of resurrection and are audible to me, in the (quieter) coastal West, only because of their presence in televised newscasts. Patterns of migration of the whales, cycles of salmon regeneration, and the huge flocks of pine siskins at my bird feeders in May and June are something I simply accept. Whales follow what the Irish poet Seamus Heaney calls the whale-roads—also an element of old Anglo-Saxon descriptions of sailing routes—just as much as coastal dwellers (animal and human) watch for changes in the tides, waves, and clouds.

Human grids in connection to music are found all over the world, and people connect to them even when traveling to a new place with unfamiliar music or trying something new in music. Musicians work with both sounds and silences, and learning a new instrument is a matter of understanding the intersecting grids that work with both the instrument (or voice) and the musical genre. For example, I had been playing bluegrass banjo and guitar for several years in high school when someone handed me a bluegrass mandolin: it used the same grid for the genre but a new grid for the instrument. Figuring out the instrument, as a bluegrass player, meant that all the bluegrass instrumental tunes were already in place as a grid in my head. Similarly, picking up the fiddle in my forties after playing mandolin meant that my left-hand fingertips went to (most of) the right places because the fingering is the same, but my bowing arm was (and remains) that of a novice. Shifting from the Central Javanese gamelan to the Sundanese gamelan degung was an adjustment between the existing grid in my head and my body. As a dancer, knowing my own physical grid of musculature and coordination meant that I could focus on the stepping and balancing patterns of villagers in the midst of a betel-nut exchange ceremony on the Indonesian island of Flores and not do too badly when I was (inevitably) pulled out into the circle to dance among the women. I was still, of course, a complete spectacle and laughing-stock to the villagers because as a white woman, I rendered their usual grid of betel-nut exchange celebrations ambiguous and entertaining by my unmis-takably bizarre presence.

Even with the advent of the mobile phone and its ability to direct users to desired destinations, a map (metaphorical or specific to location) is never just topographical. Like a grid, a map can be conceptual, settler, spiritual, linguistic, Indigenous, political, musical, archaeological, and more.[14] The settler colonial map is one version, while the map at native-land.ca features the Indigenous mapping that predated the settlers. An Alabama map of where enslaved people lived from the 1860 census connects almost pre-cisely with the voting patterns of Democratic vs. Republican voters in 2017.[15] A few minutes of playing online will connect you to musical maps specific to an area, such as at the website musicmapnl.ca, which features tracks and artists of Newfoundland and Labrador in eastern Canada. Similarly, the "Musical Explorers" curriculum through Carnegie Hall offers a world map with pinned images of musicians; one click takes you to sounds, lessons, and contextual information geared toward English-speaking children and their teachers. These are just Ione aspect of maps and their potential utility.

Digging deeper into the concept of map layers reveals that they are not just about how people can understand borders and boundaries. The Indigenous people of Australia have historically mapped the land and sky through the use of spiritual songs—"dreaming tracks" or songlines—that assist in the navigation of travel across distances. Songlines include Indigenous infor-mation about plants, animals, and natural features. However, the songs also express the profound local *relationships* to land, protocols, languages, and much more; they are complicated layers of grids. Through the aegis of the Australian Institute for Aboriginal and Torres Strait Islander Studies, a concerted effort to map out some of these songlines has been underway. Nyikina Warrwa community leader Anne Poelina—professor, poet, and filmmaker—says "When you look at those sorts of stories, you see the connectivity between all of the elements, between the sky, between the Earth, between the water, between magnificent sacred sites that are in the landscape that connect our people through this ancient wisdom and these ancient stories in song."[16] It is in the places that maps and lines converge—linguistic, religious, political, geographical, sonic—that transformations can happen. Those convergences form liminal identities and focus attention on what is important to insiders: those at the center.

The liminal place, then, is a locus of creative and generative transformation that can be navigated through multifaceted knowledge of grids and deep mapping. Places such as the shore are unstable and dangerous, but they are also beautiful and alluring as places of physical and personal transformation. The sea has a grid and the land has a grid, but the shore is ambiguous and changes quickly. People are drawn to those unstable places because they are drawn to the unknown. Liminality offers a chance to reach out, to be near greatness and beauty, to experience wonder, and to step into a larger complex of ideas. But we bring our awe with us; we are ready for moving experiences, especially if we have built up our hopes for such an experience in advance. That buildup is something that can simultaneously make one's powerful experience greater, and one's disappointment deeper. This book is an exploration of how people in specific areas of the world engage in issues such as transgression, migration, access, desire, power, and other crucial elements of human life—because they *need to*.

The Shape of This Book

Any of my academic colleagues reading this book could expand it easily into the sciences or indeed cover much more wide-ranging territory in the social sciences and the humanities. However, its purpose is to highlight the points of intersection of the performing arts with some of the most essential moments of human existence; that is one of the factors that can make this work relevant outside of academia. The significance of this project to people in the humanities as well as the arts is to bring to light a creative driving force in these fields. Some of the most enduring moments in literature, plays, and films are liminal, and include transformative events at windows, doorways, beaches, caves, crossroads, bridges, wells, and other places. Some of the most important points in medicine are the transformations—a wound, for example, is either infecting or healing—and the internal and external barriers of the body. Agricultural, mechanical, and industrial processes are transformative rather than inert. Pay attention to those liminal processes. One of my intentions, then, is to allow this book to serve as a connective point between disciplines.

Each chapter explores a particular theme in relation to music and liminality. The current chapter has explained the concept of and overarching theme of **liminality**; it has presented examples of liminal places, times, people, plants, and animals, and explains why liminal elements are sacred, alluring, and dangerous. This introduction also began to focus your attention on how performance practices around the world tend to occur at liminal places and times, and are often done by people who might be considered as "marginalized" by colonial or other powers but who are, in fact, *central* to the expression of cultural identity. It has pointed to issues of access and interdisciplinarity, and highlighted the idea of grids and maps of knowledge and understanding that enable us to think and behave in culturally bound ways. Finally, it sets up the following chapters, all of which connect the threshold with the performing arts in a deeper way.

This book moves from the sacred through the alluring and into the dangerous, chapter pair by chapter pair. Chapter 2—begins the discussion of the sacred and liminal points of communication. It examines the presence of liminal creatures and spiritual practitioners in the places between the sea and the shore and well above the land. In some religious practices, liminal elements may be used to contact the spirit world, whether through bird symbolism (feathers, fans, angels), fire and smoke (incense), spiritual intermediaries or priests (who are neither fully of this world nor of the next), and architecture (through sacred geometry, the use of water elements, and the incorporation of particular designs).

The main theme of Chapter 2 is **access**, in which the intermediaries of the sea and the sky offer access to the ancestors and to the unseen worlds "out there." In the sea, the reverence with which many Indigenous peoples of both the Pacific and the Atlantic hold the salmon has led to centuries of ceremonies to ensure the return of the fish year after year for nutritional and spiritual sustenance. The seal people of Ireland, Scotland, and farther north are an important part of local beliefs known to some Gaelic-speaking coastal dwellers, and the seals' songs lament the disruptions of fishermen to their families and lineages. People of the Pacific—not just the Hawaiian Islands but the northern-hemispheric shores of the mainlands—celebrate the whales as ancestral beings and echo their songs with songs of their own. Birds and insects are liminal creatures that swim, fly, walk, and sing; their longtime position as messengers to the spirit world—as well as their relationship to angels—closes out the chapter.

Chapter 3—continues the theme of sacred liminality through a discussion of those whose musical work and faith cross formal religious boundaries. Through the lens of **dual faith**—those who simultaneously celebrate older and newer faith traditions—the chapter briefly examines combinations of vernacular and official Catholicism in Ireland; Japanese Shintō-Buddhists; and Brazilian Candomblé practitioners with the local blend of African and Portuguese Catholic elements. It then has as its primary focus the ways in which Hinduism and Islam operate within the *tembang Sunda* ensemble of West Java as an example of being a devout believer in one faith tradition while singing, equally devoutly, the songs of another, older tradition.

Chapter 4—shifts the tone from the sacred to the alluring by focusing on the liminal connection between female-coded figures, the performing arts, sexuality, and water. It bears the theme of the **erotic** in its engagement with elusive desire. It features seven case studies of such seemingly disparate entities as the geisha of the "floating world" in Japan, the *widadari* of West Java, the "singing mermaids" and dangerous sirens of mythology and literature, the *devadasi* temple dancers of India, and others. Water is often considered to be a connective—in-between—element to both the underground, particularly in regard to holy wells and sacred springs, and to the spirit world. A particularly flexible local plant—bamboo, birch, willow—which not coincidentally can be developed into various musical instruments, often plays a significant role in the embodiment or the transmission of eroticism. The location of female-coded performers near a liminal element, such as water, is key to their musical, spiritual, and erotic power.

Chapter 5—is about migrants and the transmission of important concepts of both home and foreign-ness through music. It continues the idea of allure in that its theme is **longing**, using examples from African-American, Portuguese, Irish-Gaelic, Mexican, Arabic, and other languages and music cultures. Most migrants never fully assimilate, yet they often change so much that they are no longer truly welcome at home either. With intact memories of home, they have fluent access to each place yet they are a stranger to both. They are forever in a liminal position. Some immigrants to the United States have responded to this sense of displacement through the use of alcohol, which enhances their liminal state of being neither sick nor well, but which can render them even more powerless. But an alluring combination of nostalgia, joy, longing, and loss—for which no precise word exists in English—is facilitated through the performance of music and the consumption of food and drink.

Chapter 6—takes readers through a series of musical scenes that involve crossing over into what might be perceived as dangerous territory: the theme of **transgression**. Starting with the medieval European bilingual motet as a small transgressive step that yielded significant results in the secularization of Western Europe, the first section examines how a series of small changes in music and dance can lead to larger changes in society. A discussion follows of the performance of ambiguity in Indonesia and Japan, focusing on the staged performance of maleness and femaleness. Lastly, the chapter highlights the work of Lil Nas X and Amythyst Kiah as two intersectional performers doing their important work *right now*.

Chapter 7—wraps the book up through an exploration of the act of **resistance and reclamation** of land, identity, language, and pride. Colonization is not new or limited to the actions of governments of "the West"; nor is the suppression of language, culture, the performing arts, or personal expression by stronger powers. Yet it is often through *sound* in conjunction with *action* that resistance becomes embodied, and recovery is possible. Chapter 7 explores, among other points, the sonic traditions accompanying the canoe journey in Oceania and the Pacific Northwest; an exploration of gay Harlem, noting the importance of the Harlem Renaissance as a locus of both safety and transgression during the Jim Crow and Prohibition eras; and powerful and empowering acts of language reclamation through hip hop and the hazardous magic of using one's own endangered language when the majority wants you to use theirs.

Narratives, in which some of the information in this book appears, are an important means by which the members of a society build their individual and collective identities. They create a local "truth" that joins them with others, regardless of whether they actually believe the narratives (Wessing 2020: 76). Whether that truth concerns the connective powers of singing birds with the Otherworld, the ambiguous legends surrounding the geisha of Kyōto, or the importance of music among migrants, narratives fulfill a need and establish an identity. It is a way to gain access to what is locally essential and does not necessarily cross cultures or fill in all the facts. In addition, claiming that "among the people of X" some sort of universal truth exists without exception would be foolhardy. When spoken accents, belief systems, and musical styles can vary from village to village and certainly from region to region, it makes no sense to posit such claims. Instead, it is hoped that readers can assume that a discussion of a musical genre or concept in any one place can never speak for all of its people. Each region's diversity belies any such attempt.

Celebrating what James Seale-Collazo refers to as the "everyday extraordinary" requires noticing the moments of transformation that occur right in front of us: the small epiphany in a classroom; the cessation of a quarrel; the shift in the tide; or the call to prayer in a busy Cairo neighborhood (Seale-Collazo 2012: 188). Each one of those transformative events—large and small—indicates the possibility of connection across liminal borders, natural phenomena, humans, and seemingly disparate beings.

In conclusion, living between worlds—between the sea and the shore, life and death, history and memory—is rich territory. It isn't always something that people talk about explicitly, but it is a key part of the human experience. The quotation by the Polish anthropologist Bronisław Malinowski (1884–1942) at the entry to this chapter—"Nothing is as difficult to see as the obvious" (Malinowski 1944: 158)—reflects my attempt to highlight the obvious, but often less visible. Recalling the discussion of grids and deep maps earlier in the chapter, just as birds adhere to the (invisible to humans) magnetic lines that ring the globe for their migration patterns, so humans lean toward and perform, through their culturally bound grids, at the threshold again and again. It is a fundamental part of our emotional, social, and musical cartography.

2

Intermediaries and Shapeshifters

'Aohe pau ka 'ike i ka hālau ho'okahi. All knowledge is not learned in just one school (Hawai'i) (Pukui 1983)

This chapter calls attention to the sacred role of liminal creatures in both traditional mythologies and religious practices, and to the ways in which intermediaries can facilitate communication with ancestors and other elements of the spirit world. In sections about the sea and the sky, the issue of access is foregrounded while examining two major unknowns for humans: "down there" underwater and "out there" in the sky, beyond where we can go. For example, the salmon shifts between freshwater and saltwater; its role in multiple regional mythologies is as an essential life-giving force, with songs and performance practices to reinforce its central connective importance. The seal fulfills a role as ancestor, mysterious visitor, and point of affinity with the kingdoms under the surface of the ocean. The extraordinary oxygen-breathing whale—specifically the humpback but others as well—is a mighty singer with an enormous organ just for focusing on sound. Among the ancestors of the Indigenous people of the Pacific Northwest in North America and the Pacific Islands, whales offer and accept songs as associative currency.

Of the sky, birds are often linked to the spirit world because of their liminal status: they fly, walk, swim, and sing. Performers use fans, wings, and feathers to engage their symbolism. In many areas of the world, the shapeshifter—whether human or not—has a powerful, supportive, and potentially contradictory role in local stories and belief systems. "It is through grappling, curiosity, and critical conversations, with a willingness to be flexible, open minded, and accepting of different perspectives, that we will truly tell our stories and celebrate our connections to culture, time, and place across the past, present, and future" (Lane-Kamahele 2017: 313). This chapter includes stories and songs that connect people to their ancestors, their protocols, and

Music at the Threshold from the Sacred to the Dangerous. Sean Williams, Oxford University Press. © Oxford University Press 2026. DOI: 10.1093/9780197761762.003.0002

the heart of who they are. And of the cultural keystone species—those which loom large in oral traditional materials—this chapter focuses in particular on three types of sea creatures, three types of birds, and two types of insects. Knowing these animals means understanding a different type of agency and access to knowledge across the artificial nature of binary divisions.

> Present in every human being are two desires, a desire to know the truth about the primary world, the given world outside ourselves in which we are born, live, love, hate, and die, and the desire to make new secondary worlds of our own, or if we cannot make them ourselves, to share in the secondary worlds of those who can. (Auden 1968: 46)

As most of the world is underwater, its depths remain inaccessible to most humans. It has fired the human imagination, however, as evidenced by millennia of visual art, literature, mythologies, and rituals at its boundaries. These are elements of "biocultural memory," a type of community storehouse of traditional ecological knowledge beyond individual experience (Jacques-Coper et al. 2019: 35). The liminal creatures of the ocean in this chapter are connected either currently or historically to the shore, whether the salmon that spawns in freshwater and migrates to saltwater (and back); the seals that live half in the water and half on the shore; or the whales that once walked on land and never will again. They cannot be away from the shore, and they cannot be *on* the shore (in the case of seals, not for long). Sea creatures such as otters, crabs, and turtles are also liminal and also appear in mythologies and rituals, but this section has as its focus only the shapeshifting salmon, seal, and whale, and their long-standing connection with humans. In centralizing Indigenous perspectives and identifying the contributors through their home tribes, I do not remove the settler narratives; instead, I build them back into the mix. The section on seals connects with an older Gaelic system in both Ireland and Scotland, so I do not include the English-language songs about seals. In addition, almost all of the Irish folklore about seals has been noted in Irish-speaking communities only (Ní Fhlionn 1999: 226).

Song is a primary medium through which the ancestors communicate across the boundaries of time and space. It is also the means by which local human epistemologies focus on the timings, protocols, practices, and standards for communication, demonstrations of respect, and at its most basic level, the conveyance of what is important. As Roberta Haines (Colville Confederated Tribes) mentions, "In the lives of everyday people, spiritual traditions were kept alive and nurtured by song" (Haines 1999: 13); the salmon, seal, and whale are deeply embedded in local spiritualities, as are the condor, raven, and owl. Bruce-*Subiyay* Miller (Skokomish) writes that his siblings would learn songs, stories, and dances from their great-grandmother, appearing on her doorstep at dusk—between day and night—and learn the songs through repetition and questions about how a song, story, or dance went (Miller 1999: 30). While this section focuses on those who live in the ocean and along its shores in the Northern Hemisphere, there are similar situations in other regions of the world; see, for example, Stanbury and Clegg 1990 about whales in regard to Indigenous Australians, and Barría 1997 about the *millalobo* or seal-man of Southern Chile.

Indigenous songs in the Pacific Northwest of North America tend to be single melodies sung either by a soloist or a group; a single frame drum—often decorated with figures from the sea or sky—is the most common accompaniment, but carved rattles are common as well. The songs occur in short phrases with repetition (Olsen 1999: 109); those who are allowed permission to sing or to listen vary by region. However, songs that might seem "basic" to outsiders are rarely so. Richard Keeling points out that such songs may sound "simple and repetitive, but the semiology can be quite complex, because the songs usually have a hidden meaning or a story behind that is not expressed in the song itself" (Keeling 2012: 234). It is not so much about the precise content of individual songs as it is about the structural position of the song in the community for which it is important. Songs belong to the ones who receive them, and they are held close in families.

In addition to songs, however, are human attempts to instrumentally duplicate what they have received from the sea. The Irish instrumental air "Pórt na bPúcaí" ("Song of the Pooka") is locally understood to have been bestowed on humans by the fairies; the Pooka is one of the best-known of the local trickster figures. It comes from the island of Inis Mhic Aoibhleáin of the Blasket Islands in the southwest of Ireland. It has generally been accredited to the composer Seán Ó Riada, who later embedded it into a larger composition. Its roots and a local recording predate his efforts, however. It is said to have been heard by islanders rowing from the mainland as sounds came from below the bottom of their currach (a canvas-covered wooden-frame boat); possibly it was the song of a humpback whale. One of the islanders is said to have picked up the fiddle and played along with the tune. Some stories say that it was a woman who brought the tune back to the island. Whether it came from the fairies, the wind, or a humpback whale is regularly debated, but it is always associated with the Blasket Islands, and it is always regarded as a gift.[1]

Animal/ancestral communication can also happen through human intermediaries. Spiritual intermediaries live on all the major continents; using a map to locate some specific territory would be an exercise in futility. The word *šaman* (Manchu-Tungus, "one who knows") applies to those who have access to extraordinary ways of knowing[2]; I will refer to them here as spiritual intermediaries. Sometimes that extraordinary knowledge is gained through years of training, and other times the training comes through being specially chosen. The varied roles of such a person include serving as a storyteller, singer, scientist, prophet, priest or priestess, exorcist, meteorologist, keeper of memories, healer, and intermediary. The exceptional abilities of such spiritual intermediaries—of seeing and hearing and understanding, among other skills—have led to their depictions in petroglyphs as larger-than-life; often portrayed as bigger than other humans, images of them can include horns, feathers, or rays radiating upwards and outwards from their heads.

The manifestations of Indigenous religions are profoundly varied and correctly resistant to generalization. Rather than pretending that there is a one-size-fits-all version of these practices (and thereby doing violence to local Indigenous beliefs and processes), let us explore elements of the intermediary in very local connections with birds. In some cases, an example can illustrate a much larger concept that applies in other areas of the world; we can recognize that almost nothing applies to the whole world.[3]

The use of fans, fins, feathers, teeth, and wings—and artistic depictions of flight or of transformative animals such as whales—is not merely symbolic of communication with the otherworld; they are fundamental to the facilitation of that communication. While spirituality is deeply interwoven with culturally specific ways of understanding the world, its outward expression through performance can form the locus of healing and transformation. Part of this work includes examining the role of spiritual intermediaries, wisdom keepers, and others with practices in healing and in connecting with the spirit world. From Sápmi to Australia to Bengal to the Andes, the person who connects to other ways of seeing the world—regardless of sex, age, or race—can serve as a powerful connective figure. In that role, through the voice, ritual, and sometimes sonic objects such as bells and rattles, the intermediary is able to elicit clarification and contact with the otherworld on matters of illness or community disruption. Engaging in the liminal act of trance, in which the practitioner is neither awake nor asleep, can allow transformation to take place. And because a spiritual intermediary may draw from elements of the natural world, sometimes using images or sounds of birds, fish, and other creatures, transformative elements appear in their important connective work.

The connection of each sea creature to water fosters the fluid dissolution of boundaries beyond the surface, whether according to nation, culture, or species. It isn't just about people; it is about the reciprocal relationships built between locals on the land and locals in the sea. Shirley Roburn discusses the importance of centering the ocean, rather than the land, as an acoustic space: "Reframing the ocean as an acoustic space both highlights the speciesism inherent in human perceptions and categorizations of space, and reclassifies ocean habitats not as wild nature but as areas differentially affected by the pollution of modernity" (Roburn 2013: 107). In other words, the ocean is central; the ocean is *home.* This first section about the sea draws primarily from (northern-hemispheric) Native American and Asian/Pacific relationships with salmon and whales, and from the people of the British Isles and Ireland who have long-term relationships with seals. All three types of sea creatures have families, hierarchies, genealogies, and songs; all three share parts of their existence with humans, and bestow songs on those few liminal humans willing to listen.

Salmon Nation

The Pacific Northwest of the North America, where I live, is sometimes referred to as "Salmon Nation." From the coast of Northern California to Alaska and across to northern Japan, this border-defying bioregion comprises a conglomerate of Indigenous homelands, a legacy of settler incursions, and marine and shoreline ecosystems. It is supported by a vast network of rivers descending from the Pacific Coast ranges (and the east coasts of Russia and Japan), and those rivers have been the historical support networks of the salmon. As the most important fish in the region to dozens of Indigenous tribes and the fish most deeply worked into local beliefs and practices, the Pacific salmon lives in its own nations underwater. The salmon is also anadromous; it shifts its physiology from freshwater to saltwater and back to freshwater during a single lifetime. That liminal act of physiological transformation has determined salmonid habitats for millions of years. Of the five salmon common to the Pacific Northwest region—pink (humpback), coho (silver), sockeye (red), chum (dog), and Chinook (king)—the large Chinook salmon tends to appear most frequently in local ceremonies. Settler practices of repeatedly taking the largest fish have resulted in the unnatural selection of smaller fish able to make it back to the streams to reproduce; over time, regional salmon have evolved to be smaller than they once were. Currently weighing up to thirty pounds (more rarely up to seventy pounds) and spending up to eight years at sea, the Chinook (capitalized because it is a proper name given by the Indigenous people of the Lower Columbia River) is now far less common than the others.

> According to Makah legend, salmon were people before they were transformed into fish and, as fish, they look forward to fulfilling their duty as food for earth people, part of the sacred cycle of life. To the Okanagan people, salmon are the outward expression of God. The Tlingit name their clans and design their crests around varieties of fish. The Ainu of northern Japan call salmon "the fish of the gods." (Roche and McHutchison 1998: 12)

The Pacific salmon is not limited to the west coast of North America; its territories cover the entirety of the North Pacific, including across the Bering Strait into Eastern Russia and northern Japan. It is the broad expanse of this part of the globe in which the salmon play such a key role in local stories, songs, poetry, dances, and ceremonies. Because the Chinook (Latin, *Oncorhynchus tshawytscha*) is the central fish for Indigenous people, it is the focus of this section. The salmon use a combination of factors to navigate from their natal streams to the ocean and back, including the use of magnetic sensing organs, ocean currents, scents, degrees of safety, geospatial location from the sky, and the ability to modify behaviors depending on food, mating possibilities, and tides. They prefer colder water and will take a longer time to migrate if they can remain cool. And because the magnetic field has shifted over time, scientists can measure the changes in their migration patterns. Salmon ways of sensing are salmon ways of *knowing*.

> Key to the ongoing survival of those who dwell in the Canoe Nations are the finned-ones, especially the Salmon People who, it is said, at the time of transition, consciously chose to sacrifice their lives every year so that the transformed humans might survive. (Tuttle 2006: 202)

The many Indigenous stories about the salmon include certain families being descended from salmon; most of them connect to liminal acts of shapeshifting or personal transformation. In Khabarovsk (Siberia), one story as told by Nadyezhda Duvan (Ulchi, of the Tungus tribes) includes a salmon approaching a young woman, requesting that she cook and eat him, then later appearing as a handsome young man who gives her three children (Duvan 1998: 94–95). Jeannette Armstrong (Okanagan) describes the salmon as "the most important source of life" (Armstrong 1998: 182). Elizabeth Woody (Warm Springs) writes, "Salmon was a key element in the spiritual framework of my people" (Woody 1998b: 29). Salmon are not, however, the only beings offered gratitude as part of the network of relations. In memory of the Yakima spiritual practitioner Ellen Saluskin, also known as Hoptonix Sawyalilx (1890–1993) and her teachings to others, Virginia Beavert-Martin (Yakima) notes the following:

> When a man shoots a deer or a boy catches his first salmon, he thanks it for its life and calls it "*pyap*, older brother." When a young girl plucks a berry for the first time or is initiated into root digging, she thanks it for its life and calls it "*pat*, older sister." (Beavert-Martin 1999: 69)

And while the connection of salmon to Indigenous beliefs may practically be a trope in white people's imaginings, all of us—humans and fish—are descended from a common ancestor. Tiktaalik (several hundred million years ago)—a fish—had legs, shoulders, wrists, and a neck (Shubin, 2009, writes about it as our "inner fish"). We are all literally descended from a liminal ancestor.

Of the songs connected to the salmon in the Pacific Northwest of North America, the singers generally use vocables or non-lexical words. In some of the early published reports of local songs, the words are incorrectly described as "nonsense syllables." The syllables absolutely have meaning, but they do not form discernable words that belong to the lexicon of a specific language. Sometimes songs—not just for salmon, but for other animals—connect to the sounds of the animals to whom they refer, or to whom they are addressed (Keeling 2012: 241). Songs intended to welcome and respect the salmon are part of specific ceremonies with established protocols; these songs can be requested from the salmon themselves. From the first competition (a *slahal* or stick game) between humans and animals, Bruce-*Subiyay* Miller (Skokomish) says that the people "retained the right to eat the animal and quest for, and sing, the guardian spirit songs of the animal"—in this case, the salmon (Miller 1999: 43). Cliff Sijohn (Coeur d'Alene) writes about the songs being delivered to people from "the messengers of the Great One," including the birds and the fish (Sijohn 1999: 47).

Settler prohibitions—and violent actions—against all aspects of traditional Indigenous ways of living and believing deeply disrupted tribal connections to the songs and ceremonies (Amoss 1987: 58). The 1974 Boldt Decision, granting tribes the right to catch half of the harvestable salmon, was upheld by the Supreme Court of the United States in 1979,[4] but tensions (and legal issues) have continued between tribal and settler fishing communities. By the late 1970s, many of the salmon ceremonies were being reinstated among the tribes of the salmon region, and thrive today.

The First Fish ceremony of the Pacific Northwest celebrates the arrival of the first salmon of the season every year; the salmon is usually a Chinook salmon. The arrival is a liminal moment, worthy of celebration. Those who participate in the ceremony treat the first Chinook salmon as an honored guest, laying it out on a mat of fresh cedar, cooking it with reverence, and dividing it up so that each person present can partake of a small piece. According to Pauline Tuttle, it can be "ceremonially given a name that is validated through feasting, songs, dance, and gift-giving," and returning its bones, fins, and other parts to the water in ceremony on a bundle of cedar with blessings so that they will return home with stories of how they were shown dignity and respect (Tuttle 2006: 202). These ceremonies have been reported in print for at least two hundred years (William Clark of the Lewis and Clark Expedition noted them in 1806), but of course they wouldn't have been newly conceived simply because a white person was a witness; they are older. Songs are an integral part of the ceremony. In the Columbia Basin (part of the land and river between Washington and Oregon), those who follow the local traditional religion of Washut enact the following practices:

Upon entering the longhouse, the women go to the south side and the men go to the north. Each forms a circle, standing shoulder to shoulder. Drummers begin a series of prayer songs. To their right, the longhouse leader holds a brass bell, ringing it and using it to count the song sequences. During the service, Washut members since, dance, or move with small dignified steps. Some of the songs thank the salmon for giving its life to feed the people while others remind those gathered of the traditional laws that must be observed.[5]

Elizabeth Woody (Warm Springs, Oregon) describes her tribe's salmon-welcoming song as "phenomenal, repeated seven times by seven drummers, a bell ringer and people gathered in the Longhouse," including the drummers and bell ringer stationed in the north of the Longhouse as dancers move counterclockwise (Woody 1998a: 82). In her detailed description of the Tulalip First Fish ceremony of 1979, Pamela Amoss includes the words sung in Lushootseed at each step: "The spring salmon is landing now," "The spring salmon is coming up from the beach," and "We recognize the spring salmon" (Amoss 1987: 60). Song lyrics as the salmon carcass is returned to sea include "The spring salmon is going toward the water," "You are departing, Noble one," and "You are returning home, Noble one."[6]

The Lummi people (near what is now Bellingham, Washington) involve children as part of the welcoming ceremony in late spring; the ceremony includes an entry song with vocables, the use of cedar fronds, rattles, frame drums, and another song in the Lkungen language (a variant of Coast Salish) to return the carcass to the water (Lund 2004: 45). The songs used to welcome the First Fish are sung in unison (octaves, according to the capabilities of the singers) to the accompaniment of a drum beating single strokes at approximately the same tempo as a slow march (70–90 beats per minute). Each step of the ceremony—bringing the fish inside, sharing it, and returning the carcass to the sea—features a different melody with different vocables performed by different groups. Without the songs, the ceremony and the transformation of the fish would not follow important local protocols. The welcoming song can be heard in its context in a video created by the Northwest Indian Fisheries Commission, which connects and supports twenty tribes in the Pacific Northwest.[7]

The Siberian taimen salmon of the Khabarovsk region is the largest salmonid in the world; it can grow to seven feet in length and weigh over 200 pounds. Stories of its strength and liminal transformative power include the idea that it can exact revenge on people, walk on land, and leap from the water to catch small mammals. It has a key position in Mongolian folklore, where local Buddhists believed it to be the child of an ancient river spirit.[8] Shigeru Kayano (Ainu of Hokkaido, Japan) writes that the Ainu carry in their traditional cosmology the belief that the salmon were messengers from the divine (the *kamuy*), especially the first ones of the year (Kayano 1998: 29). As in the Pacific Northwest of the United States, the first salmon of the season is welcomed and celebrated by the Ainu. They offer adornments of shaved-wood decorations—*inawkike*—and other items such as rice and bamboo, which are then sent back to its people with gifts; in response, the salmon return up the rivers in abundance (Oda and Matsui 1998: 128). Liminal reciprocation, facilitated by song, is key to the ceremony across the Pacific Ocean.

The Atlantic salmon is connected to its own sets of beliefs and practices among people of the northern shores. In the Sámi culture of the far north of Europe, the salmon have been historically revered through ritual performance at *seite* or sacred sites that function as gateways to the spirit world, and called through the vocal performance practice of *joik*. Until recently, the joik has been sung unaccompanied, and functions as an evocation of elements of the natural world such as reindeer, salmon, bear, and others. But more than just an evocation, the joik calls others into presence; into *existence* (Ramnarine 2009: 191).

A key point of the joik, however, is that there is a specific recipient for it—rather than an abstract concept—rendering it as an actual dialogue (Hilder 2012: 167). Such dialogic performances are at least partly the territory of the *noaidi* or Sámi spiritual practitioner. Richard Jones-Bamman notes that "the reindeer, the bird, and the fish are described as 'helper' figures to the *noaidi*" (Jones-Bamman 1993: 137). In joiking to evoke the presence of the salmon (or other liminal helper figures), the noaidi are connecting across a very permeable Sámi border. The following translated text of a salmon joik was recorded in 1876:

> The Salmon, that strong and precious fish
> swimming along the bottom.
> It will follow the Tana River through the earth
> if that is the course to follow.
> Once again, it swims the long way to reach the source,
> turns black and stops eating.
> Once again, it turns back to where it came from,
> to the great ocean
> where salmon abound.
> Once again, it glistens in the water
> when it returns
> to its own seas.
> There it will find herring to feed on,
> grow fat again,
> and again look like its old self.[9]

In Ireland, where one of the most famous stories is about the hero-warrior Fionn MacCumhaill and the Salmon of Knowledge, salmon have been celebrated as the keepers of wisdom for centuries. In this story, an elderly man waits fifty years to catch a specific salmon that would grant the knowledge of all things; upon Fionn MacCumhaill's arrival, the salmon is caught. Fionn is asked to watch the salmon cooking and ends up (because it burns his thumb) tasting it before the elderly man. In breaking a protocol, he receives the knowledge (but must chew his thumb to the bone as punishment if he wishes to use that gift). On Tory Island, north of Donegal, women used to refer to their boyfriends or lovers as their "salmon" (*"mo bhradán"*). One of the primary poetry publishing companies in Ireland—in the west-coast city of Galway, with its famous salmon weir—is called Salmon Poetry Press. In contrast to the Pacific salmon and its many species, the Atlantic salmon has only one species, and most people eating Atlantic salmon in maritime Canada and northwestern Europe today are eating farmed salmon. While the farmed Atlantic salmon is still important in the fisheries of Northern Europe, it is the wild salmon that retains its exceptional communicative power and simultaneously central and liminal position in the lives and understandings of the many people who surround the oceans.

Selkies and Seal People

Seals and sea lions spend much of each day in the sea; they haul out on land to sleep, mate, give birth, and nurse their young. They are mammals, breathing with lungs, yet they cannot move easily across the land. Bairbre Ní Fhlionn describes seals as "liminal creatures *par excellence*" as "beings of both land and water, belonging completely to neither element" (Ní Fhlionn 1999: 225). As liminal creatures they gather at a liminal place: the shore. Humans gather at the shore as well, and the two encounter each other frequently. Humans anthropomorphize them repeatedly, whether in real-life sightings at the shore or at an enclosure.

> Is it the round head, is it the large innocent eyes, is it the possibility of comic movement on land (which contrasts so sharply with the weightlessness and elegance with which they glide through the water) that the zoo or seal enclosure visitor cares so much about the animals? (Wulff 2015: 29) [original in German; translation mine]

Mythologies about seals as shapeshifters are particularly focused in the areas of Ireland, Scotland, the Isle of Man, and north to parts of Scandinavia (Morris 1937: 172; Darwin 2015: 123; Christiansen 1958: 75). Sometimes referred to in English as selkies (Scots, "grey seal"), they are usually believed to have the ability to shift between human and seal form, and stories about them involve encounters with (single-shape) humans. Stealing the seal's skin or cloak allegedly binds that creature to the one who steals it as long as the skin is hidden; the folkloric motif of stealing the clothing of a maiden to capture her is not limited to this region. The tale type (AT B650) of the "animal bride" is quite widespread (Almqvist 1990: 1). As for the actual origins of the stories in Ireland and Scotland, people of the far North have used seal skins for clothing, and encounters between Inuit people and those further south occasionally took place. It is not a stretch to imagine people coming ashore, taking off their sealskin clothing, and revealing themselves to be human.

One commercial version of the basic story—depicted in the 1992 film *The Secret of Roan Inish* and set in Donegal—is that a fisherman discovers a seal woman relaxing on the shore (in human form) next to her seal skin; he steals it and "claims" her as his wife. She bears his children and, having discovered where her seal skin is hidden, slips it on and disappears back into the sea. Long before the popular film, the Irish singer and storyteller Joe Heaney (with whom I worked) repeatedly told a much older Connemara version of the story: A young man sees three seals disappear into a cove and return as three young women, leaving three shawls on the beach. He asks an older helper figure how to capture the youngest, then waits for his chance to steal her shawl. At his success, he forces the young seal woman to return to his home as his wife; over time they have five children. One day he returns from fishing, and his house is on fire. His wife has discovered her shawl when it fell out of the rafters in the fire, and she has returned to the sea. Shortly afterward, she meets him at the shore—the threshold—and promises to keep their children safe and provide them with plenty of fresh fish. More recently, the animated film *Song of the Sea* (also allegedly set in Donegal) engages the idea of a child born of a human male and a selkie woman; the child is a selkie herself.

Irish-language versions of the story usually include the stealing of a scarf or cloak, rather than a skin, and the woman herself is called a *maighdean mhara*—a sea maiden—rather than a seal (or, in Scotland, a selkie). She brings prosperity to the family in the form of abundant fish and descendants with great skills in fishing. Gregory Darwin refers to this story as one that "defines the relationship between ordered human society and the primordial wilderness, especially the sea, which is presented as unstable, liminal, and often dangerous" (Darwin 2015: 137). Other beliefs about seals include the idea that seals might actually be elderly folks under a spell, and that stories in which a man wounds a seal often end up with an encounter between the hunter and a woman—often elderly—wounded in exactly the same place on her body (Ní Fhlionn 1999: 230).

Stories about seal women tend to focus on their production of children (never mind the women's abduction and forced acceptance of motherhood); the ensuing relationship of the children and seals leans on their mutual feral nature. And because seals have families and genealogies, certain surnames are associated with the seals: the MacCodrums of North Uist, the Gallaghers of Donegal, the Conneelys of Connemara, and others (Darwin 2015: 124). Stuart Aitken notes that "The idea that child well-being is intimately related to frequent and intimate connections with nature and wild things is pervasive in past and contemporary psychology and popular culture" (Aitken 2010: 13). Bairbre Ní Fhloinn points to these family connections as possible older origin stories; the earliest Irish records of supernatural seals date to the twelfth century (Ní Fhlionn 1999: 238).

Seal men, however, are more volatile as lovers and serve as challengers to the local sense of the masculine (Dennison 1893: 172). In Iceland, the *marmennill* is a seal-man who—rather than shifting between seal and human bodies—looks mostly like a man; perhaps he is a "value-added" man because he knows things that human males do not (Erlingsson 1999: 67). In an Irish-Gaelic story that goes by different names (but conforms to aspects of Aarne-Thompson's "Beauty and the Beast" tale type #425, "The Search for the Lost Husband"), a young woman marries a handsome man who asks her whether she would prefer him as a man at night or a seal in the day. Being a smart woman, she asks him to be a man at night, and they are very happy. He is then stolen by another woman, and our heroine has to use her wits (and the assistance of three helper figures) to regain him for herself. When she does, the spell is broken and he is now—in direct translation from the Irish—"in his manliness" night and day. The Irish language uses a particular grammatical construction—I am in my sleeping, I am in my standing, I am in my manliness, I am in my sealness—that easily supports the liminal concept of shapeshifting.

The anthropomorphizing of seals, regardless of gender, is common. During my first of many visits to Ireland, decades ago, I was sitting alone at the shore on the Dingle Peninsula, watching a seal that was watching me from the water. An elderly man stopped to chat and, noticing the seal watching us, said, "Now there's your man the seal. He doesn't miss a thing." A few minutes later he cautioned me not to "go out there," jerking his chin in the direction of the seal. "He's got all his people down there." As a woman in my twenties, I initially thought his referral to the seal as "your man" was a charming quirk, but I had also read the works of the Irish writer Flann O'Brien (a.k.a. Myles na Gopaleen). In his humorous writing about "the brother," he says the following:

> The brother says the seals near Dublin do often come up out of the water at night-time and do be sittin' above in the trams when they're standin' in the stables. [. . .] Begob the brother says it's a great sight of a moonlight night to see your men with the big moustaches on them sittin' upstairs in the trams lookin' out. And they do have the wives and the young wans along with them, of course. [. . .] The seals are great family people, always were. (O'Brien 1975: 53)

As is often the case with humor, the passage is funny because it is only slightly off-center. While the idea of seals lumbering up the steps of an urban tramway to sit in the moonlight is comical, everyone locally knows that the seals are, in fact, "great family people," and the stories of the seal people highlight that special feature. Because so many families are associated with seals in Ireland, family taboos against killing seals are common.

Some of the stories include songs: not to lure men away, as discussed in Chapter 4, but to enable the seal maidens to sing of their plight or to tell the story from their own perspective. Barbara Hillers points out that "music functions almost as a marker of fairy-otherness; their pursuit of music earmarks the fairies, just like their deathlessness, or their ability to shapeshift, or their diminutive stature" (Hillers 1994: 59). Both songs sung from the perspective of seal people here are performed solo, by humans, in free meter. The song "An Mhaighdean Mhara" ("The Sea Maiden") is sung widely in Ireland, and has its roots in the northwest—in Donegal (Figure 2.1). It is a song of the *sean-nós* or "old style" genre, which focuses on love songs and laments rather than narrative content. In this song, which includes the children's voices as well, the mother laments her fate.

Figure 2.1 "An Mhaighdean Mhara" ("The Sea Maiden")

Is cosúil gur mheath tú nó gur thréig tú an greann

    It seems that you have faded away and abandoned the love of life

Tá an sneachta go frasach fá bhéal na trá

    The snow is spread about at the mouth of the sea

Do chúl buí daite is do bhéílín sámh

    Your yellow flowing hair and little gentle mouth

Siúd chugaibh Mary Chinidh is í i ndiaidh an Éirne shnámh.

    We give you Mary Chinidh to swim forever in the Erne.

'A mháithrín mhilis' dúirt Máire bhán

    'My dear mother,' said blonde Mary

Fá bhruach an chladaigh is fá bhéal na trá

    By the edge of the shore and the mouth of the sea

'Maighdean mhara mo mháithrín ard'

    'A mermaid is my noble mother'

Siúd chugaibh Mary Chinidh is í i ndiaidh an Éirne shnámh.

    We give you Mary Chinidh to swim forever in the Erne.

Tá mise tuirseach agus beidh go lá

    I am tired and will be forever

Mo Mháire bhruinneall is mo Phádraig bán

    My fair Mary and my blond Patrick

Ar bharr na dtonnta is fá bhéal na trá

    On top of the waves and by the mouth of the sea

Siúd chugaibh Mary Chinidh is í i ndiaidh an Éirne shnámh.

    We give you Mary Chinidh to swim forever in the Erne.

Tá an oíche seo dorcha is tá an ghaoth i ndroch aird
The night is dark and the wind is high
Tá an tseisreach 'na seasamh is na spéarthaí go hard
The Plough can be seen high in the sky
Ach ar bharr na dtonnta is fá bhéal na trá
But on top of the waves and by the mouth of the sea
Siúd chugaibh Mary Chinidh is í i ndiaidh an Éirne shnámh.
We give you Mary Chinidh to swim forever in the Erne.

When Joe Heaney, the Connemara sean-nós singer, described singing this song, he referred to the phrase *ar an bharr na dtonnta* (literally "on top of the waves") as referring to the space "between the water." He said to imagine oneself standing in the tide as one sings, with the water up to one's chest, feeling the push and pull of the water to engage in feeling simultaneously of the land and of the sea. He further explained that the seal woman is forever *in between*, but never fully at home in either place.[10]

Similarly, the Scottish-Gaelic song "Òran an Ròin"[11] ("Song of the Seal") is connected to North Uist of the Hebrides. Whereas in Ireland the seal people are known family members, in Scotland, the seal people are a separate species.[12] The lyrics, translated by gifted singer Julie Fowlis, reveal the seals to have their own hierarchies, genealogies, and griefs. The story of this one, according to Fowlis, is that when some young men had killed their share of seals and were cooking seal meat for dinner, they heard this song "coming from an offshore reef."[13] It is from the perspective of a female seal (Figure 2.2).

Hò i hò i hì o hò i
Hò i hò i hì o hò i [sound of the seal]
Hò i hì o hò i ì
Hò i hì o hò i ì
Hò i hò i hì o hò i
Hò i hò i hì o hò i

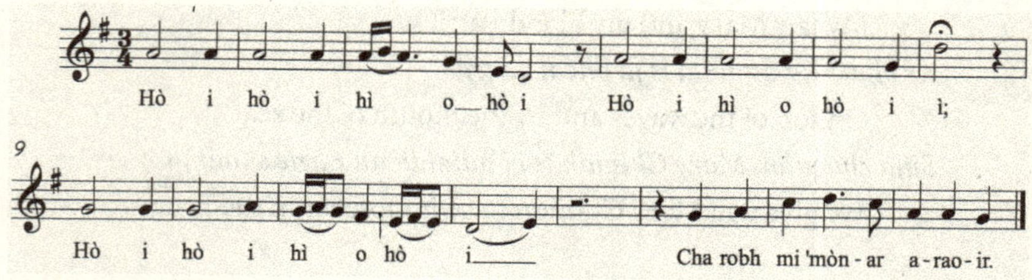

Figure 2.2 "Òran an Ròin" ("Song of the Seal")

Cha robh mi 'm ònar a-raoir.
　　I was not alone last night.

'S mairg san tìr seo, 's mairg san tìr
　　Pity to be in this place
'G ithe dhaoine 'n riochd a bhìdh;
　　Where people are eaten as food
Nach fhaic sibh ceannard an t-sluaigh
　　See the chief of the people
Goil air teine gu cruaidh cruinn.
　　Boiling hard on a fire.

'S mise nighean Aoidh mhic Eòghainn,
　　I am the daughter of Aoidh son of Ewen
Gum b'eòlach mi mu na sgeirean;
　　I was knowledgeable about the reefs
Gur mairg a dhèanadh mo bhualadh
　　Pity the person who would hit me
Bean uasal mi o thìr eile.
　　I am a noble woman from another land.

Thig an smeòrach, thig an druid
　　The thrush comes, the starling comes
Thig gach eun a dh'ionnsaigh nid;
　　Every bird returns to its nest
Thig am bradan thar a' chuain
　　The salmon comes from the sea
Gu Là Luain cha ghluaisear mis'.
　　Until Doom's Day I will not be moved.

In each case, the song comes from a seal to mortals, warning of the danger *to themselves* from the mortals who dared to force marriage on them or kill them for meat. The songs are laments. The connection itself is dangerous. A song from a selkie is a gift in its transmission; humans do not give songs back to the selkies (Hillers 1994: 66). Some seal people teach songs to their children, as on the Orkney Islands north of the Scottish mainland (Dennison 1893: 174). The seal person has a family and a firm presence in Ireland, Scotland, the Isle of Man, and other places in the region. Crucially, she is sometimes depicted as having a singing voice that she may lose forever if she goes to land with a man. The liminal selkie is forever positioned between worlds.

Whale Ancestors

In the case of salmon and seals, at this point we know that humans imbue their own stories and songs with the sense that the salmon and the seal have elements tied to humans and can shapeshift. Whales, on the other hand, are renowned by all, including scientists, for their voices and their songs. Toothed whales (sperm whales, orcas, and belugas) vocalize in clicks, grunts, and high-pitched whistles, while baleen whales (humpbacks, minkes, grays, fins, and blues)—especially humpbacks—produce sustained songs with a very broad pitch range. There are specific historical and biological reasons for the whales' appearance here as shapeshifting leviathans. It is common knowledge that these mammals once walked on the land (approximately 50 million years ago), shifting to the water through stages of evolution as their ability to swim grew more effective over millennia. Even now, the whale fetus briefly has legs during its gestation (and has the vestiges of a pelvis and femurs) but is born with flippers and a fully functioning tail, ready to swim.

Whaling was one of the first global industries; there was trade in whale meat, oil, and blubber by the first millennium BCE. By the start of the Industrial Revolution, whale products were used for lubrication, lighting, and women's products such as flexible boning for corsets (baleen is made of keratin). Whaling technology included steam-powered whale boats and harpoon cannons; the initial techniques for settlers' harpooning and butchering in North America were learned from the Wampanoag people.[14] The widespread adoption of this technology boosted the United States into the position of the world's first superpower, so much so that profits from whaling had helped to finance the American Revolution at the end of the eighteenth century. After the 1859 discovery of petroleum—as the decomposed and compressed remains of marine and freshwater organisms, fossilized with mud into oil shale—the entire whaling industry went into a decline by the early 1900s. In fact, if fossil fuels had not been found to be useful, whales would be a distant memory preserved only in poetry and such literature as Herman

Melville's *Moby-Dick* (1851, prior to the discovery of petroleum), visual arts of the era, and songs.

Whales have been considered mighty creatures for millennia; the leviathan of the Bible and the Talmud includes significant depictions of a great sea monster, but other written and oral epics document their importance from the beginning of the creation of the world.

> And God created great whales, and every living creature that moveth, which the waters brought forth abundantly. (Genesis 1:21, King James version)

> *Hanau ka palaoa noho i kai*—Born is the whale living in the ocean. (the *Kumulipo*, the native Hawaiian genealogical creation *mele* chant)

The *kētŏs* of Ancient Greece, from which the scientific term *cetacean* (aquatic mammal) is derived, is an element in the myth of Perseus and Andromeda. In Indonesia, the whale is known as *ikan paus*, the "pope fish." In Siberia, the whales that washed up onshore were historically offered a drink in Yup'ik communities (Bogoras 1904–1909: 407). In Hawai'i, the *koholā* (whale) is the embodiment of Kanaloa, the ocean deity—one of four primary sacred beings (Aikau and Aikau 2015: 659). The fact that whales are forever between land and sea (as sea mammals) distinguishes them as liminal. While knowledge of whales and their songs and stories is always local, their biology and their ecosystem are international.[15]

Sound, as a physical property, behaves as a wave and propagates as a wave in a medium; in the case of whales and sound, that medium is water. As sound moves through salt water, it encounters points of reflection and intensification depending on whether it meets the surface of the water, the seabed, and water of different density (i.e., higher or lower temperature or salinity). In deep salt water, light does not penetrate well, so animals that live primarily in darkness rely on sound, smell, and touch. Toothed whales (including sperm whales, which figured prominently in the whaling industry) have small eyes but a large organ called a melon in their foreheads, connected to their nasal passages, specifically for sonic communication. Think of it as a sound lens. The beluga whale has the ability to physically alter the shape of its melon to detect and produce sound.

Whales sing by inhaling deeply, then passing air across folds near their lungs as they exhale. The sounds can be heard above water, and although the humpbacks are the most famous for their songs, the other baleen whales sing as well.

> Humpbacks' songs are the most complex; blue whales' may remain stable for decades, scientists have observed. Bowhead whales have one shared song in each population that changes over the mating season. Fin whales produce the simplest songs. Australian experts wondered for 50 years what made a reverberating, blasting sound—until they linked it to the singing of minke whales. (Welch 2021: 60)

The underwater sound channel is at the same level around the world (1,000 meters below sea level); it is of the exact density and salinity to allow sound to travel quickly across thousands of miles with no loss of energy. It is the basic radio frequency of whales and, since the 1940s, underwater military technology. The sound channel is where whales accomplish their transmission and reception of sound. They have just as many hair cells in their ears as humans do, but three times the number of neurons in those hair cells. The chaos of underwater sounds—shifting ice, waves, seismic events, vulcanism, explosives, traffic, drilling—all makes it harder to hear the songs of one's own species.

When male humpback whales sing, they draw from a large repertoire of sounds and arrange them in patterns. The songs are picked up by all the other males in the region, and they change over time—usually across several years—so that certain sounds or patterns are added or dropped. Songs can last from fifteen minutes to up to twenty hours, and the oceans have nine populations with different songs.[16] Occasionally the whales will abruptly change parts of a song and create a new one altogether. Their musical culture stretches across 6,000 miles of ocean sonic channels. In her work on humpback whale song hybridization, Ellen Garland (et al.) noticed that some whales spliced specific song phrases from other whale cultures into existing songs as an element of cultural contact and song evolution (Garland et al 2017: 7822–7829). There are dialects, communities, and arrangements of patterns regardless of the type of whale (Welch 2021: 66). However, whales do not just sing among themselves, and humpbacks are not the only ones to communicate.

In 1986, an Iñupiat whale hunter, Harry Brower, Sr., was lying in a hospital near death—in a deeply liminal state—when he was visited by a bowhead whale calf, which brought him to witness the hunting and killing of its mother by members of Brower's own family in Utqiaġvik in the far north of Alaska. He recovered, correctly identified who had struck the killing blow and who had the meat stored in a locker, and subsequently succeeded in changing the local laws about harvesting female whales with young offspring (Langlois 2018). This level of communication between humans and whales during a liminal time of coma, dream-state, or other out-of-the-ordinary experience is very specific to Indigenous coastal communities of the Pacific Northwest, where months of ritual practices intended to show the whales the respect they deserve would take place before a hunt. Songs are a key point in requesting a single whale to offer itself to hunters in support of the human community.

Hunting has historically been important to the region. However, the whales are also the ancestors, and their yearly migrations offer a chance to check in across many generations. As a speaker from the Kwakwaka'wakw Nation of British Columbia noted, "When the whale comes back, he is coming home. He is the ancestor, returning, making sure all is right; and that we are taking care of the land, and we are taking care of the water, because this is our responsibility as human people. And that's why the ancestors return."[17] As part of the Kwakwaka'wakw performance of the whale dance (accompanied by a song, a frame drum, and a wooden rattle carved into the shape of a whale), the mouth of the whale mask opens to reveal a carving of a human head inside. Whale-shaped rattles and whistles carry the voices across the liminal boundary from the other world (Haines 1999: 24).

Multiple regional tribes—the Makah, the Quileute, the Kwakwaka'wakw, and many others—have had songs and strict protocols regarding whales; songs are connected to hierarchies and reflect ownership of creative work within communities. In many cases, the songs are understood as a gift from a whale to members of the community. The Quileute people tell a story about a twelve-year-old (liminally pubescent) boy swept into the sea during a whale hunt; he survived but said this: "The whale told me to crawl down the rope to him. As I did this, a bubble of air from his blow hole surrounded me. Then the whale began singing a beautiful song. I hung on and listened. When we started toward the surface, we came through different layers. Each layer was of a different color and had a different song. Each song was more beautiful than the last. Then, when we surfaced, I fell asleep" (Smyth 1999: x). Helma Swan (Makah) discussed the use of songs for inviting whales, pointing out that "most songs connected with hunting, fishing, whaling, and warfare have faded from memory," but stressed the importance of music in maintaining the balance and function of tribal society (Goodman and Swan 1999: 84). Whales also appear vividly in regional visual arts, such as button blankets, drums, rattles, prints, and carvings.

Kirk Oviok (Iñupiat) of Point Hope, Alaska, is quoted as saying "Like my aunt said, the whales have ears and are more like people. The first batch of whales seen would show up to check which ones in the whaling crew would be more hospitable . . . Then the whales would come back to their pack and tell them about the situation" (Roburn 2013: 115). In Hawai'i, the whales migrate to give birth and nurse their young in warmth and safety, but also to visit those who honor them as part of the liminally reciprocal pantheon of ancestor spirits or 'aumākua.[18] The perceived near-humanity of whales—the essence of their liminality because of the fact that they breathe, sing, carry messages, and connect to humans at times of vulnerability—includes their ability to communicate with their own kind across thousands of miles. The reciprocal offering of their songs and bodies to those people who follow careful protocols on land is a powerful, sacred combination that sustains coastal communities. It points to a profound network of whales and humans, and the transcendent combination of spirituality and science in the sacred singing body.

Winged Messengers to the Spirit World—Birds, Angels, and Insects

All types of birds are considered to be spirits of the heavens. (Duvan 1998: 91)

Creatures with wings have inspired humans in our dreams of flight, wishes for a different view of the world, and hopes of access to a unique understanding of what's "out there" beyond our comprehension. Nadyezhda Duvan (Ulchi of Siberia) situates the birds in a significant local animist cosmology in which "everything in existence [functions] as living beings endowed with reason, spirit and power. Mountains, rivers, lakes, oceans, rocks and forests all have their own spirit master" (Duvan 1998: 91). She is not alone in this belief. Because birds can fly anywhere, and because they are the *only* creatures with the natural ability to walk, swim, fly, and sing, they receive considerable notice and incorporation into human spiritual practices and oral cultures in many areas of the world.

When birds are recognized for their spiritual significance, the powers they embody can imbue a family with a sense of the bird's ongoing presence and protection or assistance. The sound of these birds' voices reverberates along channels of inter-species communication beyond the limits of human hearing, for these voices are apprehended at a deep level that connects ancestors with their descendants and with the spirit beings of forests, mountains, and waters. (Sault 2020: 60)

As we imagine birds' greater capacity of knowing the world (a "bird's-eye view"), we ascribe to birds the ability to see and understand the things we cannot, placing them as a mediating force in the liminal place between seen and not seen. And that leads directly to our sense that they must have capacities for perception, in the larger sense, greater than our own. That, in turn, enables birds to connect to places and beings that are beyond us, such as the ancestors, the spirit world, the past, and the future.

> The two-wing animals.
> They are the ones that fly above us.
> They are the ones that see above us.
> They are the ones that see the future in front of us.
> —Alex Gwinn, Mandan-Hidatsa elder (Chandler et al. 2016: iv)

This information falls under the category of ethno-ornithology, "the comparative study of the knowledge of birds held by human communities throughout the world" (Hunn and Thornton 2010: 182). Birds are among the first creatures to appear in many stories of the Creation, and ethno-ornithologists point out "that people first learned to talk from birds, and that birds are the intermediaries with the deities" (Sault 2020: 65). In the context of communicating with elements of the spirit world, the birds—like the sea creatures from earlier in this chapter—occupy a powerful liminal role that transcends the normal capabilities of humans. The Romans developed what was for them the practice of ornithomancy—divination through birds—which we still have today in the word *inauguration*: obtaining the favorable sanction from the spirit world by reading omens in the flight of birds. But the Romans were late on the scene in terms of the larger systems at work across the globe.

This section of the chapter features the condor, the raven, and the owl.[19] As the renowned folklorist—and my beloved late professor—Alan Dundes has written, using threes as a system of organization "is part of the nature of culture" (Dundes 1980: 159).[20] The eagle, the crow, the swan, and many others have importance as well, but the birds in this section are significant in large portions of the world. Even if I have limited the bulk of this section to just three examples, however, birds appear nearly everywhere as a key element in local beliefs and practices. In his discussion of the KhoeSan of the Kalahari, Chris Low describes a type of "potency" as a near-shorthand for the more vague sense of magical agency ascribed to birds; he identifies a network of potency along which birds and spiritual intermediaries travel to communicate messages, cure or cause sickness, and do other extraordinary things (Low 2011: 297). Birds are celebrated in representation as well. "At the national level birds are represented in flags and statuary, such as the eagle on the cactus of the Mexican flag. At the local level birds are honored and celebrated, expressing totemic relationships to ancestors belonging to descent groups like clans or as members of extended kind networks" (Sault 2020: 59). In Panama, for example, the bird songs and calls appear "between the invisible and the human worlds as they inform people of new birth and impending death. Because songs and calls depart and are distinct from the avian bodies that produce them, they can travel across the space of the imagination as well as physical space" (Kane 2015: 35). Birds are both liminal and important everywhere.

In the great flyway of the North American plains, John James Audubon (1785–1851) was one of the earliest settler record keepers of the birds (and the best-known), but the Indigenous people had long been well aware of the patterns and individual species of birds, and had built an extensive oral culture about the birds as messengers and communicators with their own agency. This agency "transcends human-bird reciprocation; it extends this sociality to human-object (bird parts), human-landscape (bird habitats and features associated with bird trapping), and bird-ancestor (bird reincarnations of human souls) 'entanglements'" (Chandler et al. 2016: 2). And yet, bird talk goes both ways; people receive their avian communications and can respond individually, but also "address birds in ritual contexts officiated by local leaders" (Sault 2020: 65). It is the ritual performance of music and movement that is the most closely documented of these interactions.

Birds are often assigned human characteristics as parts of stories; referring to them as people who have conversations, play tricks, learn morals and good behavior, and function as community members is common. The stories serve the greater function of conveying information about "social proprieties, morals, relationships, landscape and the law" (Tidemann and Whiteside 2010: 154). Understanding bird language (both sung and embodied) for something as common as reading weather patterns or as complex as taking advice on one's next move in battle has been part of the historical training of young people (Davidson 1988: 187, in reference to the *Edda*, the Icelandic poetic saga). People in many areas of the world use bird imagery, as well as actual body parts of birds, to enable designated representatives from different cultures to more fully grasp something of what birds themselves experience, and to convey that experience through stories, songs, movement, and other elements of oral tradition.

The Condor

In the Andes, the condor (a large vulture whose English name derives from Quechua, *kuntur*) has a wingspan that can extend beyond ten feet; its very large size helps it to loom large in Andean mythologies.[21] The national symbol of Peru, Bolivia, Argentina, Ecuador, Chile, Venezuela, and Colombia, condors are associated with the sun and the heavens. The fact that, once they are in the air, they generally rely entirely on soaring for hours rather than ever flapping their wings has given them a kind of extra-avian status, as if they are exempt from flying like "normal" birds. They are documented as flapping their wings just 1 percent of the time they're aloft. The image of the condor appears on stamps, coins, flags, shields, and t-shirts.[22]

> From the mountains of Machu Picchu to the coast of Paracas, condors are depicted in textiles, ceramics, carvings, astronomy, medicine, place names, kinship and politics. (Sault 2020: 63)

The condor plays an important role in local oral narrative traditions. For example, in the story of Quni Raya—an Incan creator deity, also known as Huiracocha—the condor serves to assist Quni Raya in locating Qawi Llaqa, the human mother of his child. In response, Quni Raya praises the condor along with other highland creatures that assist him, calling the condor a "master of the animals" and the "chief of birds" (Harrison 1989: 105). And even though Christianity has been present for several hundred years in the Andes, it has not altered the fact that the secular and spiritual worlds are joined in daily life. The *apus* or mountain deities populate the highlands, take the shape of animals or humans, and can speak to secular humans directly, including in the shape of a condor (Sáenz 2017: 444). As a primary intermediary, the condor is the supreme authority that connects the three Andean worlds of sky, earth, and underworld (Jacques-Coper et al 2019: 36).

Though they do not sing, they nonetheless are believed to have voices. "Condors are prominent in Andean songs, dances, dreams, and ceremonies, for they represent the spirits of mountain deities or *Apus*. Condors are the embodiment of these deities, sent as their messengers" (Sault 2020: 63). Because healers have a close relationship with the mountain deities, both the healer and the condor serve as the intermediaries; the mountains themselves can transform into condors in order to enter a house with the assistance of a healer (Sáenz 2017: 449). This rich and complicated system of transformation happens with the assistance of one or more small bells, spoken words, and ritual actions leading to spirit possession and, ultimately, resolution of an issue or illness.

Even without a voice that sounds particularly musical to human ears, the body of the condor contributes to musical spiritual practice. Its feathers, in flight, produce a distinct hissing sound that can be heard up to a kilometer away. In addition, condor bones have been used to create flutes and panpipes (Sault 2020: 62). The use of wind instruments made with condor bones dates to at least 2500 BCE from Caral, Peru (Barber et al. 2009:94); while the voice, the bell, and ritual practices connect humans with condors, the condor bodies themselves also serve this important purpose.

All of this ignores the fact that Christianity has had a significant impact on the transmission of local knowledge. Speaking directly to a condor is less likely when one has been raised in a Pentecostal situation, for example (Jacques-Coper et al. 2019: 41). Instead, the evangelical surge in the Andes is likely to view the Apus in the mountains as representations of the Devil. Over time, the local sense of the condor as a powerful intermediary has begun to devolve to more of a two-dimensional generic symbol of local Andean (or national—Chilean, Venezuelan, Peruvian) identity than as a real-life conduit to the other worlds of the Andean sacred topography.

The Raven

The raven and the crow are usually distinguished by size, with the raven being the larger of the two. The sacred raven appears in the Bible and the Qur'an, in Celtic and Nordic mythologies, and in some Indigenous Australian and Chinese stories as an ancestor; in Alaska, the raven has specific marked territories where great scrapes and geological features abound. In Bhutan, the raven is the national bird and appears prominently as a Hindu-Buddhist protector figure, Mahākala ("Great Black One"). He also appears as Kutkh among many Indigenous groups of coastal Siberia, such as the Chukchi, Itelmens, and Koryaks, bringing light, fire, language, sex, and other elements to the world (Bogoras 1902: 637). In the traditions of Chinese oral narratives, the raven has been deployed to justify expanding agriculture, facilitate invasions, and function as both a driver and resilient respondent to political and environmental change (Thornton and Thornton 2015: 74). The Norse god Odin is often depicted with the two speaking ravens Huginn ("Thought") and Muninn ("Memory")—one on each shoulder—as special advisors.

Raven is a significant character in the Indigenous stories of the Pacific Northwest of North America, Asia, and elsewhere. To the Tlingit of southeast Alaska, the local social structure divides into two matrilineal clans: Raven and Eagle. People acknowledge their historical affiliations with each (Hunn and Thornton 2010: 184). Raven brought the drum (Thornton and Thornton 2015: 75) to the people as well; it is the central instrument of the region. To the Tsimshian, Haida, Nunivak, Kwakwaka'wakw, and many other regional tribes, he is a powerful liminal trickster figure who exhibits human characteristics. Tricksters generally inhabit two worlds simultaneously—the spirit world and the human world—and draw advantages from both. In many cases, they emerge as a "culture-hero, specifically as a transformer who makes the world habitable for humans by ridding it of monsters or who provides those things (such as fire or various ways of capturing animals) that make human society possible" (Carroll 1981: 305). They can also make mistakes with significant consequences to themselves or others. Raven mediates "between the non-material and the concrete" (Jensen 1980: 161), and when he isn't flying, he can be spotted primarily in two liminal places: the beach (between sea and shore) and the tree (between earth and sky).

For the Yup'ik (a larger category encompassing numerous local groups) of Alaska and the Bering Strait, Raven created the first woman, brought the sun, created the land forms, communicates with all the other creatures, sings, dances, and features prominently in moral lessons (Fienup-Riordan 2017: 220). Raven was once renowned for the beauty of his feathers and for his fine singing voice, but—being a trickster—his deeds (including releasing the sun, moon, and stars into the sky) resulted in his feathers becoming blackened by soot and his voice becoming harsh from the smoke of a fire.[23]

> His [Raven's] stories illustrate, above all, the animistic moral-ecological world that Tlingits inhabit in which non-human actors, whether they are Brown Cormorant, 'the Old Woman of the Tides' or Brown Bear, respond to other actors according to a covenant of reciprocity and respect, which when violated can produce personal, social and even cosmic repercussions. (Hunn and Thornton 2010: 185)

In terms of raven intelligence, their brains contain more neurons than many mammals; their cognitive capabilities mirror those of the great apes (Olkowicz et al. 2016: 7255). Recognizing the exceptional skills of the raven in locating food, communication, play, and complex behaviors, the people consistently used stories about them "as a way to code knowledge and stimulate memory in ways that aided in their survival" (Pierotti 2020: 50). As they did this, whether in song, movement, or storytelling, the ravens continued to bestow their gifts of access to the sky, to other animals, and to the ancestors.

The Owl

The very specific liminality of the owls—hovering between good and evil, healing and illness, or life and death—renders them simultaneously powerful, honored, and feared. Prohibitions against killing owls are widespread, at least partly because of the sense that they may be messengers to the ancestors or to the gods. Owls have been described as the "master messengers" in Indigenous traditions of North America, and can be "at once a fearful creature and a healer, a messenger, and the tool of a trickster to get around a strict taboo" (Chandler et al. 2016: 53). Their many names can reflect their capabilities, as in the Yup'ik (Siberia to Alaska) names for birds that can transform into humans, speak with human voices, and other skills (Krupnik 2017: 190); they do not necessarily have Latin names. In the Missouri River area, owls and their calls indicated misfortune, yet they also appear in local origin stories as teachers, healers, and protectors (Chandler et al. 2016: 43–45).

The Ainu of northern Japan perform *kamuy yukar*, a type of song that features a nature spirit speaking in the first person; these songs are sung by women. In the song "Silver Droplets Fall, Fall, All Around," the owl—through a woman serving as an intermediary—sings about how it was respected and, when received with honor, bestowed riches upon those who received its presence in their midst. As the guardian god of the village, the owl god conveys important lessons through his song as he tells his own story.[24] The lyrics begin with the point of view of the owl.

> "Silver droplets fall fall all around me
> Golden droplets fall fall all around me." So singing
> I went down along the river's flow, above the human village
> As I looked down below. (Yukie 2015: 131–136)

The owl takes note, in the song, of the ways in which paupers have become rich, and the rich have become paupers. It relates the story of visiting a poor family who treated him with deep respect and honor in words and deeds. In return, the guardian owl god rewards the family with riches, and points out that their relationship continues in reciprocity through the years that follow.

Owls are often associated with women in mythology. In Bengal—India—the goddess Lakshmi is often depicted with a white owl. As she is associated with abundance and wisdom, so is the owl. As her *vahana* or sacred vehicle, the owl is a smart and strategic hunter. In Ancient Greece, the owl is associated with Athena, the goddess of wisdom and the patron deity of Athens. Depictions of the owl have appeared all over Athens (on coins, vases, and other media). In Rome, the owl was the favorite bird of the goddess Minerva, the goddess of music, medicine, and other essentials. The owl, in connection with the goddess, is very much about providing access: to wealth, to knowledge, to music.

Some members of the Indigenous people of Australia include owls as messengers to the "Skyworld" (Clarke 2007: 142), and their prominence across multiple language groups signals the presence of the owl as part of a larger system of local beliefs. Its nighttime flight and its night vision are elements of Australian traditional beliefs that it is primarily malevolent and assumed in some areas to be an agent "of the supernatural, sickness, and death."[25] Yet its presence can also be connected to the role of assistant totem, in anthropological terms, wherein it serves alongside a local healer. In North America, a Blackfoot elder was quoted discussing owls teaching him songs to heal people: "They said, 'Now, watch us and we shall give you power to cure disease.' So they taught me songs and how to use them when doctoring the sick. I have used these songs to cure many people" (Wissler 1912: 81). As messengers, healers, and singers, owls are among the most prominent and celebrated in their liminal connection to the spirit world.

Among the mainstream religions, birds (and their counterparts, angels) have long performed communication with the divine. In Buddhism, Jainism, and Hinduism, the mighty Garudas are hybrid shapeshifter birdmen with the body of a man and the head, wings, and talons of an eagle. As a singular god-being, Garuda carries the Lord Vishnu through the sky and serves as a powerful protector figure, about whom songs are created and sung. In both the Qur'an and the Hadith—the most important written texts of Islam—birds receive special mention. Muhammad expresses sympathy for the feelings of birds, encourages his followers to set birds free, and mentions them as being supported in their flight by Allah (Qur'an 16:79).

Judeo-Christianity has been rich in stories about birds and their liminal messaging. Part of the Old Testament—sacred to both Jews and Christians—builds ample support for both birds and—see below—angels. The dove appears repeatedly as the bearer of an olive branch (a sign of land during the flood), and as a harbinger of peace. In Job 12:7–9, the passage "But ask the animals and they will teach you, or the birds in the sky, and they will tell you" indicates the degree to which levels of understanding the natural world have been facilitated through religious protocols involving birds. King Solomon, the son of King David, is said to have received significant wisdom and guidance from birds, especially the hoopoe (with its spectacular feather crown); it told him about the Queen of Sheba's wealthy land in the east.

The eagle has seen particular importance in both the Old and New Testaments. In Exodus 19:1–6, God tells Moses that "I carried you on eagles' wings" to safety. This passage in Isaiah 40:31—"Those hoping in Jehovah will regain power. They will soar on wings like eagles"—is a clear indication that believers will gain access to power and (metaphorical) altitude. It serves as a metaphor for the resurrection of Christ (rising to the sky as an eagle does), so the implication is that others can be resurrected as well. Of the four Evangelists, St. John is associated with the eagle, a symbol of the sky (and, generally, the king of birds in European traditions). In depictions of the *Tetramorph* (Greek, "four shapes," referring in this case to artistic renditions of the four Evangelists), St. John and the other three Evangelists are shown either with their animal symbols or physically blended. The eagle of St. John, depicted alone, sometimes holds a book representing the Logos—the Word, central to Christianity. St. John's gospel takes more of a bird's-eye view of

Christ (the Ascension, the divine nature, etc.) than that of Saints Matthew, Mark, or Luke.

A number of birds are said to have tried to help Jesus while he was on the cross by pulling at the thorns in the crown and the nails in his hands. St. Francis of Assisi (b. 1182 CE) is the patron saint of ecologists,[26] and is said to have ministered directly to the birds by reminding them that God "made you free and gave you the purity of the air," chastising himself afterward because he had previously neglected to communicate with them (Armstrong et al. 2004: 330). In turn, birds would flock to him to express their devotion to God, using him as an intermediary. Finally, St. Kevin of Glendalough (498–618 CE, Ireland) is famously said to have had his arms outstretched in prayer when a blackbird landed and laid its eggs in his hand.[27] As someone renowned for his wish to isolate from other humans, St. Kevin's performance of "green martyrdom" (joining the company of nature rather than the company of other humans) was amply illustrated by his relationship to the blackbird. He stayed in a praying position so the bird's eggs could hatch, grow, and fledge, even though an angel told him he had already done his duty (Swartzlander 1988: 478).

Angels

Mainstream religious traditions—Judaism, Christianity, Islam, Buddhism, and Hinduism—all celebrate the power and importance of subdeities in communicating across the liminal boundaries between life and death, and boundaries between humans and the divine. In the Old and New Testaments, the presence of angels as protectors and messengers is strong. The etymology of angel makes their messaging task central to their definition: *angelos* (Greek, "messenger, envoy"). Cherubim are animal–human hybrids charged with guarding duties (Ezekiel 10:20–21), while the Seraphim were the singers, surrounding God with songs of praise (Isaiah 6:3). Angels appeared to the shepherds at the birth of Jesus, singing (Luke 2:13–14). But these are not the only avian humanoids.

In Hinduism, the deities such as the *gandharvas* (sacred musicians), *apsaras* (sacred dancers), and so many others are not seen as a path to a central deity. Instead, they are worshiped directly and propitiated through ritual and other performative acts, gestures, and sayings. Music and dance are often a direct way of engaging with the deities (see the section on the *apsaras* in Chapter 4). In Hinduism, it is the embodiment of the arts that serves as the intermediary. In Buddhism, *devas* or spiritual subdeities have different gradations depending on how far they have come along the path to enlightenment. Unlike Judeo-Christian angels, however, they are not immortal; they sometimes serve in a protective function.

Gabriel also features strongly in the Old Testament Books of Daniel and Ezekiel as a messenger and guardian angel of Israel; the one who announced to Mary that her life was about to change (Luke 1:26–38); and the one who is popularly believed to blow a trumpet to announce the resurrection of the dead. Although Gabriel is never actually assigned to that task anywhere in the Bible, as one of the most important messenger angels, he would be the one to play the music announcing the transition. Islam features Jibrīl (Gabriel), the *malāk* (Arabic, "messenger"), as the direct source of the holy Qur'an from God.

While they have many other roles in the various holy scriptures, this discussion centers on the angels' links with birds, who also sing and communicate across the same boundaries. Because birds have historically fulfilled the messenger role to and from humans and the divine in many areas of the world, the fact that birds would eventually be depicted as winged creatures with human heads should not surprise anyone. As liminal bird-people whose function is to communicate with the divine, angels fulfill a very old role. Whether their function is primarily one of communicating news, teaching a song or augury through their songs and movements, or contacting the gods and ancestors, birds and angels loom particularly large in the world's spiritual traditions.

Insects

Bees, especially honeybees, are renowned liminal messengers, and this chapter would see diminishment without a mention of them. The most obvious form of communication that honeybees practice—dancing to indicate the direction of flower pollen availability—reveals that even without the spiritual element, they communicate effectively among themselves. That may have prompted the first people to tell the bees when someone has died, in the hopes that they will pass on that information to the spirit world (Burnside 2015: 29). In my own childhood in Berkeley, my best friend's grandmother (an African-American woman from Alabama, born in the nineteenth century) talked about telling the bees any kind of news so that they would carry it home to Alabama where her family members remained. A quick perusal of folk and literary sources online will reveal plenty of stories about "telling the bees"[28] with greater and lesser degrees of accuracy. However, the truth of a story is not nearly as important as the fact that *the story is told*.

Cicadas—according to the Ancient Greeks—were once singing humans. They praised the Muses and were so caught up in their singing and dancing that they forgot to eat or sleep. They died in their ecstasy. The Greek gods rewarded their devotion with immortality, so they arise from dormancy periodically to sing and dance once more. In China, they are a symbol of resurrection; corpses were buried with a jade cicada placed on the tongue. In Japan, they have come to symbolize the sound of summer. Any TV show or film set in the summer includes the ringing song of cicadas in the background. The poets Basho, Issa, and Shiki all dedicated poems to the cicada; the larger connection of the sound of the cicada with the ephemeral, liminal nature of life isn't lost on the reader.

> The cry of the cicada
> Gives us no sign
> That presently it will die.
> > —Matsuo Basho (1643–1694)

> While a cicada
> sings softly
> a single leaf falls ...
> > —Kobayashi Issa (1763–1828)

> As thunder recedes
> a lone tree stands illuminated in sunlight:
> applauded by cicadas
> > —Masaoka Shiki (1867–1920)

The Hawaiian quotation at the beginning of the chapter ("All knowledge is not learned in just one school") points to the fact that drawing from many different resources can build a structure that houses a larger point. In each case visited by this chapter—whether thinking about techniques of communication; engaging contact with specific liminal creatures; or being in touch with the ancestors through songs, movement, and imagery—we come to the issue of access across the binary of *here* and *not-here*. While humans long for access to knowledge, food, health, natural resources, or the divine, they cannot cross those borders without an intermediary. The cultures and sea and sky creatures that form part of this work are highly localized but still-living traditions with boundary-crossing intermediaries.

3

Liminalities of Faith

Music is the language of the spirit. (Kahlil Gibran, Lebanon)

This chapter is an exploration of the liminal experience of belonging to one faith tradition and simultaneously following or incorporating another, performing the music associated with both. The other faith tradition might be very local, or a mystic (or vernacular) sect of a mainstream one, or a different mainstream tradition altogether. What makes the experience liminal is the coexistence of two faith traditions in one person. Is it an expansion of the primary faith? Is it the ability to recognize the spiritual validity of more than one tradition? Is it about the importance of music in spiritual practice regardless of the location? Hinduism and Buddhism have easily coexisted in various parts of the world, for example, because Hinduism is more absorptive than exclusionary. The primary focus of this chapter is the simultaneous performance of Islam and Hinduism within a single genre from Indonesia called *tembang Sunda*. Yet Indonesia is not by any means the only place where it can happen. This chapter also includes discussions of musical encounters between Catholicism and other faith traditions—in Ireland and Brazil—as well as the connections between Shintōism and Buddhism in Japan.

Before entering a discussion of those regions and faiths, however, it is worth pointing out that multiple faith traditions feature a liminal state of suspension—and sometimes, spiritual cleansing—that occurs immediately following death. Note the qualifier of "some," because not everyone believes the same way, even when it is a matter of doctrine. Each one of these is much more complicated than what could be covered in a single chapter. Where the faiths differ is what happens *after* the liminal state is complete: some go to a version of a better/worse place for eternity, while some transition to a new being or a higher plane of existence. However, the existence of a liminal state after death is a normal occurrence and an expectation for many. Because this

Music at the Threshold from the Sacred to the Dangerous. Sean Williams, Oxford University Press. © Oxford University Press 2026. DOI: 10.1093/9780197761762.003.0003

liminal state does not generally feature the presence of live music, however, it does not appear in the chapter.

The human voice—whether chanting or singing or reading in a type of heightened speech—is a part of every mainstream faith tradition and many minor ones. In its communicative and connective role, it serves as an exemplar of sacred liminality. Just as people use their faith to help make sense of the world, people use their voices to facilitate their faith practices. It moves fluidly through the human body and follows the breath. As mentioned in Chapter 1, the root source of the English word spirit—*spiritus*, from Latin—means "breath." Spirit *is* breath. And because the human voice must appear as an element of breathing, it is often venerated in the belief that it is connected to the spirit. Inspire (breathe in), respire (breathe again), transpire (breathe across), perspire (breathe through), suspire (breathe under [sigh]), and expire (breathe out) are all related. Conspire (breathe together) is what humans do as they speak, recite, chant, sing, and pray.[1]

The voice appears later in this chapter as a way to highlight the appearance of Indonesian Islamic modernism in an older Hindu-based musical genre. Before that featured section, however, the chapter explores blended musical situations from Ireland, Japan, and Brazil to get a sense of some of the ways in which two seemingly contrastive spiritual ideas can exist side by side and in the body of the same person or community. As Marc Gidal writes in connection with Brazilian syncretic faith practices, "Music can help explain the coexistence of multiple religions and practices within individual worship houses and a larger multi-faith community" (Gidal 2016: 163). It is precisely the moving-at-the-edge boundary works of performing arts practitioners that enable two or more faiths to thrive in one community, or in a single person.

Dual Faith Traditions

To be of dual faiths is to lean confidently into more than one faith tradition, knowing that each one offers fulfillment, structure, context, safety, and confidence in one's beliefs and actions. These faith traditions are often complementary and inclusive; other times they are radically different. In many ways, it is a simple version of syncretism, in which more than one system interweaves and become something different ("greater than the sum of its parts," as some of us learned in school). Because the existence of *any* pure type of faith would be a challenge to prove or maintain, it is simply easier to recognize that—as in music—exploring the manifestation of a religious tradition in the richness of its many contexts is more likely to yield interesting fruit than simply exploring the scripture (or music theory) isolated from context.[2] In doing this work, musical elements tend to be central to the act of syncretism and to the engagement with the divine.

The Old (and New) Ways in Ireland

Ireland is famously Catholic,[3] and its home celebration of the most famous of its three primary saints—Saint Patrick—has historically been eclipsed by chaotic celebrations in North America, Australia, and elsewhere. From the arrival of Patrick in the fifth century CE, Ireland developed a rather specific branch of Catholicism that has sometimes existed in oblique opposition to the expression of Catholicism as it has been espoused by Rome. In its first several centuries, Catholicism in Ireland was rather like the existing—pre-Catholic—systems of spirituality that functioned with regional variations. For example, the reverence for the natural world and the belief that all things have agency are built into the Irish-Gaelic language, which only sometimes places human beings as the subject of a sentence, and is just as likely to regard a cat, a stream, or a boat as capable of experiencing agency, emotion, and decision-making skills. Similarly, the belief in chthonic entities—spirits, fairies, and giants—has persisted in ways that have led some Irish people to foreground rituals and customs designed to appease those beings and to ensure a sense of order and rightness, beyond what mainstream Catholic beliefs require. Over the centuries, Irish Catholicism has been drawn more closely into line with Rome during two specific occasions: the twelfth century, when a set of structural reforms took place, and the nineteenth century, when Ireland experienced its Devotional Revolution (1850–1880).[4]

Catholicism was outlawed in Ireland in the seventeenth century as part of English colonialism; while it lasted, a number of penal laws were instituted—such as placing a bounty on priests' heads—that caused mainstream Irish Catholicism to shift out of power and visibility, and priests became scarce. An array of pre-existing, vernacular, independent, female-driven set of Irish-Gaelic devotional practices revived to fill the space. Among those practices included patterns (pre-Christian processions and social celebrations), rituals connected to sacred springs and wells, and seasonal celebrations, among many other activities. Most of Ireland's rivers are named for goddesses, and the land itself is gendered female; Ireland (modern Irish: Éire) is named for the goddess Ériu. In addition, although the penal laws aimed against the practice of Catholicism had faded by the nineteenth century, and the Devotional Revolution appeared to fully reinstate an orthodoxy that would disavow any vernacular practices, the folkloric elements of Irish traditional religious practices have persisted, particularly among Irish-speaking people.

A series of devotional songs developed over several hundred years in direct opposition to the official disapproval of Irish-Gaelic vernacular Catholicism. These songs "spoke to the heart of local spiritualities, persisting into the 20th century, despite continual hostility from the reorganized Catholic Church after 1850" (Williams and Ó Laoire 2011: 93). Vernacular devotional song has focused primarily on the life and suffering of Mary, the mother of Jesus, as a representation of lay motherhood. Because private religious singing—not scriptural recitation—has been one of many tasks that fall within the purview of women, the public expression of Catholicism in the twentieth and twenty-first centuries has generally been through the male viewpoint. Currently, approximately one-fourth of Catholics actually attend weekly Mass in Ireland; of those attendees, two-thirds are women. Yet these public matters of who attends Mass do not reflect private practices; plenty of Catholic women maintain their spiritual practices outside the walls of the churchyard.

Three Irish-language songs form a central focus of vernacular spiritual practice; though each one is connected to events in the lives of Jesus and Mary, they are emphatically outside the mainstream of Catholic doctrine. The songs—"Caoineadh na dTrí Muire," "Dán Oíche Nollaig," and "Amhráin na Páise" (Lament of the Three Marys, Poem of Christmas Eve, and Song of the Passion of Christ)—refer to events in the life of Jesus largely from the perspectives of both Mary and Jesus. Mary's own words in the Bible are limited to four occasions: the Annunciation (when she speaks to Gabriel—Luke 1:34–38); her Magnificat or recitation of the goodness of God (to her cousin Elizabeth—Luke 1:46–56); her scolding of Jesus when he is found in the temple (Luke 2:41–52); and when she points out the lack of wine at the wedding at Cana and tells the servants to do what Jesus tells them (John 2:3–5).[5] In Irish-Gaelic song tradition, the three vernacular songs place Mary directly in the position of suffering, and "Caoineadh na dTrí Muire"—"Lament of the Three Marys"—in particular connects to that (Figure 3.1).

Figure 3.1   "Caoineadh na dTrí Muire" ("Lament of the Three Marys")

A Pheadair a aspail, an bhfaca thú mo ghrá bán? (Ochón, is ochón ó)

Chonaic mé ar ball é dhá chéasadh ag an ngarda (Ochón, is ochón ó)

Cé hé an fear breá sin ar Chrann na Páise?

An é nach n-aithníonn tú do Mhac, a Mháithrín?

An é sin an Maicín a d'iompair mé trí ráithe?

An é sin an Maicín a rugadh in sa stábla?

An é sin an Maicín a hoileadh in ucht Mháire?

A mhicín mhuirneach, tá do bhéal 's do shróinín gearrtha.

Is cuireadh calla rúin ar le spídiúlacht óna naimhid

Is cuireadh an coróin spíonta ar a mhullach álainn

Crochadh suas é ar ghuaillí arda

Is buaileadh anuas é faoi leacrachaí na sráide

Cuireadh go Cnoc Chailbhearaí é ag méadú ar a Pháise

Bhí sé ag iompar na Croiche agus Simon lena shála

Buailigí mé féin ach ná bainidh le mo mháithrín

Marómuid thú féin agus buailfimid do mháithrín

Cuireadh tairní maola thrí throithe a chosa agus a lámha

Cuireadh an tslea trí na bhrollach álainn.

Éist a mháthair, is ná bí cráite

Tá mná mo caointe le bre fós a mháthairín.

Oh Peter, apostle, did you see my loved one? (Alas, oh, alas)

I saw him some time ago, tormented by his enemies (Alas, oh, alas)

Who is that fine man on the Cross of Passion?

Don't you recognize your own son, mother?

Is that the son I carried for three trimesters?

Is that the son that was born in the stable?

Is that the son that I reared on my knees?

My dearest little son, your mouth and nose are bleeding.

They dressed him in purple and spat on him with scorn

They put a spiny crown on his beautiful forehead.

They lifted his mother up high on their shoulders
And threw her down on the flagstones of the street.
He was taken to Calvary Hill to hasten his Passion
He carried the cross and Simon helping him
Beat myself, but do not touch my mother
We'll kill yourself and we'll beat your mother
There were blunt nails put through his hands and feet
There was a sword put through his beautiful chest.
Listen, Mother, and don't be grieving
The women who'll weep for me have yet to be born

This song features ritualized lamenting words—*óchón, is óchón ó*—at the end of each phrase; the use of the word *óchón* (alas) was common for centuries among older women—*bean chaointe*—whose position was to mourn the dead. The Irish wake, at which members of the family and community come together to keep the deceased person company for a period of time, featured these women in small groups, chanting or reciting *óchón* ("alas") and expressing the grief of the community. Described by Patricia Lysaght as maintaining a central position in lamenting the dead (Lysaght 1997: 65–66), these women appear in every depiction of this important death ritual. In the 1841 painting "The Aran Fisherman's Dead Child" by Frederic William Burton (Figure 3.2), the keening women to the right are expressing the grief of the community. "In this worldview, religious experience is not something cool, detached, and intellectually discrete. Rather, it is an embodied, verbal, and musical rhetoric of emotional expression, ecstatic and transformative in delivery" (Williams and Ó Laoire 2024: 5). Women who sing "Caoineadh na dTrí Muire" are engaging in their own grief process, privately connecting their sung words and lives with Mary's herself, who has been rendered nearly silent through the public, male, enduring authority of the Bible and Catholic Church hierarchy.

When my teacher Joe Heaney (also known as Seosamh Ó hÉiniú), the *sean-nós* (old-style) singer from Connemara, died in 1984, local divisions between male and female, public and private, and official and vernacular came to the fore. At his funeral mass in Carna, County Galway, it was a woman who wished for people to sing "Caoine na dTrí Muire." The priest disallowed it. After a significant argument between the two, the lament was sung inside the church, at the front, by a small group of men and women.

Figure 3.2 "The Aran Fisherman's Dead Child" (1841) by Frederic William Burton

This song in particular was multiply transgressive at that event: as a symbol of vernacular female-based Catholicism, it had no role in a standard funeral mass. As an Irish-language song, it was out of place in a Latin-based genre of music even though mass in that village is carried out in the Irish language. As a song well outside the metered hymns that might be played or sung in a church, it is in free rhythm. As a song associated with women and their hereditary position as keening figures at a wake, particularly with its refrain of *óchón*, it stands out as a symbol of their powerful role in society.

Women have been the mainstays of both vernacular Catholicism and regular church attendance and continue multiple forms of spiritual practice that lie well outside church doctrine (Williams and Ó Laoire 2024: 1–14). Their liminal position—precisely between vernacular and semi-official, singing and wailing, and often postmenopausal, which some might regard as outside the boundaries of "normal" femalehood—reflects the simultaneous mirroring of historical conditions of the Catholic Church in Ireland. When the mainstream religion was outlawed, it persisted through the efforts of women for several hundred years. With the dominant position of women in attendance and practice, it is logical that the strength of that vernacular practice would remain undiminished even as mainstream Catholicism has long functioned as the primary religion of the Republic of Ireland.

Japanese *Shinbutsu-shūgō*

In Japan, Buddhism and Shintōism are so deeply intertwined that a recent poll saw 70 percent of Japanese following Buddhism and 70 percent following Shintōism. Shintō is Japan's indigenous religion; it celebrates the ancestors and connects its practitioners with the many nature spirits known as *kami*. It is profoundly connected to Japanese spiritual practices; the name means "Way of the Gods." Shintōism gave rise to thousands of very localized village rituals and performing arts practices across the Japanese archipelago, including *kagura*, entertainment for the gods. Because of the very long history and local sensibilities connected with Shintōism, together with the lack of a central deity or holy scripture, there are few nationwide practices to which everyone adheres.[6] Buddhism, imported to Japan from China and Korea by the sixth century CE, slowly gained a foothold alongside Shintōism. The most enduring sects of Buddhism—Zen, Nichiren, and Pure Land— were fully established by the Kamakura period (1185–1333), with the central text being the *Lotus Sutra*, based on the words of the central deity, Buddha. In Buddhism, the premise is that all life is capable of compassion and the renunciation of desire; prayer, chant, and meditation are efforts to release all sentient beings from the cycle of birth and death (Williams 2006: 182).

The word *shinbutsu-shūgō* ("syncretism of *kami* and *buddhas*") describes the centuries-long conglomeration of Shintōism and Buddhism in Japan. From the early days of Buddhism in Japan, Japanese people incorporated the two faith traditions to the point that Buddhist temples and Shintō shrines were often in the same locations, sharing certain points of design and architecture. For example, the Zeniarai Benzaiten Ugafuku Shrine, not coincidentally inside a cave entrance at Kamakura, features the Shintō figure Ugafukujin, the kami spirit of water, who later integrated with the Buddhist figure Benzaiten (connected to Saraswati), goddess of music, good fortune, and water. The presence of a Buddhist musician—Benzaiten in this case, at the lower right of the picture at this Shintō shrine (Figure 3.3), right next to a circular wooden rendition of an *inari* (Shintō fox kami), is normal. The theory of *honji suijaku*, meaning "the prime entity and its manifestations," supported the idea of kami being folded into Buddhism (Asai 1997: 52). This idea ultimately conflated Shintō kami and Buddhist buddhas and *bodhisattvas* (compassionate beings who delay nirvana to help others). Initiation rituals simultaneously involved elements of both traditions to pass on esoteric knowledge from masters to disciples, such as the use of specific *mantras* (chanted phrases) and *mudras* (codified gestures), specifically from the Shingon and Tendai sects of Buddhism, in conjunction with the purification steps of the *torii* gates and invocations to the kami of Shintōism.

> The metaphorical structure underlying the ritual—a passage from the profane to the sacred, from ignorance to wisdom, from the human realm to that of the deities—is a direct adaptation/translation of esoteric Buddhist imagery [. . .] with the substitution of appropriate *kami*-related items. (Rambelli 2002: 271)

This syncretism lasted until the Meiji Restoration beginning in 1868, at which point the "Kami and Buddhism Separation Order" (Shinbutsu Hanzenrei) enforced the importance of (much more codified and nationalist-serving) State Shintōism and the worship of the emperor as a "living god" (Kamusella 2014: 34). At that point, Buddhism was firmly suppressed, and Shintōism became celebrated as the state religion until 1945.[7] Today, the two operate side by side again in a pluralist society, and people visit shrines and temples regularly without being strict adherents to either faith. Without a particular "conversion ceremony," people might keep both Buddhist and Shintō objects in their homes, and visit both temples and shrines around New Year's Eve (temple) and New Year's Day (shrine) to ensure good luck, health, and happiness the following year.

Some of Japan's least-mainstream ritual traditions, such as those paired with the spirit world, are carried out by women known as *itako*.[8] Blind

Figure 3.3 Benzaiten (below right) next to a wooden rendition of a Shintō *inari* at the Zeniarai Benzaiten Shrine (photo credit: Ethan Doyle White)

initiates learn a number of important local practices such as purification, healing, channeling the dead, exorcism, and ceremonial duties; these feature specific Buddhist scriptures, such as naming the 33 temples dedicated to Kannon, the goddess of mercy, and Shintō prayers for purification (Sasamori 1997: 87). Historically, itako would have been wed to a deity through a ritualized experience of spirit possession, and served as an intermediary (Kawamura 2003: 265–267). Chants are short and repetitive regardless of whether the influence is of either faith.[9] The bells, drums, bows, and prayer beads drawn from both traditions are used in combination with other sound-making objects to drive away evil, emphasize the syllables of the chant, and make sounds that attract the spirits (Sasamori 1997: 92). The incorporation of Shintōism and Buddhism into itako practice again reflects Japanese pluralist ideas about religion in theory and practice.

Both Buddhism and Shintōism use performative elements as aspects of worship: chant, dance, and drama. Buddhist chant—*shōmyō*—is sung in multiple languages, reflecting Buddhism's multisource origins of development. It occurs in a temple. In general, a solo chanter begins, followed by the voices of the others present; the chanters start at their own pitch level. The inclusion of several kinds of percussion, such as a wooden slit-gong in the shape of a fish mouth (*mokugyo*) and others, such as a bell and chimes, allows various philosophical elements to appear in conjunction with chant. For example, the importance of *ma* (silence), the use of the "earthquake" pattern of gradual acceleration, and bodily control of one's breath are larger forms that appear elsewhere in Japanese music. The great suspended temple bell—*o-gane*—is struck at the beginning and ending of the service.[10]

Shintō chant—*kami uta*—is divided into songs done to praise the gods and those intended to entertain the gods. Shintō music also appears at seasonal *matsuri* (festivals) across Japan, accompanied by an ensemble of several drummers and a bamboo flute player. The lack of specific regular services for groups of people, the very local connections to the kami, and the ritualized but individual ways in which people visit shrines (to drop money in the box, bow twice, clap their hands twice to call the attention of the spirits, bow once, and pray for various reasons) are all part of what make Shintō intimate. William Malm notes that at least partly through the level of ease with which Buddhism and Shintōism have coexisted, Buddhist priests sometimes served as Shintō priests (1959: 42); Jennifer Matsue recalls the offerings to Shintō kami in one of the Buddhist temples of Kōya-san (2016: 21). Both are connected to two major liminal moments in human existence: Shintō rites are associated with birth-related ceremonies, and Buddhist rites are tied to funerals.

Kagura, the "entertainment for the gods" in Shintōism, creates a type of sacred space through the use of songs, instrumental music, and dances that lead to purification; local traditions vary. Kagura is performed in many regions of the country—including at the court and in the rural areas connected to harvests and seasonal festivals—but it reflects "shifting emphases in religious thought, absorbing ideologies from a variety of sources" that readily feature Buddhism (Lancashire 2001: 27). Nagasawa describes the key feature of a local performance of *kagura* as the moment at which the (transient) appearance of a Buddhist deity (*gongen*) in the form of a Shintō *kami* appears (Nagasawa 2011: 107); it is part of engaging the spirit of the local mountain. In her work on *nōmai,* a masked dance drama of northern Japan, Susan Asai highlights the assimilative abilities of religious practitioners operating within both Buddhism and Shintōism, such as the use of Buddhist song melodies and Shintō instrumentation of flute, drums, and cymbals to accompany the drama (Asai 1997: 59).

The interweaving of Buddhist and Shintō beliefs and practices is not a deliberate, publicly stated experience in Japan, and in fact, attempts by outsiders to point out their *separate* elements is a well-worn exercise in futility (Gilday 1993: 274). It is instead the result of centuries of recognition that the local moral code extends to welcoming related and/or sympathetic deities. It is also a way of making immanence (the presence of the spiritual world in the physical world) manifest through ritual and sound. It isn't something discussed in school or at work; instead, it primarily comes up as an aspect of life-cycle events (e.g., marriage and death). Visiting a (Shintō) shrine or a (Buddhist) temple is a moment of peace in a busy working life, done largely by people who may not consider themselves to be devout.

Brazilian Candomblé

Brazil is one of the world's most visible nations for religious and musical syncretism. Where half of the population is partly or wholly descended from the five million people forcibly imported from Africa, liminal combinations of beliefs and practices that vary sharply by location, heritage, and class are the norm. This section has as its focus the musical practices of the religion of Candomblé, currently practiced by approximately five percent of the population. In selecting this particular genre to highlight as part of a chapter on liminalities of faith, I wanted to direct attention to what happens when this type of musical and religious syncretism arises in a challenging climate of oppression, resistance, and discrimination.[11] While popularly (and too-simply) described as a blend of Portuguese, African, and Indigenous people and cultures, Brazil's liminality crosses many borders, including class, gender, race, religion, and politics.

It would be simple to assume that Brazil has become post-racial because of its colonial policy (*blanquamiento*) of encouraging Portuguese-descended men to have children with African-descended women (thereby lightening the collective skin of the nation after a dozen generations); however, the presence of over a hundred named racial designations beyond Black, white, and mulatto reveals a local need to pay close attention to race (Sterling 2010: 73). While Portuguese is the official language of Brazil, and Brazil is the largest Portuguese-speaking country in the world, several hundred other languages—including two hundred Indigenous languages—are in regular currency across the country. Samba, its biggest musical export and the genre featured during its Carnaval (pre-Lenten) celebrations in Rio de Janeiro, combines Portuguese and West African drums and rhythms. These combinations are just a few of the ways in which Brazil's liminality appears, but an examination of the Candomblé tradition goes a little deeper.

At its most basic description, Candomblé is a local blend of West African traditional religious practices and Portuguese Catholicism; it divides into denominations depending on where the African traditions originated and how it has developed in its current location. Yet, given its combination of musical practices, ethnobotanical knowledge, and political issues both external and internal, its presence can serve in some ways as a representation of Brazilian social history. It is emphatically *not* simply a straight-across import from Yorùbá (or Bantu, or Fon) country of several hundred years ago; it is wholly *Brazilian* with all its internal diversity and regionalism. Its Catholic influences derive from the forced conversion to Portuguese-inflected Catholicism that Africans had to face as part of their enslavement. Candomblé also receives constant renewal from various sources, including continuous contact with changes in contemporary West Africa (Díaz 2021: 17) and developments in Brazil. Candomblé has thrived in multiple places in Brazil; its spiritual home may be in Bahia (northeast Brazil), but variants of it have their own homes elsewhere in Brazil as well as in Uruguay, Paraguay, and other South American nations.

Candomblé is an oral tradition practiced in *terreiros* or temples. In practice, religious leaders guide their followers in the celebration and propitiation of *orixás* or spirits, with Olodumare as the principal deity. In many cases, these orixás are connected, one way or another, with the saints of Portuguese Catholicism, and individual practitioners are connected to their own orixás. Using one of the best-known examples, the very powerful goddess of the sea, Yemanjá/Iemanjá, is connected to the Virgin Mary *and* to Yemoja of Yorùbá tradition as one of the major orixás. Importantly, though, she is *neither Mary nor Yemoja*. She is herself. Through the use of highly specialized sound, ritual gesture, spirit possession, offerings, objects, plants, and specialized knowledge, practitioners can effect healing, community bonds, empowerment, and other specific goals.

The use of restricted ethnobotanical knowledge is a key element in Candomblé. Knowing the leaves, their uses, their modes of preparation, and their ceremonial function is the domain of the *babalorixá*, the healer (Voeks 1990: 120). Without the plants, the ritual, ceremony, initiation, or celebration would be incomplete. The necessary herbs are sold in markets; some were imported directly from West Africa, while others are local substitutes. The *cantos* used for invocation and instruction are in the form of hundreds of very specific verses with the intention of calling out the spiritual power of the leaves with smoke, tea, and baths. In the Catholic Church, incense is used to evoke the prayers of heavenly saints, and to convey prayers upward into Heaven. Smoke of various kinds is a normal feature of all the mainstream religions as both a liminal conduit to the divine and a symbolic offering.

The figure of the Baiana—Black women dressed in billowing white dresses associated with Candomblé who sell *acarajé* (fried cakes of black-eyed beans) on the streets and in kiosks—is part of the public face not just of Candomblé, but of Africanness. Juan Diego Díaz has stated that Candomblé has been almost continuously celebrated for the purity of its Africanness (Díaz 2021: 20); there have been social, cultural, and political reasons for doing so. As a very public persona, the Baiana-who-sells-*acarajé* is locally considered one of Brazil's own intangible cultural heritages. The sacred food *acarajé* (*akará*, "ball of fire" + *jé*, "to eat," both from Yorùbá of West Africa) is an offering to the orixás. The body of the Baiana herself is further noted frequently as a symbol of Mother Africa, and groups of Baianas are a key feature during Carnaval each year, leading the samba schools in parade.[12]

Cheryl Sterling's work on these women in the community indicates that "Afro-Brazilian women create an alternate social and cultural space in which their Africanness, their blackness, generates powerful narratives of identity to interrupt the social forces that negate them" (Sterling 2010: 72). With Candomblé as a locus of power for Black women, the racist, sexist, and classist dynamics of Brazilian society at large are turned on their heads, making white male participants subservient to the matriarch. Entering a *terreiro* means entering a liminal space in which the divine as it appears in mainstream patriarchal and Catholic Brazilian society is subservient to a different system. Still divine, still powerful, and still engaged in a chain of command, the orixás come to their followers through a radically different system than contemporary Brazilian power structures might support.

The very public Catholic hymn in honor of Nosso Senhor do Bonfim (Our Sir [Saint] of the Good Death) is a sonic signifier of the region of Bahia. Composed in 1923 by Arthur de Salles and João Antŏnio Wanderley, "Hino ao Senhor do Bonfim" is in 4/4, without a trace of the musical syncopation for which (Afro-)Brazilian music is so famous. It marches. It commemorates Bahian Independence, the victory of which is attributed to the saint. It is sung at *fútbol* matches, religious processions, and on the airwaves to the accompaniment of various Brazilian instrumental combinations (samba, bossa nova, etc.), where the blend of its straightforward melody and deeply syncopated accompaniment is obvious. The originally Catholic regional festival in the saint's honor is now "the most important celebration besides Carnival" (Roca 2005: 182) and includes Baianas dressed in white bringing water, flowers, and other offerings in their role as festival organizers. Of the many videos available online, the one indicated in the footnotes is a point of access for the reader.[13] Oxalá—the representative of the supreme deity Olodumare on earth (and the creator of humans)—also has white as his color. White happens to be the color of the saint himself.

> "Nosso Senhor do Bomfim"—Our Sir [Saint] of the Good Death.
> *Glória a ti neste dia de glória*
> *Glória a ti, redentor, que há cem anos*
> *Nossos pais conduziste à vitória*
> *Pelos mares e campos baianos.*
> Glory to you on this day of glory
> Glory to you, redeemer, who for a hundred years
> Our parents carried to victory
> Across the seas and lands of Bahia.

The public presence of thousands of primarily Black people—dressed in white—praying, singing, dancing, tying up strips of cloth that have touched the image of the saint, and other performative activities so deeply tied to Candomblé has resulted in the festival shifting from a primarily Catholic to a primarily Afro-Brazilian one.

In private—inside the terreiro—the experience of Candomblé is more than just the performance of specific rhythms dedicated to specific orixás, just as the cultural context of Candomblé is more than just religious practice. The purpose of the musical experience is to summon the orixás. By using carefully adorned and baptized conical drums (*atabaques*), a double bell (*agôgô*), and a gourd with beads strung in a net around it (*xequerê*), the ensemble carefully engages the attention of the spirits, the dancers, the supplicants, and the primary religious leaders (the *mai-de-santo* and *pai-de-santo*) through the guidance of the master drummer. The balance of signaling between orixás, dancers, and drummers comes through specific rhythmic patterns. "Cutting across the established beat with the rhythm of a particular orixá, he is able to trigger in the dancer's brain the learned response that expresses itself as the state of 'possession'. From that moment on, the dancer *is* the orixá, and behaves accordingly" (Fryer 2000: 20).

One of the problems of liminality in combination with racism and sexism (or nationalism, as in the Japanese formation of "State Shintō," above) is that those in power often feel the need to isolate that which is liminal into one form or another. In a place where people of African descent have been profoundly scrutinized, it has historically been safer to claim that one is a mainstream Brazilian Catholic than that one follows Candomblé. "The slaves appeared to be praising Jesus, Mary and the saints when they may have been honoring Oxalá, Iemanjá, and other divinities from African religions either instead of, or in addition to, the other Catholic figures" (Gidal 2016: 164). Because of the power of the Catholic Church, anything outside the mainstream was regarded with suspicion, and Candomblé was legalized only in the 1970s.[14] Practitioners of Candomblé have been almost continuously under surveillance, proscription, and downright attack throughout its several-hundred-year history.

Each of these three traditions so far—in Ireland, Japan, and Brazil—builds a network of the local and the national with international roots of mainstream faith. Whether Catholic or Buddhist, the followers of each tradition have managed to work within a larger umbrella of a mainstream faith tradition in a way that not only speaks to them personally but connects them to others locally. In the following section, which comprises the remainder of this chapter, a particular form of local music serves as a powerful connective point between the Sundanese Muslims of West Java, Indonesia, and the vestiges of their Hindu-Buddhist roots from hundreds of years prior. The details of this particular tradition are laid out through the use of song lyrics, sonic clues, and the results of my own ethnographic research; a previous version of the section was published in the *Yale Journal of Music and Religion* (Williams 2018: 43–59), the editors of which have kindly allowed me to reprise my work here.

Hinduism and Islam in the Songs of West Java

The Sundanese sung poetry of West Java has long represented a rich set of elite values that often reflect Hindu, Buddhist, and animist ways of understanding the world. In a region known for its strong adherence to Islam, the continuing presence of songs that directly reference and celebrate Hindu deities and narratives from hundreds of years ago seems like both a startling anachronism and a commentary on the ways in which song can transcend contemporary religious and political identities. Here the focus is on the changing relationship between Hinduism and Islam as manifested in the performance of two Sundanese songs—"Ceurik Rahwana" (The Tears of Rahwana) and "Hamdan" (The Praised One)—over thirty years of studying *tembang Sunda*, a genre of sung poetry primarily associated with the hereditary aristocracy. In examining a song that reveals an older local connection to Hinduism ("Ceurik Rahwana") and contrasting it with a contemporary popular song reflective of Muslim beliefs ("Hamdan"), this segment highlights the overall changes in a musical genre and the ways in which those changes are indicative of changes in a particular society.[15] Furthermore, singers who perform the songs reflect a liminal level of engagement with both Hindu and Muslim cosmologies, respectively, in both lyrical and musical materials.

In their introduction to *Divine Inspirations: Music and Islam in Indonesia*, coauthors/editors Anne K. Rasmussen and David D. Harnish note that "[some communities] embrace unique mixes of select Islamic principles with Hindu-Buddhist or indigenous animist practices" (Harnish and Rasmussen 2011: 7). Though Islam came to the Sundanese region hundreds of years ago, it encountered a foundation of Hindu-Buddhism deeply connected with local animism (Wessing 1984: 730). As is often the case in

Indonesia, the practice of Sundanese belief tends to be layered, with little separation between religions, leading to easy justification for their coexistence. These codependent systems of faith allow multiple points of access to the sacred.

The Sundanese are Indonesia's second most populous ethnic group. Inhabiting the island of Java, just south of the nation's capital, Jakarta, they bear some similarities in language and culture to their neighbors to the east, the Javanese. Historically associated with Hindu-Buddhist practices (Van Zanten 1989: 45), the Sundanese became adherents to Islam in a gradual process that remains somewhat incomplete, based on some of their folk-loric and ritualistic practices. Since the end of the twentieth century, however, much of western Indonesian—and, by extension, Sundanese—culture has tended to emphasize the influences of Islam and de-emphasize the vestiges of Hinduism and Buddhism. As the Sundanese have come to lean on increasingly outward expressions of their Islamic faith—through the use of the *hijab* and specific kinesthetic cues to one another, as well as through musical means—it has been Sundanese women who have consistently provided the most public expressions of West Java's increasing Islamization. Among those women who sing, regardless of the genre, the presentation of beliefs, priorities, and faith traditions is on full display through both the lyrics and the musical elements of the songs. As Anne Rasmussen points out, Indonesian women are significantly involved in public and popular expressions of Islam (Rasmussen 2010: 16); as visual signifiers of Islamic identity in both rural and urban regions of West Java, women publicly delineate boundaries of belief.

Locally sung poetry of various types tends to highlight elements of Sundanese history (animist and Hindu-Buddhist), the natural world, spirituality, and heartache. With a landscape that features volcanoes, rice fields, bamboo and conifer forests, and significant rivers and hot springs, it is a small step to imagining the ways in which some of these important natural resources might appear in songs, and how they might connect with an older spirituality that includes ancestor worship and reverence for the natural world, including animals such as tigers and birds (Wessing 1986). This is the Sundanese foundational belief system, overlaid with layers of other religious traditions and practices. Influences from Hinduism began to appear by the first century CE, and Buddhism was established locally by the sixth century. In general, the influence of Hinduism is part of a larger syncretic pattern that affected all of Java by the tenth century (Tarling 1992: 178). Islam is estimated to have arrived in Sundanese territory by the fourteenth century CE (Ricklefs 1993: 4), becoming established by the eighteenth century.

The golden age of Sundanese cultural history is locally believed to have arisen during the Hindu kingdom of Pajajaran (1333–1579). This was a time of economic interdependence and strength for the Sundanese, as the area's pre-Islamic highland regions developed a rich trading culture. Although the area's leadership was continually in competition and sometimes conflict with Majapahit, the East Javanese Hindu kingdom, the era is seen as a time of considerable health and prosperity, and of connectedness with both the spirit world and the ancestors. In short, it is the time that people remember most fondly as their historical Golden Age through the performance of *tembang Sunda* songs (Van Zanten 1989: 71).

Javanese rulers colonized the Sundanese highlands after a battle (Pasunda Bubat) between Majapahit and Pajajaran in 1357. The later collapse of Pajajaran in the sixteenth century occurred just as Islamic ideas and beliefs were becoming established in Central Java in the kingdom of Mataram. The Dutch East India Company gained control over the Sundanese highlands in 1677, when the Javanese ruler of the Mataram kingdom ceded the region to them. That territorial gain provided the company with much-needed plantations for tea, indigo, coffee, and other trade goods. One of the ways in which the Dutch (who ultimately nationalized the Dutch East India Company in 1800) furthered their aim of colonization in the region was to support local performing arts and the layers of social hierarchies, including in West Java (Heins 1977: 36). This support—financial, social, and political—kept the Sundanese class levels in place. The hereditary aristocrats learned to speak Dutch as well as Sundanese, and many were able to function fluidly in colonial society as local rulers under colonial law. Because the Dutch were interested primarily in local natural resources rather than in large-scale religious conversion, the Sundanese maintained their layered religious practices of animism, Hindu-Buddhism, and Islam for several hundred years.

By the late nineteenth and early twentieth centuries, many of the forms of Sundanese performing arts that are still performed today were becoming established and codified; among them were genres that tended to celebrate animistic or Hindu-based mystic spirituality side by side with those more closely aligned with Islamic viewpoints. This musical syncretism reflects a local blend of both religious traditions—with deep influences from much older animist beliefs—that work specifically in a Sundanese context. For example, the Sundanese play several types of gamelan (bronze gong-chime) ensembles, which date from pre-Islamic days. They also play tuned bamboo rattles called *angklung*, which invoke the rice goddess, Dewi Sri, in order to ensure the continuing fertility of the rice fields upon which their lives depend. The rice goddess functions as a liminal figure between animism and Hinduism; she simultaneously features prominently in the earliest Sundanese origin myths (Wessing 1988: 52).

In understanding contemporary Sundanese usage of *tembang Sunda* and its inclusion of frequent references to the Hindu kingdom of Pajajaran, however, it is helpful to remember that many adherents to Sundanese Islam continue to appreciate aspects of their collective past that help them to feel strong, locally vibrant, and sophisticated. That includes references to a sense of longing for the glorious time of Hinduism and the celebration of the Pajajaran kingdom as a uniting element among the Sundanese.

When Indonesia declared its independence in 1945, the old system of arts patronage under the Dutch collapsed; many instrumentalists and singers moved into the regional colonial capital city of Bandung to find work. As a result of that dramatic shift, formerly royal genres became associated with the city, including *tembang Sunda*. The hereditary aristocracy that had supported the performance of sung poetry since at least the nineteenth century set down new roots in the postcolonial regional government, and in that chaotic milieu, its performers and enthusiasts celebrated what they remembered of their aristocratic Hindu past through performances of *tembang Sunda*. By the end of the twentieth century, much of Indonesian society was moving toward an increasingly conservative Islamization that called its long-standing syncretic religious practices into question.

Tembang Sunda—the genre featuring aristocratic sung poetry accompanied by the boat-shaped *kacapi* zither and *suling* bamboo flute—is one of the primary sonic tools used for remembering—and commemorating—the feudal era of Hindu Pajajaran. The proper performance of *tembang Sunda* includes local customs of politeness, standards of performance that are upheld by competitions and specific teachers, and the use of precisely detailed systems of vocal ornamentation, instrumental choices, and behaviors. *Tembang Sunda* simultaneously reinforces the Hindu-based class divisions between members of Sundanese society, and celebrates the highest classes as the people most deserving of the past spiritual glories of Pajajaran, transmitted to the present.[16]

Sundanese societal divisions are reflected in musical choices, and *tembang Sunda* is most closely connected to the upper classes. In its contemporary context of connecting the upper classes to the time of Hindu gods and, further back, a spiritual connection with animist elements such as tigers, *tembang Sunda* embodies the continuing stratification of Sundanese society without necessarily making it explicitly Hindu.

In its intimate, late-night performance contexts with just a few insiders present, *tembang Sunda* is intended to celebrate all that is good about the Hindu past—for the upper levels of society—even as it laments love lost in the present, which on the surface level represents a risk for the members of society as a whole. On a deeper level, love lost reflects a type of longing for spiritual connection with one's ancestors and with God.

An evening of *tembang Sunda* often begins with the performance of a formal introductory piece, to ask permission from the Hindu ancestors for the ensuing performance. Next, before beginning the first set of songs in *pélog* tuning, the singer—usually female—sings, "Daweung ménak Pajajaran" ("Now we will consider the noblemen/god-kings of [Hindu] Pajajaran"). In other words, the evening performance is set in a context that celebrates and honors the Hindu past, not the Muslim present (Van Zanten 1989: 77).

What follows the initial invocation is a series of sets of songs: one or more free-meter songs, often focused on Sundanese history (both literal and myth-ological), followed by a single fixed-meter song that usually connects heart-ache with an aspect of the natural world. For example, in the song "Salaka Domas," a very powerful man wants to fight against every weapon or oppo-nent he encounters. Sundanese instrumentalists and singers both describe this man—like them, the descendent of the very powerful King Siliwangi—as "the modern Sundanese man, hampered by his current circumstances but ready to spring into action at a moment's notice to defend himself and his *nagara*, or Sundanese nation-state" (Williams 2001: 221). More directly, on several sepa-rate occasions I heard Sundanese men in positions of power referring to *them-selves* as "King Siliwangi." King Siliwangi was the last ruler of Pajajaran, and his disappearance—rather than his death—has led generations of Sundanese to believe that he will return one day, as strong as ever. Van Zanten (1989: 78) states that "most noble families claim to descend from King Siliwangi."

In the performance of *tembang Sunda*, both the lyrics and the perfor-mance practices reflect an outer manifestation (*lahir*) of a deeper and more important inner life (*batin*). The subject of many lively Sundanese discussions, these two concepts revolve around the idea of public and private belief systems. When the Islamic holy month of Ramadan comes to a close, many Sundanese people send cards with the phrase "*mohon ma'af lahir dan batin*"—asking forgiveness not only for one's physical and emotional wrongdoings, but also for both intentional and unintentional errors. In these words and actions, there is an understanding that humans have an inner life and an outward manifestation of that inner life, and that the two may be different in character. Because so many songs celebrate both the mundane and the spiritual, the corporeal and the emotional, and the power of the natural world, it is clear that Sundanese composers and musicians acknowledge the connection between the two. That the sound of the instruments and the sung poetry serve to weave those two concepts together is an important transcendent liminal function for the genre.

The *kacapi* zither serves as a type of spiritual gatekeeper or *kuncen* in that by supporting the work of the singer, it connects contemporary urbanites with aspects of their rural past (Williams 2001: 212). Its boat shape, referred to as an "ancestral ship" by kacapi player Rukruk Rukmana, is said to carry people back to the time of the ancestors when they listen to it, regardless of the context. In referring to it as a kuncen, or key-bearer, players note that it serves the function of a guard of a sacred place. Someone who plays the kacapi is the one who—together with the singer—serves as a liminal connective go-between.

An evening of *tembang Sunda* goes through several different subgenres (*papantunan, jejemplangan, dedegungan,* and *panambih*) and several modes (*pélog, sorog,* and *saléndro*). It is the songs of the papantunan subgenre—the oldest, most historical of the subgenres—that tend to highlight the Hindu past, the golden era of Pajajaran, and the connection of the Sundanese rural past with the present. They are considered very difficult to sing in terms of technique, vocal pressure, and ornamentation, and are quite serious in content. The modes of *pélog, sorog,* and *saléndro* reflect the time of night, mood, lyric content, instrument tuning, and song choices.[17] Papantunan songs are always performed in the *pélog* mode, at the beginning of the evening. Songs from the other subgenres tend to highlight love and loss; they are saved for later performance in the evening. However, only the papantunan songs reflect an orientation toward or acknowledgment of Hinduism.

The incorporation into *tembang Sunda* performance practice of a popular song celebrating Islamic elements has begun not only to alter the specifically Hindu aspects of the genre, but also to cause a shift in genre-based class distinctions. Just as women form the foundation of the Sundanese home—celebrating the Hindu rice goddess with small shrines in their kitchens, and dominating the interiors of houses and stages in this matrilocal society—women are the ones making the change in this Hindu-based repertoire through the musical incorporation of Islam.

The two great Hindu epics—the *Mahābhārata* and the *Rāmāyana*—are performed all over Southeast Asia, and West Java is no exception. The *Rāmāyana* in particular appears in various Sundanese performing arts in a variety of ways, one example of which is in *tembang Sunda*. In the story, the king Rama and his brother chase after a golden deer that Rama's wife, Sinta, desires, leaving her vulnerable. She is tricked and abducted by Rahwana, and—after a significant battle—is reunited with her husband.[18] It is a very popular story and, like the *Mahābhārata*, is often divided into small pieces, performed in sections because everyone is familiar with the entirety of the story.

The *tembang Sunda* song "Ceurik Rahwana" (Tears of Rahwana) highlights the moment in the *Rāmāyana* Hindu epic when Rahwana, struck down by King Rama, comes home at the edge of death and apologizes to his wife, Banondari. Rahwana (known as Ravana in India) begs her forgiveness for the fate that led him to pursue another woman. After Rahwana's death, Banondari sings a lament, "Kulu-Kulu Bem," in which she begs him not to leave her. Within the *tembang Sunda* genre, "Ceurik Rahwana" is an important song requiring both a male and a female singer with significant vocal skills. Its presence—and the presence of other specifically Hindu songs—in Sundanese musical life has colored the ways in which *tembang Sunda* performers and audience members think of the *Rāmāyana*, yet it is *only* in Sundanese music that Rahwana experiences regret, asks for forgiveness, and weeps. In every other rendition of the *Rāmāyana*, he dies after the battle with Rama.

"Ceurik Rahwana" (along with "Kulu-Kulu Bem," Banondari's lament that follows it) was written by a woman, Saodah Harnadi Natakusumah (1922–1981). In the lyrics, Rahwana says that he is fated to die, but before he perishes, he begs to be forgiven, body and soul. He says he was drawn to another, enchanted by Sinta, and—in a nod to the Hindu belief in karmic retribution—that the suffering one inflicts on others returns to oneself. The fact that Ms. Natakusumah led the *tembang Sunda* ensemble at Radio Republik Indonesia in Bandung from 1950 to 1958, and was not only a respected composer of many songs but an accomplished performer as well, meant that her compositions and choices of songs to perform had a strong impact on the development of the genre during the middle of the twentieth century.

In the accompanying transcription of "Ceurik Rahwana" (Figure 3.4), assume that there is much more than meets the eye in terms of vocal ornamentation. Sundanese vocal music has five named types of vibrato, each of which occurs in specific places in this song.[19]

Figure 3.4 "Ceurik Rahwana" ("Tears of Rahwana")

Rahwana:

Banondari anu lucu, bojo kakang anu geulis (geuning, duh anu geulis)

Kadieu sakeudeung geuwat, akang rek mere pepeling (aduh geulis, mere pepeling) Geura sambat indung bapa, samemeh akang pinasti.

Banondari who is beautiful, wife of mine who is lovely (oh, who is lovely)

Here, just a second, emergency, I wish to give a message (oh lovely, give a message)

Go summon mother and father before I perish.

Banondari:

Aduh engkang buah kalbu sembaheun lahir jeung batin (geuning, lahir jeung batin)

Aya naon pengeresa tara-tara ti sasari (aduh geuning, ti sasari)

Nyauran ragrag cisoca, abdi mah saredih teuing.

Oh beloved fruit of my heart, dedicated body and soul (oh, body and soul)

How should one feel from now on? (oh, from now on)

Calling, streaming down tears, I am far more than sad.

Rahwana:

Aduh Enung anu ayu nu geulis pupujan ati (geulis, pupujan ati)

Akang tangtu ngababatang, samemeh akang pinasti (aduh geulis, akang pinasti)

Arek menta dihampura, lahir tumeka ing batin.

Oh Darling who is so delicate, who is so lovely, praiseworthy heart

I am fated to die, but before I perish (oh my lovely, I perish)

Let it be that I ask to be forgiven, body as well as soul.

Banondari:

Duh engkang panutan kalbu, teu kiat abdi wawarti (geuning, abdi wawarti)

Ulah sok ngumbar amarah antukna kaluli-luli (aduh, geuning, kaluli-luli)

Nu matak mawa cilaka, kaduhung ngajadi bukti.

Oh you object of my heart, I am not strong, I warn you (I warn you)

Don't so follow anger, resulting in forgetting all (oh, forgetting all)

Which apparently leads to catastrophe, regret becomes proof.

Rahwana:

Kaduhung kakang kaduhung, kataji nu lain-lain (geulis, nu lain-lain)

Kaiwat goda rancana, kagembang ku Sintawati (aduh geulis, ku Sintawati)

Geuning kieu karasan, malindes malik ka diri.

Regret, I regret, I was drawn by an extraordinary other (an extraordinary other)

Ensnared seduced temptation, enchanted by Sita (oh lovely, by Sita)

This is how it feels, the suffering [that one inflicts] returns to oneself.

Banondari's lament, "Kulu-Kulu Bem," follows; it is very challenging to sing because of its broad range and vocal ornamentation, but the women who know it and listen to it have told me that they could only wish for such a heartfelt apology from their own straying husbands. In this lament, Banondari uses liminal imagery from the natural world, such as the rays of the dawn and flashes of lightning, to describe Rahwana's presence, his abrupt end, and ultimately his disappearance from her life. She hopes only to be remembered with love. The lyrics are added here because "Kulu-Kulu Bem," in its historical connection with "Ceurik Rahwana," is another point that sets the Sundanese version of the *Ramayana* story apart from all other (non-Sundanese) performances.

First verse:

*Geuning bet siga balebat, sumping teh ngan sajorelat sumping teh ngan
   sajorelat*
Padahal ditunggu lami, dianti-anti ti wengi manis dianti-anti ti wengi
*Engke ulah waka angkat, ulah waka kebat ngejat dunungan, ulah wakada
   kebat ngejat;*
Just like dawn-rays, his presence was only brief, his presence was only brief
After all I waited for long, waiting since last night, love, waiting since last
   night
Wait, don't just leave, don't just hurry to depart my lord, don't just hurry
   to depart;
Horeng ari nu nungguan tetela ambon sorangan
*Sugan teh rek dipitineung, sugan teh rek dipiheman, dunungan
   Manis, duh, horeng ngan ukur saliwat, ngan ukur matak tibelat.*
Here is one who waits for one-sided affection
One would hope to be remembered, one would hope to be loved, my lord
Beloved, oh, here [and gone] just like lightning, just like a memory
Manis, ke heula atuh ke heula iklas teh kabina-bina
Lah, alah … ulah miyuni balebat endah basa samemeh liwat
*Ke heula atuh antosan, ulah waka luluasan, ayeuna mah geuning, ulah
   waka luluasan.*
Beloved, oh, first wait, oh, first wait; apparently I have been too nice
Ah, oh … don't become like dawn-rays: beautiful just before they depart
First wait oh wait, don't just go onward (Lord sir), now don't just go
   onward.

Second verse:

Cimata abdi saksina yen abdi lama satia (duh), yen abdi lama satia
*Yeuh badan abdi buktina, kapan sakieu resakna, manis, kapan sakieu
   resakna, geuning*
*Hate teh awut-awutan ku lami puyang-payengan, dunungan, ku lami
   puyang-payengan.*
My tears are my witness to my long loyalty, to my long loyalty
Oh my body is the proof, when it's breaking, sweetheart when it's breaking
My heart is all confused because we are long torn apart, lord, long torn apart.
Kapan saur ti kapungkur, dagoan satutup umur

Ayeuna abdi ngantosan, sugan nu nilar rek mulang, geuning
Manis, duh, sugan teh jangji rek jadi, mo gajlig, ti saur tadi.
When it was said from before, [we would be as one until] the close of life
Now I wait; maybe the one who left will come home
Sweetheart, maybe the promise will come true, you can't go back on your
   promise.
Manis, kukupu gegeleberan sugan teh anu ngiberan
Lah, alah … Rek sumping nu diantosan jangji teh rek ditedunan
Sataun abdi ngantosan, geura paparin putusan (panutan)
Ayeuna mah, geuning, geura paparin putusan.
Sweetheart, a butterfly flutters past, maybe someone might come
Ah, oh … He who is awaited will come [and the] promise will be kept
A year I have been waiting, let it pass quickly, this separation (immediately)
Now let it pass quickly, this separation.

In discussing this song with various Sundanese artists, nothing seems unusual about the fact that Rahwana offers an abject apology to his wife; in fact, a number of Sundanese men privately mentioned that "men have plenty to apologize to their wives for." Because the image of a man weeping is locally considered undignified, it is clear that Rahwana has been destroyed and is dying; those tears are the sign of his final defeat.

The related genre of *kawih*, which is also accompanied by a zither and (sometimes) other instruments, is believed to be older than *tembang Sunda* at least partly because the term is mentioned in some of the earliest texts, written on palm leaves (Danasasmita and Danasasmita 1981). While the original meaning of kawih was close to the idea of knowledge or skill, and it was the earliest word used to refer to Sundanese singing, in contemporary usage it denotes (primarily) fixed-meter popular sung poetry performed primarily by women. It is locally considered in contrast to the more refined genre of *tembang Sunda*, and its performance practices accordingly use less elevated language, vocal skills, and imagery. Furthermore, the genre is open to new compositions, lively kacapi playing and singing, and a continual infusion of popular influences. In its lyrical content, it is much more flexible in that it can refer to contemporary themes outside the traditional boundaries of *tembang Sunda*. In doing so, the genre of kawih speaks to a much larger Sundanese population than the much more closely circumscribed upperclass performers and audience members of *tembang Sunda*.

In recent years, the more contemporary kawih song "Hamdan" (The Praised One), written by the composer Koko Koswara (1917–1985) and containing both Arabic words and Arabic melodic markers, has gained popularity to the point that it appears in contexts formerly associated only with *tembang Sunda*. As a composer of pop songs, Koswara was well acquainted with both the kawih and the *tembang Sunda* social and musical worlds. The song illustrates in every way what the Sundanese ethnomusicologist Deni Hermawan describes as *musik islami*, Sundanese music with an Islamic flavor. It has a simple melody, like many kawih songs, and is easy to sing (particularly its chorus).

While "Hamdan" is not entirely in Arabic, it contains enough Arabic words to firmly locate it *outside* the genre of *tembang Sunda*. By performing "Hamdan" with its Sundanese and Arabic words—rather than Sundanese and Sanskrit, as in aristocratic *tembang Sunda*—the song bears multiple signifiers of the middle class, of Islamic practice, of group prayer, and of contemporary Islamic popular song. It is a twentieth-century middle-class Muslim song located now *within* a several-hundred-years-old aristocratic Hindu-based genre which is itself located within a diverse contemporary Muslim societal context.

The late *tembang Sunda* vocalist Euis Komariah—my teacher—was frequently asked to teach "Hamdan" to groups of women who would not normally have anything to do with either *tembang Sunda* or its aristocratic context. They would come to her house, wearing conservative clothing and *hijab*, and cluster in groups of ten or more as she led them through the song phrase by phrase. She also traveled to gathering places where she would teach groups of women to sing it. As she explained, "Hamdan" was for women who could not see themselves singing popular Islamic songs with electric instruments and plenty of hip swinging such as they saw on television; it was more dignified and "sounded older" to them than *tembang Sunda*, even though it is a mid-twentieth-century composition (Figure 3.5).

Figure 3.5 "Hamdan" ("The Praised One")

The lyrics for "Hamdan" are ones of praise for God, and they describe His attributes as the Hearer and Knower, blessing Muhammad the Messenger, his family, and his companions.[20]

First verse:
Hamdan lirobbil 'alamin
Allohu rohman warrohim
Qod koruba fatul mubin
Innahu huas samiu'l alim
Praise to Lord of the Universes
God the Most Gracious and Merciful
Qod koruba, the sign of victory
For Him, He is the Hearer, Knower

Second verse:
Puji kagungan pangeran
Nu Maha Welas tur (tus) Eman
Gusti mangka buka pura bahagja
Alloh ya Robbi Mantenna Maha Uninga
Praise to the Lord
Most gracious and Most Merciful
The Lord will open happiness
The Lord who understands

Chorus:
Solawat, solawatan
Barokat barokatan
A'la Muhammad Rosulih
Wa'ala alih wasohbih
(recitation of praise)
Bless Blessed
For Muhammad the Messenger
And his companions

Third verse:
Salam sinareng solawat
Muga netes ka Muhammad
Natrat ka para Karabat
Para ahli jeung sahabat
Peace and praise

> Descending to Muhammad
> And also for his family
> And his companions

The performance of "Hamdan" in a Hindu-based *tembang Sunda* setting speaks not only to the idea that it is welcoming to people outside of a *tembang Sunda* performance, but also to issues of class. In performances, members of the audience, including the sponsors of the evening (but not the instrumentalists), are assumed to have once belonged to the hereditary aristocracy. Euis Komariah spent considerable time discussing exactly how "Hamdan" was a necessary addition to the aristocratic context, even as it remained outside the genre of *tembang Sunda*. First, its status as a kawih song meant that it belonged to a much larger proportion of the Sundanese populace, and could cross social and class boundaries in a way that a song such as "Ceurik Rahwana" could not. As she put it, "Many more Sundanese people have become Muslims these days, and they want to know that there is a place for them too" (Euis Komariah, personal communication). In fact, locating a song of the *musik Islami* type in a Hindu-based genre is simply a reflection of larger movements taking place in Sundanese society that emphasize public expressions of Islamic faith, such as attending mosque on Friday, dressing in a more Islamic way than they did in the late 20th century, and using more Arabic-based conversational customs such as the expression "*Ālḥāmdulill āḥ!*" (الحمد لله, "Praise God!") when, for example, one is grateful for the cooler temperature inside one's home on a hot and humid day.

"Hamdan" is sung at a comparatively high pitch register, which is not at all consonant with *tembang Sunda*. Many kawih songs such as "Hamdan" are performed in a high register, which is a signifier of a lower class on the part of the singer and her audience. Whereas "Ceurik Rahwana" peaks at middle A (A4), the highest pitch of "Hamdan" is nearly an octave higher, on the pitch of high G (G5). If the higher register of the song—particularly its middle section—indicates lower class, then it is alien, in many ways, to the *tembang Sunda* context. The aforementioned composer and singer Saodah Harnadi Natakusumah may well have established the importance of the lower range of *tembang Sunda* songs; in her many performances on Radio Republik Indonesia, she always preferred to be accompanied by lower-pitched instruments (Van Zanten 1989: 116). "Hamdan" also differs from most *tembang Sunda* songs, however, in its melodic material. Several Sundanese musicians with whom I spoke said that the "Arabic sound of the melody gave them chills" and reminded them of the "importance of Islam," particularly for those who do not pray regularly. Its ease of singing allows outsiders a type of new access to *tembang Sunda* social and musical circles.

Singers performing "Hamdan" enjoy imitating the Arabic language as they sing, emphasizing the accents and back-of-the-throat sounds that Arabic affords them. For example, they might imitate what they perceive to be an Arabic accent while speaking Sundanese or Indonesian, the national language, or say "Allah" (God) with the double l's in the back of their throats, accompanied by conspiratorial grins. *Tembang Sunda* singers of the upper classes jokingly tease one another about how Arabic they sound and imitate each other, but only within earshot of those who understand the jokes as insiders. Since the 1980s, the song's strong increase in popularity has reflected an increasing societal interest in, and outward expression of, Islamic faith through the use of specific clothing (including hijab), the popularity of Islamic music of various types, and in conversational topics. Yet, as Anne Rasmussen points out—in her book on women and Islamic music in Indonesia—women who become more outwardly Islamic are not retrenching or experiencing some kind of revival of Islamism (Rasmussen 2010: 20). Instead, the women who perform "Hamdan" are choosing to transcend *both* religion- and class-bound rules of participation.

Because "Hamdan" has no connection to colonial feudal days and the strong divisions in societal hierarchies associated with those times, it is much more contemporary and close to the emotional surface in terms of how people regard it. Knowing it well allows one to play at being aristocratic in the liminal Hindu-Islamic context of *tembang Sunda*, without abandoning Islam as a central faith tradition. The combination of crossing class levels to be part of *tembang Sunda* and crossing faith boundaries while singing an emphatically Islamic song is immensely freeing for some of the women performing the song.

In a series of conversations I engaged in with women learning to sing "Hamdan," several comments I heard were quite revealing. One older woman said, "I have wanted to sing *tembang Sunda* ever since I first heard it as a little girl, but my father refused to allow me because it wasn't Islamic enough." Another, who enjoys singing pop Indonesian songs, said that she was learning "Hamdan" so that she could perform an Islamic song that would please her family. A third said, "I am a good Muslim and I want to sing a song that reflects the strength [*kekuatan*] of my beliefs without swinging my hips." They all agreed that "Hamdan" was easier to sing than any other song in the *tembang Sunda* repertoire.

During my two years of continuous study of *tembang Sunda* in West Java, I was asked to be part of a ritual used to initiate performers into the esoterica of the genre. Called a *tawajuh*, it involved a local *dukun* or spiritual intermediary who came to my house. I was required to bring certain items to the ceremony, including water from the four directions, bitter coffee, palm sugar, flowers, a cigar, rice, bananas, and other things. He praised Allah and the local Sundanese Hindu god-ancestors such as Prabu Siliwangi, described himself as a son of Pajajaran, and spoke in a combination of Arabic (Muslim), Sanskrit (Hindu), and Sundanese (local). He used Arabic to open and close the ceremony. It may be worth pointing out that this kind of Pajajaran-era ritual—particularly its use of water from the four directions—is very much tied to early Hindu traditions. It was held on Jum'at Kliwon (an auspicious Friday of the 35-day Sundanese calendar), *just prior to the start of Ramadan* (Williams 2001: 213–216).

Expressing Wa'as

If there were ever a more liminal sensibility than *wa'as*, one would be hard pressed to find it. *Wa'as* is the perfect balance between the emotions of happiness, wistfulness, joy, longing, nostalgia, and bitterness. English has no word for it, though "bittersweet" might account for how someone might experience wa'as; Chapter 5 features an entire section on this exact sensibility. Multiple Sundanese performing artists described it specifically, over time, in this way: One feels wa'as at the rural sights and sounds of sunset over terraced rice fields, as the farmer walks his water buffalo back home and a young child sitting on the water buffalo's back plays the *suling* bamboo flute, with the Islamic call to prayer in the background. One feels wa'as during a late-night performance of *tembang Sunda* as the conflicting thoughts of colonial memories, the lost kingdom of Pajajaran, heartache over a once-urgent love, youth, and old age converge in one's mind. Wa'as surges up in one's heart as one experiences the scents and sounds of one's childhood—the foods, the neighborhood, the sounds, the voices—that one feels torn at having left behind for mixed reasons. Neither happy nor sad, but genuinely both and more, wa'as is precisely the feeling that *tembang Sunda* is supposed to generate. Each of these descriptions arose from instrumentalists, singers, and composers during late-night performances of *tembang Sunda*, and collectively they represent a very local way of understanding the world.

In the late 1980s, I was living in West Java, Indonesia, doing research for my doctoral dissertation on *tembang Sunda*. My voice teacher—Euis Komariah—was part of a performing arts troupe or *lingkung seni* called Jugala, and she allowed me to tag along at her gigs; she usually had me sing just one song for the novelty of it. One time we went to a performance location straight out of a liminal dream: we were at an outdoor pavilion surrounded by terraced rice fields just after a heavy afternoon rain. The young rice was a vivid green, even at twilight, and the newly set sun allowed the fields to retain a warm glow. Fireflies had begun their nightly dance patterns above the waters in the fields. About eighty urban people were in attendance, chatting and eating. To the sound of the strings and flute, my teacher sang songs about the inextricable links between joy and heartache, and between past and present. People sighed and exclaimed, "Wa'as!"

For the urban people at that open-air pavilion—with a roof but no walls—at twilight, at a terraced rice field with dancing fireflies, listening to nineteenth-century court music from the rural past, eating foods central to Sundanese cuisine (steamed carp in bamboo leaves, rice, spicy vegetables), it was excruciatingly moving and almost painful in its beauty and power. An elderly local Sundanese composer of sung poetry smiled as he leaned over to me and said, slowly, "This is who we are." I was deeply honored that he chose to use the inclusive word *kita*—all of us, including you [an insider]—rather than the exclusive word *kami*—all of us except you [the outsider].

"Ceurik Rahwana" and its accompanying lament, "Kulu-Kulu Bem," create and express *wa'as* lyrically through the deliberate expression of simultaneous commitment and betrayal. In the lyrics, Rahwana's apology, expressions of love, and recognition of *karma* are reflective of his continuing commitment to his wife into death, in spite of his fate of being "drawn by an extraordinary other." Rahwana's death at the very moment of his sung apology profoundly represents one of two great liminal moments: birth and death. In Banondari's lament, she simultaneously expresses her joy in him and her despair in his violent passing. Musically, the shift back and forth between Rahwana and Banondari is a continuous repositioning of perspective from male to female and back, again and again. At no point in "Ceurik Rahwana" does the listener feel settled with one single perspective, but must always be unstable. The exceptionally wide vocal range of "Kulu-Kulu Bem," and its challenge in effective performance, puts it well out of the capability of anyone other than a committed practitioner of *tembang Sunda*. As is often the case with this genre, listeners hearing Banondari's lament feel her heartache in their own lives, no matter how happy they might otherwise be. The result, in performance practice, is that many of the listeners are moved to tears by both "Ceurik Rahwana" and "Kulu-Kulu Bem": *wa'as* (longing, nostalgia, sadness, joy) has been achieved.

The Sundanese characterize themselves as cheerful and fun-loving. They enjoy practical jokes, double entendre, and wordplay. Yet at their most private times—the late-night sessions when the children and the outsiders have long since gone to bed—this elite subset of Sundanese society *revels* in historical and mythical songs that awaken what they regard as their true Sundanese selves. The heartache celebrated in so many songs leads to tears of understanding during the evening, as they feel the loss of the Hindu Pajajaran kingdom as keenly as the loss of love in their own lives. The term *kasundaan*—the essence of Sundanese-ness—is every bit as important to them as the deeply Sundanese sense of wa'as, and achieving that Sundanese-ness through performance practice is a powerful pathway to personal and regional identity. By being simultaneously cheerful and deep, fun-loving and weepy, and public and private, the hereditary aristocracy of the Sundanese live their experience of liminality at all times, but feel and discuss it most keenly during all-night performances of *tembang Sunda*. For descendants of King Siliwangi and, prior to the emergence of the Hindu kingdom Pajajaran, the mythical tigers that roamed the forests, it is the expression of wa'as that allows and supports the liminal place in which one sings in the tumultuous present, yet lives at least part of the time in the stable, feudal past. Indeed, performing that stable, feudal past is a way of connecting to, and receiving the approval of, the ancestors.

The relationship of "Hamdan" to the experience of wa'as is tied primarily to the Islamic calendrical cycle. At certain times of the year, such as the Prophet's birthday and the first and final days of Ramadan, all Sundanese are more mindful of being Muslims. By singing "Hamdan" during these times, feelings of wa'as in connection to one's family, childhood, and one's deceased relatives are common. Romantic heartache is not a part of this array of feelings, whereas it *is* deeply connected to *tembang Sunda*. What one feels at this time both *is* and *is not* wa'as. In the climate of increasing Islamization—socially and politically—the aristocratic Sundanese find themselves in the liminal place of being caught between regional identity issues that allow for variation of belief and the presence of multiple musical genres, and the national "project" that requires allegiance to the state and at least some kind of public allegiance to Islam in the name of political/personal advancement.

In 1987, "Hamdan" was still relatively new—about twenty years old. A few people sang it, but they were thought of rather dismissively by those who sang *tembang Sunda* because it is so easy and has such a (low-class) high vocal range. At the time, almost no Sundanese women wore Islamic clothing, preferring skintight blouses and skirts. By the mid-1990s, approximately 20 percent of women dressed more conservatively than before, and most older women wore hijab, the traditional Islamic head covering. In 2007, "Hamdan" was often performed toward the early part of the evening in a *tembang Sunda* session, and about half the women singing wore hijab and other signifiers of Islamic clothing, at least when they were outdoors. By 2017, most women were dressed modestly, wore hijab both indoors and outdoors, and sprinkled their conversations with Arabic words in the midst of any normal conversation in Sundanese. "Hamdan" had become a *tembang Sunda* standard, linked with the gradually increasing Islamization of Sundanese society.

Tembang Sunda is a nineteenth-century genre in a twenty-first-century context. Many of the song lyrics, the instruments, and the formal clothing and hairstyles date from the nineteenth century. Most importantly, the hierarchies that divide the singers, especially, from the instrumentalists and everyone else are from a much earlier time. That time, referred to as *zaman feodal*, or "the feudal era," is enthusiastically celebrated by those who stand to benefit from it the most. The performances of both "Ceurik Rahwana" and "Hamdan"—often in a single evening of *tembang Sunda*—reflect the development of a liminal regionalism in Sundanese culture, in which multiple genres of music and multiple levels of society represented in the music have begun to coexist in the same performance venues, performed by the same people. In particular, performing "Hamdan" has become a means by which middle-class Sundanese women may enter the rarefied air of the musical elite. Sundanese women's musical performance practices are not only open to outside influences but also include specific places in which those influences may be revealed. Both the Islamic nature of "Hamdan" and the fact that "Ceurik Rahwana" contains the specifically Sundanese apology of a major Hindu character to his wife reflect the importance of a simultaneously Hindu-Islamic balancing act for the Sundanese.

Accessing the Spirit Through the Cracks and Borders

Different factors have driven each one of these musical and spiritual intersections. Irish women's inclusion of Mary-centered song reflects a larger division of public and private—doctrinal and vernacular, male and female—religious expressions, and their coexistence as part of current spiritual practice is an important aspect of what it means to be Irish. In the case of Japan, the fact that Japanese people themselves have blended Shintōism and Buddhism for centuries set the stage for the integration of the two after World War II, as well as the incorporation of Christmas and Santa Claus in recent years. Brazilians of African descent had no choice about their resettlement in Bahia; the elements of African and Catholic religious practices that appear in Candomblé are a result of conscious choices, political expediencies, and active engagement with the spirit world.

The more in-depth examination of Sundanese Hinduism as performed by Muslims connects to older ways of relating to the rural past, and newer ways of incorporating changes to existing traditions. By performing (Hindu) "Ceurik Rahwana" and "Kulu-Kulu Bem" in a modern context, Sundanese Muslims find an unbroken line to the *local* at a time when their former political and cultural power has fallen under the heavy influence of modern Indonesian nationalism. By performing (Muslim) "Hamdan" during a night of *tembang Sunda* performance, the context is welcoming to those at different societal levels where the shadows of an older Hindu caste system remain.

Evidence of the ways in which musical systems belonging to the followers of two different faith traditions can be found in numerous places around the world. These examples appear here, in a book about music and liminality, specifically to illustrate the idea that some of the most powerful moments of intersecting musical sounds occur at a deeper level than simply, for example, combining two forms of music. Combining two faith traditions in sound can engage one's euphoric sense of community, of participation, and of reaching something greater than oneself. It is at precisely those moments of sonic ecstasy that one has the potential to connect with the divine.

4

Erotic Currency

Amach as an uisce a bheirtear an duine. Out of the water a person is born. (Ireland)

This chapter shifts into the territory of the alluring, with women, water, eroticism, and sung performance as a means by which *people*, more generally, can focus attention on ambiguous places, acts, and beings. The element of water is so fundamental to human experience, and so normal, that its ubiquitous presence in mythology, folklore, and performance is often overlooked. Yet it can be deeply and simultaneously connected to female-coded singers as eroticized beings, across many cultures. The transformative unpredictability of water, along with its simultaneous possibility of offering life or death, looms large in the liminal space it occupies. The addition of music through the feminized body of the singer in or on the water connects a liminal place, liminal act, and liminal person in alluring combinations. The "floating" or "willow world" of the geisha of Japan may be a familiar metaphor, as are the sirens of ancient Greece, who lure men into dangerous or deadly territory through song. Rivers named after goddesses and holy wells associated with female saints are just further evidence of those connections. That female performance is so often carried out in proximity to water, or even *in* water, is part of that affiliation. The *cortigiane* (courtesans) of Venice—performing artists, intellectuals, politically savvy powerhouses—served not just as a form of male-tempting siren, but also made a practice of disrupting male systems of power and privilege as they traveled the canals of the city.

But who are these "women"? For the purposes of this chapter, the women in reference are not necessarily heteronormative cisgender females. Some are not even human. As you read through the case studies, keep in mind the idea of erotic currency driving interactions between humans of all sexes, between mortals and gods, and between gods and goddesses. That erotic currency is much more about what is represented—danger and desire—than the

Music at the Threshold from the Sacred to the Dangerous. Sean Williams, Oxford University Press. © Oxford University Press 2026. DOI: 10.1093/9780197761762.003.0004

specifics of a person's (or a deity's) biology. While the case studies discuss specific female elements, the women and female-coded spirits represented here comprise just a fraction of each culture area under discussion. The case studies of female water spirits in this chapter, then, might be relevant to just a portion of the people in any given place. Assuming rich diversity within each area referred to in this chapter is key.

Neither the concept of nor the English word "liminality" automatically applies to each potentially in-between situation straight across all cultures, and not every encounter with water, for example, will evoke the female element, the erotic, death, or singing. Some of the details outlined in this and other chapters were selected because of their resonance in specific places; however, the contents of the sections here are not intended to imply a "theory of all things." Instead, they represent more of a collection of liminal congruences that appear repeatedly in specific areas of the world.

Water, so tied to the earth through gravity, is associated with the underworld in various regions of the globe. Humans, being unable to live without water, are drawn to it through stories, folklore, and songs. The allure of water extends to being drawn to everything connected to it, including a sense of welcome and well-being (White et al. 2010: 482). As a source of life, particularly in regard to holy wells and sacred springs, it is also recognized as a source of death. Even though it can be considered an undifferentiated mass, water nonetheless changes constantly. Its seemingly fickle nature (running dry, flooding, misting, freezing) makes it an element about which there is vigilance; its dangers in terms of drowning are obvious. As will be shown, women, in association with the powerful, alluring, dangerous, and sacred nature of water, absorb some of that power—and apparent need for vigilance—through localized mythologies. That connection can lead to their frequent depiction in mythology, for example, as wringing abundant water from their hair, which ensures fertility and protects the people in the region against drought.[1]

Described as "subversively transcendent" because of their ability to control men through their singing voices (Braham 2018: 149), the figure of the mythological siren may inhabit the body of a human or of a hybrid woman-serpent or woman-fish. They are connected to water, whether singing siren or singing human. In reference to the many manifestations of *Mami Wata* in Africa, "She is a transcendent, transformative, transcultural, transnational, transgendered, and trans-Atlantic being" (Drewal 2006: 295). These figures do sing, but they may also dance; they can imbue musical instruments with powerful voices of their own. As Austern and Naroditskaya point out, "However diffuse or improbable their bodies, with or without souls, the song of the sirens has often been the most memorable aspect and principal locus of their tremendous power" (2006: 3). Singing and dancing is, in fact, the manifestation of their erotic power and the engagement of creative play.[2]

In Russia, the *rusalki* represent a type of liminal young spirit woman, simultaneously alive and dead; she is responsible for the growing fertility of the fields and is deeply connected to the moment between betrothal and marriage. She represents a kind of pause during what is now known as the (Russian Orthodox) feast of Pentecost, when work must cease and men must not approach water for fear of being lured into it by the song, laughter, and dancing of the rusalki (Dynda 2017: 103). The power of the erotic in song is sustained by the draw of water as a basic human need; it is also essential for the perpetuation of farmlands.

The mermaid as North Americans know it is all about the body—"the wholesale displacement of vocal seduction on the enticing body, a shift simultaneously reflecting modern culture's transfer of fascination from verbal to visual forms and its fetishization of female flesh" (Goscilo 2007: 58). While the generic mermaid may be ubiquitous—from the image on your cup of Starbucks coffee (from a nineteenth-century Nordic woodcut) to the figurehead of a ship to the Disney films *The Little Mermaid* and *Splash*—it is the ambiguous yet alluring water-woman and (primarily) her song that is the focus of this chapter.

Part of the joy of being familiar with a trope is that when it is used in comedy, the comedy is even more entertaining. In the popular film *O Brother, Where Art Thou?* (2000), the lead characters are escaped convicts who encounter some women stationed at the edge of a river because the men hear their singing voices as they drive past. The men stop, irresistibly drawn to the sound. The women are (of course) scantily dressed in wet white clothing, singing in harmony, and washing white cloth. Alcohol is involved. Naturally, our gents are helpless against the sirens' overwhelming erotic, spiritual, and vocal power. The ensuing hilarity is made funnier by the fact that the audience is expected to know something of the source being parodied by the film: Homer's *Odyssey*. The Coen Brothers, makers of the film, never actually read *The Odyssey*, but they know the high points as well as any layperson who has heard of it: Man goes on a trip and encounters dangerous beings while his wife fends off annoying men at home. Movie critic Roger Ebert had this to say about the film:

Another sequence almost stops the show, it's so haunting in its self-contained way. It occurs when the escapees come across three women doing their laundry in a river. The Sirens, obviously. They sing "Didn't Leave Nobody But the Baby" while moving in a slightly slowed motion, and the effect is—well, what's it's supposed to be, mesmerizing. (Ebert 2000)[3]

Several excellent sources drew me toward writing this chapter. *Music of the Sirens* (Austern and Naroditskaya 2006) reveals the hybridity of the singing water-woman. In its multiple chapters drawn from several places and in its mixture of classical and traditional sounds, it brings us again and again to the idea that there is no stable sense of security in this key liminal figure of mythology and culture. *The Courtesan's Arts: Cross-Cultural Perspectives* (Feldman and Gordon 2006) offers a rich and detailed sense of courtesan culture from Europe to Asia. While noting that part of the courtesan's work is sexual, the focus on the arts ties in to how power and eroticism are traded across class, gender, and political boundaries. The links between water, the erotic, and the power of song become clear. *Sacred Waters: Arts for Mami Wata and Other Divinities in Africa and the Diaspora* (Drewal 2008) is rich in multi-authored profiles of African and diasporic water spirits across thousands of miles. *Water and Womanhood: Religious Meanings of Rivers in Maharashtra* (Feldhaus 1995) goes deeply into the feminized topography and geography of the Mumbai region of India, exploring the festival traditions, mythologies, and other elements that bring the water and the women into contact with each other.

Another source drew me in, though. Decades ago, I was raised on the many gory murder ballads favored by my Kentucky-born mother. In the British Isles and across Scandinavia and their respective diasporas, the ballad "The Twa Sisters" (Child ballad #10) features an older sister drowning her younger sister out of jealousy over a man. The body of the younger sister is discovered in the water by a man (often a miller or fisherman), who creates a harp out of her breastbone and strings it with her hair (Figure 4.1). In some cases, the tuning pins are made of her finger bones. When the harp is brought to the wedding between the older sister and the lover of the younger sister, it is placed at the hearth (the threshold of fire and connective point to the Otherworld) where it plays and sings the story of its (the younger sister's) murder. In the case of this song, the water spirit of the murdered younger sister has been borne downstream before its transformation into that most popularly feminized of Western instruments, the harp, and freed to sing its story only at the mighty threshold of the hearth, with all its elemental power.

The earliest published version of "The Twa Sisters" (sometimes called "Binnorie" or "The Cruel Sister") is as a broadside from 1656 (Child 1882: 119); its popularity continues to the present in various places and through folk and folk revival performances such as in the band Pentangle's song, "Cruel Sister." It also conforms to the classic "truth comes to light" motif (#780) of the Aarne-Thompson tale index (Aarne and Thompson 1961: 269–270), in which a musical instrument is fashioned from the body of a victim, and thereby enables the victim to tell their story. I mention "The Twa Sisters" here not to highlight the deadly cruelty of the sister, but to point out that without the water, there would be no story. And without the liminal moment of the body being transformed into a harp, the spirit of the woman would have remained silenced forever. As Amanda Lalonde describes it, "the human body and the instrument come together to create a grotesque, living-dead amalgamation of breath and metal, wood, sinew, and string" (Lalonde 2015: 602). Only through water, and the liminal transformation into a new living-dead hybrid being, may the story be told.

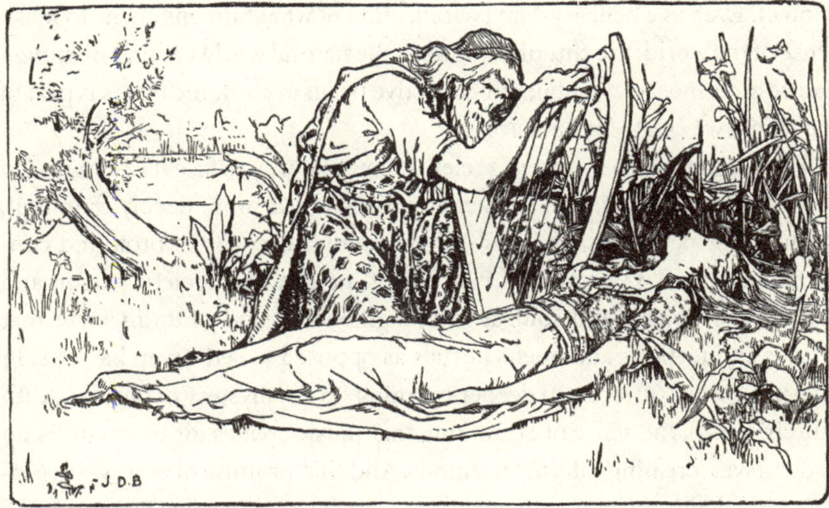

Figure 4.1 "Binnorie," illustration from *English Fairy Tales* (John Jacobs), 1895: 45

The Waters and the Goddesses

Many rivers of the world are gendered female. In Europe alone, the Shannon, the Loire, the Danube, the Volga, the Po, the Tagus, the Thames, the Moselle, the Don, the Vistula, the Elbe, and many others are all considered female in local gendered languages and mythologies. Most of the rivers of India are female as well (Feldhaus 1995: 40). Out of such an elemental sacred force comes the replenishment of water for the survival and fertility of humans, of animals, and of plants in the fields and forests. Humans have brought gifts to both shore and riverside for millennia to ask for help from the female spirits of the water; some of us in the twenty-first century toss coins in the water of a fountain or a well in the hope that a wish will be granted. It is a form of contagious magic, also known as the law of contact; bringing something of our own as a gift connects us to the power of the water and the female spirit in it.

It is belief in and connection to the chthonic forces—the powerful spirits of the underworld, of water, of the earth—that drive the development of these localized beliefs about women and water as a type of erotic currency. They are associated with life and death, fertility and abundance, and esoteric knowledge: *access*. Gaining access to those forces through female principles, water, song, and/or eroticism is a way by which people—often men—gain a type of reflective or associative power for themselves; again, it's the law of contact. Even as a belief system is a reflection of what humans create to make sense of the world, the chthonic forces of the natural world are part of *human* nature at its most elemental; our collective belief in chthonic forces is part of the reality we create for ourselves.

The German verb *stimmen* is relevant here. At the surface it can mean "to be in tune or correct," but its meaning runs much more deeply than that. Its noun form, *Stimmung*, is also used to indicate a type of profound concordance between person and instrument, person and society, person and nature, and person and soul. It is a heightened mood of *attunement* that reveals connections and opens portals as opposed to setting up barriers. In offering a sense of access to deeper meaning, to the mystery of life and death (and beyond), the sense of Stimmung that music creates for us opens us up to ourselves, creating internal harmony. And that promise of access—to esoteric knowledge, to nature, to ourselves—can be made available through the voices of the women of the water.

In a brief survey of women associated with water, one could easily explore the sea-mother of the Inuit, Sedna, who was drowned by her father; a spiritual intermediary has to journey underwater to ask for her blessing. Atargatis, an ancient sea goddess of the Middle East, gives fish and life. Ireland is the home of Brigid, the goddess of healing, holy wells, and fire. In Brazil, Yemanjá is the sea spirit and source of all life; people bring offerings to her at the shore, with the greatest offerings arriving at twilight and carried by fishermen in boats. Ganga in India has her manifestation in the holy waters of the Ganges river. Isis, the "star of the sea," and Nut, the goddess who brought rain, are omnipresent in Ancient Egypt. Oshun, the Yorùbá goddess of rivers, divinity, and fertility, carries a fan. The thermal springs of Bath, England, were associated with the goddess Sul, linked with the Roman goddess Minerva. The winged maiden-harp of Ireland[4] was used in the eighteenth century to simultaneously represent the nation, galvanize several political movements, and serve as the figure at the prow of a ship.

While the ocean is not universally gendered as female, some of the earliest female deities are associated with the ocean. Mazu (China), Tiamat (Babylon), Nyai Roro Kidul (Java), Nammu (Sumeria), and many other named local goddesses are tied to saltwater and creation stories. Olokun of West Africa—particularly in Yorùbá communities and the diaspora—is variously gendered as female, male, or androgynous, depending on local custom.

Amphitrite, the Greek goddess of the ocean and partner to Poseidon, gave birth to fish, dolphins, and seals. Most of the ocean mammals—whales, dolphins, manatees, and dugongs, the latter two of which belong not coincidentally to the *Sirenia* family—are matriarchal or at least matrilineal (Rendall et al. 2019); their liminality in particular came under discussion in Chapter 2. One could even take note of the sultry (read: dangerous) women singing alluring jazz standards in tight slinky dresses at "watering holes" in old black and white films. Sultry is closely related to swelter, meaning "to faint (or die) from the heat." The presence of the dangerous goddess and the water is seemingly ubiquitous.

What is also quite common (and long-standing), though, is the use of these figures as a way to affirm political, spiritual, or sexual power for the men. So this chapter is not just about the linkages between women and water; it deals with the special combination of women, water, sexuality, and performance, and the examples are drawn primarily from that subsection of a very broad pantheon with regional variations and generally in relation to their simultaneous relationships with the natural world and with the world of men. Note, however, that each of these case studies includes something of an objectification of the female; as the object of desire, her alluring agency can sometimes be subsumed under the mantle of the dangerous—the *femme fatale*, the siren, the diva, or the sex worker.

How does liminality figure into this discussion? Women who are removed from society—whether isolated in a specific district (or temple, or island), and perhaps existing between life and death (as in the *rusalki*) or between the past and present (as in the *geisha*)—are perpetually in between. Sexual activity breaks the boundaries between people, even without actual penetrative intercourse. Its sacred nature is acknowledged in major religions, its allure is a biological imperative, and its danger is connected not just to sexually transmitted diseases and risky pregnancies but to violence caused by the need to possess. One of the most famous conflicts over a woman is the Trojan War (Greece, twelfth or thirteenth century, described at length in Homer's *Odyssey* and *Iliad*), but between honor killings, the use of rape as a weapon of war, and jealousy-fueled crimes of passion, women often bear the brunt of male violence. Water is sacred, between its appearance in holy water, sacred springs, and its necessity for life. It is alluring in the way it draws people to the shore, to waterfalls, and to water views. It is dangerous in that it can kill in an instant. We can't stay away from it. In combination with the erotic power of the women in these examples, those drawn to them don't stand a chance against their songs.

Seven Case Studies

This chapter features seven case studies of different culture areas—from Greece, Japan, Russia, India, the Andes, Indonesia, and Central and East Africa—to make a larger point. Women and water are both fundamental to the continuation of life. Eroticism, whether humorously connected to women and song as in the film *O Brother, Where Art Thou?* or in a more deadly sense of being lured to one's death by the singing voice of a siren, is an element of the connection between women and water. Eroticism energizes all of these case studies to a greater or lesser degree. Some are not indigenous to the area in which they currently reside; the Andean *sirenas* are an indigenized colonial import with local precedent, for example. Regardless of their respective origins, though, each figure is entrenched in the folklore and mythology of the location. In most of these case studies, many ethnomusicologists and other scholars did the initial fieldwork and analysis; I also did some of it.

What follows is at least partly drawn from and expands on the excellent work of my colleagues in both music and academia, with respect and credit.

The Sirens of Ancient Greece

Draw near, illustrious Odysseus, man of many great tales, great glory of the Achaeans, and bring your ship to rest so that you may hear our voices. No seaman ever sailed his black ship past this spot without listening to the honey-sweet tones that flow from our lips, and no one who has listened has not been delighted and gone on his way a wiser man. (cited in Nugent 2008: 48)

Our most consistent early representation in the West of the conceptual cluster of women, water, sex, and song appears in the form of the sirens and is represented to us through Homer's oral epic, *The Odyssey*. The sirens appear in Book 12 of the epic and are just one of Odysseus's many encounters, yet their influence and skills at using alluring song are known in the present (more so than, e.g., the competition among Penelope's suitors to try to string Odysseus's bow in Book 21). They are described in a warning by Circe as the bearers of wisdom and foreknowledge; they may kill those who find them irresistible, but they may also render that person immortal. They are liminal in the possibility of being simultaneously death-dealing and life-giving. Painting the various women of Odysseus's adventures as deadly distractions not only gave Homer a way to extend his model of the Greek hero, but it affirmed, over and over, the masculine rightness of following a true path against the temptations of women, while bonding with other men in the process.

In Book 12, Odysseus is told to block his sailors' ears with beeswax so that they won't hear the song of the sirens; Circe suggests that he have his men tie him to his mast so that he can hear the song, but to charge his men with not unbinding him no matter how much he begs.

Who draws near in ignorance and hears the sound of the Sirens, him wife and innocent children shall not meet on his returning home, nor shall they have joy of him, but the Sirens beguile him with clear-voiced song, sitting in their meadow; but all about is the great heap of the bones of rotting

men, and their hides waste away around them. (cited in Holford-Strevens
2006: 16)

He begs, of course, but they don't release him until they are safely past the
danger that the sirens pose to the ship (which would have broken up against
the rocks near one of the islands, and the men would have been killed by the
sirens). Helena Goscilo refers to the chaotic, liminal, deadly moment when
any man tries to resist the sirens' song of adventure, distraction, or fulfillment
away from home as "the polarized dyad of roam/home" (Goscilo 2007: 51).
The binding of Odysseus to his ship's mast to resist the deadly allure of the
sirens would not be the first or last time that a phallic image (and all that it
implies) has been the only thing a man could consistently rely on to resist (or
dominate) female power.

Leofranc Holford-Strevens presents the possible etymology of *siren*:
"... from a West Semitic (Phoenician?) *šir-ḥēn*, 'bewitching song', parallel
to Hebrew *'eben-ḥēn*, 'magic stone, talisman, charm'" (Holford-Strevens
2006: 17). Note also that in English we use the word "siren" to describe
the loud and urgent sound of the fire truck, ambulance, police car, or
approaching tornado; we know immediately to take shelter, to figuratively
tie ourselves down, and to stop our ears. We do not actually have a sense of
what the sirens looked like from *The Odyssey*; we know only what we *imagine* them to be.[5] It conveys on us, the listeners of *The Odyssey* in recitation,
the absolute authority to imagine their allure for ourselves and to create the
sight and sound of irresistibility.

It is also possible that our own imaginations are far stronger than any literal description of what was embodied by the sirens. This imaginative power
and the allure of song, women, and water may be precisely why so many
visual artists have attempted to capture the appearance of the sirens, and why
they appear, repeatedly, in the popular imagination. The actual sound of the
sirens—their song—is unknown, but is described as being simultaneously
beautiful and full of important knowledge that could have helped Odysseus.
Furthermore, because their singing surpassed that of any other creature,
Homer would have had to avoid depicting the songs with any precision, lest
they surpass his own creative work.

The sirens are usually seen in ancient Greek iconography as hybrid
creatures, with the head and torso of a woman, and the body, tail, and feet of
birds. Their looks are nearly identical to the Ba-bird of ancient Egypt from
a thousand years earlier; the bird aspect represents the fact that the soul,

following the death of the body, is connected to the Otherworld. In Spain, the seventh-century archbishop Isidore of Seville wrote that sirens were "harlots, who, because they would seduce passers-by into destitution, were imagined as bringing shipwreck upon them. They were said to have wings and talons because sexual desire both flies and wounds. They have lived among the waves because the waves gave birth to Venus" (Blarney 2010: 245). The idea of the siren as a *fish*-woman does not appear until the eighth century CE (in the *Liber Monstrorum*, an anonymous catalogue of monsters). Until that time, the sirens of ancient Greece were bird-women.

Homer uses the word *thespesios* ("divinely sweet") to describe the voices of the sirens in his tale; the prospect of the sirens actually singing *about him* (Nugent 2008: 50) might not only have been irresistible to him, but might possibly serve the larger purpose of emphasizing his own masculine power in the presence of powerful, sacred, erotic, knowledgeable women. "This memorable section of Homer's oral epic registers the danger posed to teleological homosocial machismo by mysterious females who reside in unknown, turbulent waters—that is, outside the blueprinted, stable terrain of patriarchal regulation, logic, and self-affirming activity" (Goscilo 2007: 51). Any woman who transgresses the patriarchal power dynamics and uses her voice, her brains, and her body in an empowering way—Beyoncé, anyone?— is disruptive to the social order.

The Floating World of the Geisha

The image of the Japanese *geisha* has a well-worn place in the Western popular imagination: she is exquisitely dressed and coiffed; she plays a musical instrument and sings; and she inhabits a (semi-tragic) world outside the realm of the ordinary. The image of the geisha is also frequently depicted in popular culture as being frozen in time in the Edo Period (1600–1867), rather than functioning as a living, breathing—though highly symbolic of traditional life—human being of the present with full autonomy and agency. Although some of these case studies focus on the nature spirit or water nymph element of the local mythology, some, including the geisha, are fully human. But as a full human being whose public persona is elaborately costumed in layers of kimono, historical hairstyle, and very specifically coded makeup, the geisha carries the symbolic weight of several hundred years of Japanese traditionalism within Japan itself.[6]

Anyone who becomes a geisha has undergone years of dedicated training in the arts. The word geisha comprises *gei* (arts) and *sha* (one who does); as professional artists of music, dance, theater, comportment, and conversation, these women are standard bearers of excellence. As is the case with the others in this chapter, they also bring a deep allure of the erotic to everything they do. In particular, the geisha of Kyōto are believed to represent the heights of sensual elegance; Jennifer Matsue describes Kyōto as "steeped in erotic imagery" and that "the refined sexuality and importance of tradition are captured in the arts" of the geisha or *geiko*, as they are known in Kyōto (Matsue 2016: 158).

It is too easy for non-Japanese people to assume that someone gifted in erotic temptation is a sex worker only. The actual culmination of allure and eroticism in physical sex may well be present, but it is not what being a geisha is about. The value of the geisha in contemporary Japan lies instead in what she represents: Old Japan, nostalgia, and access to a different way of life, as well as the elegance of tea, exceptional skills in traditional arts, erotic temptation, and flirtatious conversation; what Lesley Downer describes as the "eroticism of concealment and mystery" (2006: 236). In the chaos of cutthroat urban living, such a person can be an oasis of calm, joy, and pleasure.

During the time that I worked in Japan as an exchange faculty at the University of Hyōgo, I visited many *onsen* or hot springs. Bathing and soaking in very hot water is an important aspect of being Japanese. In a conversation about this exact subject with several Japanese colleagues at the university, I learned that there was a popular sense that *all* the hot springs were connected underground, and that the network of hot springs was itself at least partly connected to the underworld. An entire class of geisha work in *onsen* towns in Japan; though their clients are usually temporary rather than long-term patrons as in the cities, they too are professional artists (Downer 2006: 224). Even in towns such as Kyōto and Tōkyō, river travel was the way to reach the geisha districts, and a man in transition to those districts would be in a different mindset by the time he arrived (Screech 2006: 256). In Japan of the Edo Period, visiting a geisha was associated with crossing water to what was sometimes referred to as "The Willow World." Willow trees have their roots in water, at the edges of streams; they are strong, but flexible. Another common term for the district of the geisha during the Tokugawa period (1603–1867) is *ukiyo*, 浮世, "The Floating World." But *ukiyo* is also a homophone for "Sorrowful World," a Buddhist term indicating the suffering under which one bears the cycle of death and rebirth. That ephemerality, associated with water and transitions, connects to the ambiguity of the geisha.

In 1661, the writer Asai Ryōi (1612–1691) wrote about the nature of ukiyo: "Living only for the moment, savoring the moon, the snow, the cherry blossoms, and the maple leaves, singing songs, drinking sake, and diverting oneself just in floating . . . " (Hickman 1978: 6). In their own way, each of these ephemeral pleasures connected to water and floating are the world of the arts, and are located in the urban milieu. As for the singing voice one might hear in the ukiyo, this lush description from the *Tokugawa Bungei Ruiju* serves only to heighten the sense of stepping away from one's normal activities.

> The sound of [her] voice when she greets you is like the mysterious first call of the nightingale as it flies forth from a valley recess . . . and when she begins to sing, one's heart is buoyant and one's spirits rise to heaven's heights with the sounds of her voice in song. And even though one returns on the morrow to the dust of the temporal world, for now there is the rapturous dream of the floating world. (Kokusho 1914: 339–340)

In keeping with the many gradations of the profession, there are specialists. Geisha who specialize in music are known as *jikata*; they play instruments or sing in contrast with those who specialize in dance or other arts. The *kouta* or "short songs" of the traditional repertoire are an essential element of the quality of *iroke*—sensual understatement (Dalby 2000: 11). It is never obvious, because to be outwardly sexual or bluntly sexy would be crass. In its very subtlety lies its intense eroticism, as a language that an informed insider would speak, but which might be lost on an outsider.

The geisha of the twenty-first century live between worlds. By existing outside both the realm of Japanese wife/mother and working woman role (since professional geisha are sponsored by the state), the liminal existence of the geisha represents pure dedication to the arts (Foreman 2008: 83). This arts-focused dedication is precisely what gives her agency, rather than serving only at the whim of a male patron. Well beyond the most obvious dichotomy between Old and New Japan—in which a geisha in full Edo-era dress might wait for a traffic light to change while texting away on her *keitai* (cell phone)—the subtleties of ambiguity pervade the in-between culture she represents.

The Rusalki of Russian Rivers

Among the several major female figures in Russian mythology—including the terrifyingly powerful Baba Yaga, the forest-dwelling bird-woman (*sirin*), and the water-dwelling *rusalka*—it is the *rusalka* that is the focus of this case study. Derived from the name of the spring festival at which the figure appears—*Rusalia* or Pentecost, the name appears to be a post-Christian imposition on multiple older, localized names (Dynda 2017: 86–87). At its most basic level, the rusalka bears a similarity to the siren of Greece in that *rusalki* (plural) are water-women who lure men to their deaths through their songs; they may well derive from Greek beliefs. But there are complications specific to Russia that make the rusalki an interesting point of focus. Her fluids—"amniotic fluid, menstrual blood, maternal milk, or, in folklore, the revivifying 'water of life'" (Goscilo 2007: 64)—are a potent combination, against which men who stray near water are helpless. Vodka, so deeply tied to Russian identity,[7] translates as "little water" (*voda + ka*). In northern part of Russia, the rusalka is referred to as the *vodyanitsa*, the water spirit. As another one of Russia's powerful and alluring liquids beyond those embodied by the rusalki, vodka features prominently at life-cycle rituals such as weddings, funerals, and post-baptism celebrations.

Many scholars describe the rusalki as the souls of drowned woman who "live in rivers and cascades and lurk near unwary bathers" (Schultze 1982: 77). They have usually been disappointed in love (falling for the wrong man, a weak man, or a cheating man) and are considered objects of dread and pity. The soul of a drowned person is considered unclean (Warner 2011: 156); it occupies a type of liminal existence as a *revenant* with one foot in each world of the living and the dead. Others who occupy this category include unbaptized children, suicides, those who died in violence, and those who die just before a wedding (Dynda 2017: 88). That sense of uncleanliness about the improper dead has deep roots in local beliefs about spiritually powerful women, thought of as witches. Those beliefs "imbued community members with an understanding of evil, deviant social behavior and the dangerous sexual nature of women" (Worobec 1995: 166). With such beliefs fully in place regarding both the danger of those who have died an unclean—*ne svoja*—death and those whose actions are regarded as sexually uncontrolled (through marriage or other means), the development of local customs, arts, sayings, and practices to ensure safety makes sense.[8] Rusalki generally sing and dance to attract adult men; their actions can include tickling them to death, dancing them to death, and seduction in a river, which leads to drowning (Dynda 2017: 90). And yet, they are essential in the fertility of the fields.

For the villagers of southern Russia, the image of a young woman dressed in white or naked, combing and moistening her long, unbraided hair in the moonlight, is a classic sign of spiritual and physical danger. Leaving one's hair unbraided would be distinctly outside the norm, and could cause immediate suspicion (Dynda 2017: 92); since hair is unbraided just before a wedding, the rusalka's unbraided hair meant she died in mid-ritual. Her hair would have been braided just after the wedding, but at that moment of her death, with her loosened hair, she belongs to no one and is potentially available to anyone.

Because the rusalki are generally believed to have been spurned, they are in limbo between courtship and marriage (Moyle 1986: 234). Yearly springtime rituals purging an area of its rusalki spirits include the presence of young village girls with their hair down, dressed in white, being noisily chased out of the village and through fields of rye, back to the waters (Warner 2011: 163). Only then, with the dispersal of the unclean spirits, can the fertility of the fields be ensured through the symbolic transmission of water from Mokosh, the great moist-earth mother figure to the fields.

During late spring [. . .] the rusalka performs the sacred rites of cyclical resurrection: she emerges from the water so as to moisten the earth, swing on birch branches (invoking fertility by symbolically enacting the rhythms of procreation), participate in the round dances (*khorovody*) that likewise symbolize continuity, and promote vegetative growth. (Goscilo 2007: 63)

This cycle follows the seasonal patterns of the water: in the winter, the rusalki live underneath the river ice, emerging as the ice melts in the spring. By the summer they have come out of the water as the sap rises (Matossian 1973: 332) to sit or swing on the trees (Figure 4.2). Their appearance coincides with the flowering of crops, and it is the only time of the year that they are visible (Dynda 2017: 96). The rusalki are associated with the birch tree—one of the trees closely tied to Slavic mythology—whose Proto-Indo-European root word *$b^herH\acute{g}$-* means "to shine white." Birch trees are known for their flexibility and strength; they are used for home, furniture, and musical instrument construction. The Russian birch thrives in very moist soil, and when a rusalka figure is depicted in a river, it is usually a river banked

Figure 4.2 "Rusalki," by Konstantin Makovsky, 1879

with birch trees. As the national tree of Russia, the birch also appears in love songs because of its connection to women.

In her discussion of the persona of the rusalka in Russian poetry and opera, Inna Naroditskaya points out that they are "half-magic and half-human—once-earthly women inflamed by love and burned by betrayal" (Naroditskaya 2006: 219). She also notes that the rusalki in both poetry and opera has had to appear powerful at the beginning, but end up being both narratively and musically suppressed in favor of celebrating the figure of the masculine hero, representing the nation. That the rusalki would serve as an element of Russia's national mythology in the nineteenth century has to do with the importance of establishing the *male* heroic figure in the context of cultural romanticism. It means celebrating *male* folk characters and the traditional beliefs of the Russian people as a means by which Russia could affirm its unique in-between position as simultaneously European and Slavic.

Through centuries of Christianity, these water sprites came to represent unrestrained and irresistible sexuality, illegal paganism, and the chaos of creation. (Naroditskaya 2006: 219)

The erotic nature of the rusalka is very much a part of her allure. Because she exists between living and dead, between the courted and the married, and between human and spirit, it is her very ambiguity that sets her apart as both liminal and extraordinary. She transgresses the norms of what is expected (even to the point of her scandalous refusal to braid her hair like a "normal" Russian woman). The "tired and tiresome imperative of envisioning the rusalka as fatal temptress" (Goscilo 2007: 67)—or, for that matter, the *femme fatale*—reduces her power to one merely of sex = death. But it is her singing voice, ultimately, that proves fatal: men might be able to resist a beautiful woman, but they cannot resist a voice.

The Apsaras and Devadasis of Indian Temples

India's religious and cultural diversity precludes the idea of examining a single type of celestial female spirit/human who is engaged in the performing and erotic arts across all of its major religious practices. Instead, this case study has as its focus both the *apsara* (Sanskrit: "water flow"), an important figure in Hindu-Buddhist belief whose primary performance mode lies in both dance and song, and the *devadasi*, a type of living counterpart as a sacred courtesan. Apsaras are always associated with the clouds and water, wherever they are; their connection to the natural world is central to their existence. Usually married to the *gandharvas*—male celestial musicians who perform at the heavenly court of Lord Indra—the apsaras figure prominently in Indian court dances as well as in local iconography. In addition to being important in many regional traditions of India, their influence on the performing arts has spread across all of Southeast Asia. Where Hindu-Buddhism has gone, so have the apsaras and their human counterparts. As approximately 80 percent of Indians follow this path, the currents of Hindu-Buddhism have historically comprised a significant proportion of social norms in India and its diaspora in Southeast Asia and elsewhere.

The presence of the apsaras in so many myths, creation stories, and iconographic works reveals their centrality to Hindu-Buddhist identity. The Churning of the Ocean myth features the gods and demons churning the ocean to extract an elixir of immortality and, in doing so, led to the creation of the world. The apsaras—along with the goddess Lakshmi and other powerful beings—are said to have emerged after the churning. In this story, "everything produced (except the poison *kālakūta* which appears in some versions) was of an auspicious nature, connected to fecundity, prosperity, abundance, eroticism, fertility, and immortality" (Cohen 2021: 6). As in the other case studies in this chapter, the apsara is traditionally associated with a plant, the *śāla* tree; another word repeatedly connected to apsara is *śālabhañjikā*, the one who breaks the śāla tree.

Part of the nature of the apsaras is that they have been historically regarded as a type of sacred temptress. In some of the stories of the *Mahābhārata* epic, for example, they are sent to distract the focus of ascetics because the Lord Indra worries about the men's growing spiritual power (which might disrupt his own). In several stories, an apsara ends up being turned into a river because of the curse of an ascetic (Feldhaus 1995: 41). In river form, the erotic allure of an apsara is somewhat mitigated. Because most of the rivers of India are gendered female, the socially recognized link between the rivers and, for Hindus, the performing apsaras is widespread. Apsaras are often depicted in the act of wringing water out of their hair; rather like the rusalki, their presence brings fertility to the soil and life-giving water. The abundance and lush fertility associated with both lies in direct contrast to what it means to be an ascetic: a system of self-denial and abstinence. If a man is denying himself the pleasures of life to attain spiritual and/or political power, that power would be seen as a direct threat to the deity.

The apsara has a living counterpart in the *devadasi*, a woman whose life has been dedicated to serving the god at a temple as a singer and dancer; local terminologies prevail for the specific title. Living in "the borderline between the embodied present and the historicized past" (Soneji 2012: 6), devadasis have been largely and forcibly separated from the status that once elevated them to the sacred level of the apsaras. First mentioned in the second or third century BCE (Roy 2009: 49; Srinivasan 2006: 162), the devadasis' ambiguity as powerful religious women outside of patriarchal control made them simultaneously revered and reviled (Srinivasan 2006: 166; Soneji 2012: 2). Being able to support a devadasi allowed a male patron greater status, as she was considered auspicious (Shingal 2015: 109). In the position of being married to the god Vishnu (and therefore not capable of being widowed), the devadasi engages in eroticism as part of the sacred performative act of worship. At the time, devadasis were associated with the goddess Lakshmi; within her domain are wealth, beauty, and fertility. Connecting sexually with the devadasi means knowing the divine; to dance is *also* to know the divine. To quote Frédérique Marglin, "The dance is a divine sexual intercourse" (1990: 224).

Before the Christian missionaries of the nineteenth century and the post-colonial conservatism of Indian society turned the livelihood and devotion of the devadasis into one akin to sex workers (Dalrymple 2008), the high-ranking women who embodied worship at Hindu temples had a unique type of ambiguous, sacred power. In the introduction to *The Courtesan's Arts*, Feldman and Gordon (2006: 13) note that "The female life force of the sacred Indian devadasi could render her extraordinarily powerful because she literally took God, and other men who partook of God, into her body and incorporated that divine force into her own fluids, thus inspiring a sacred transformation." And connected to the powerful waters of Indian rivers are the life-giving waters of the female body: her sexual fluids. "The creative powers released by this life force assure prosperity, fertility, and well-being of the land" (Srinivasan 2006: 169). However, that changed dramatically as an aspect of colonialism.

> Colonial ethnography, the legal surveillance of sexual morality, and the disciplining of sexualized bodies were central to the new order represented by empire. (Soneji 2012: 6)

While most of the other figures in this chapter primarily deal with song, the practices of song and dance became separated in the devadasi traditions after Indian Independence in 1947 (Sarah Morelli, personal communication). However, the British had already established the Bombay Devadasi Protection Act by 1934 (one of several state-wide acts by the colonial government), which was intended to prevent women from being part of the system.

The respectability of the voice—with its importance in religious practices—is very different from patriarchal and colonial notions of the disrespectability of the female body. The physical embodiment of the sacred through the devadasi has been suppressed since its outlawing in 1947, and women who would have been supported by the temple are now subsisting primarily on the wages gleaned from sex work (Soneji 2012: 3). Though many of those who fulfill this function are still referred to as devadasi or its variants, the overwhelming majority of current public opinion pieces in the Indian press reveal a sense that the tradition is a type of shameful embarrassment in the twenty-first century, as if the women (and the fulfillment of their traditional sacred role) shouldn't exist at all.

The Widadari of West Java

After I had been living in (predominantly Muslim) West Java for a couple of years during my doctoral research in Indonesia, I was driving past one of the local hot springs of Lembang, a highland village north of the regional capital city of Bandung, with my primary teacher and person *in loco parentis*, Euis Komariah. We noticed some women (both cisgender and trans) dressed as sex workers, waiting for clients near the entry to the springs. "Too bad," Ms. Komariah said. "Long long ago they existed as singing *widadari* [nymphs], but now they've fallen. Of course, if they stray far from the springs, they'll turn into regular prostitutes [*pelacur biasa*]." I put that information away, mentioning it in my field notes, only to have it resurface while drafting the first ideas for this chapter. Those Sundanese Muslim women at the springs were part of a much older legacy steeped in local—Sundanese Hindu-Buddhist—mythology. Hindu-Buddhism predates Islam by many centuries in the region, and blended in upon the arrival of Islam.[9]

The apsaras of India, above, have many local manifestations across Southeast Asia. In Java, they are usually called *widadari* or *bidadari*. Their constant movement between worlds, luring men through sacred erotic dance and song, is a source of creative energy, musical composition, and continuous engagement. In Sundanese culture of West Java, the bamboo flute (*suling*) and zither (*kacapi*), along with the aristocratic Hindu-based songs they accompany (*tembang Sunda*), are profoundly connected to the Hindu past (Williams 2018: 43–59). The zither itself is an embodiment of the widadari, a manifestation of the rice goddess, Dewi Sri. Any man who wishes to engage the creative energy of the goddess through music—as embodied in those musical instruments—must unclothe the body of the goddess by removing the cloth covering the instrument (Van Zanten 1989: 97) and "marry" it by playing it.[10] That marriage, then, produces music as the child of man and goddess (Rukruk Rukmana, personal communication). "When I want to play the kacapi, I marry it directly," he said. The verb for "play," *main*, is used for both musical instruments and sexual intercourse. The verb he used for "marry," *kawin*, is a form of unconsecrated marriage, implying more of a direct sexual connection than *nikah*, the formal, legal one.

At the edges of springs and caves in the forested highlands of West Java, the Sundanese ancestors and gods are poised between the underworld and the world of humans. The Sundanese term *ngambang*, which is more than simply "in between" but very close to suspended or floating in its meaning, applies to this sense of hovering between worlds. In his work on chthonic forces in the Sundanese highlands, Robert Wessing links wet rice cultivation with the underworld and with the goddess (Wessing 1988: 55). For the Sundanese, rice is the *only* real food. Its consumption makes us human. The inner sanctum of a Sundanese home is the kitchen, where the rice is stored; only women may enter the traditional kitchen, because that is where the Hindu rice goddess and widadari Dewi Sri is honored. She is responsible for the fertility of the Sundanese rice fields and for the appearance of rice in the first place; Dewi Sri and others brought rice to people to help them avoid starvation (Wiyatmi et al. 2020: 18). Widadari figures can engage sexually with humans ("marry," as in *kawin*, above), which ties them to the earth just as much as they are tied to the heavens. Because the widadari can bring either fortune or collapse—rather like the sirens of Ancient Greece with their life-giving advice or death—Dewi Sri's ambiguity is one of her most important aspects and why she needs to be continually propitiated.

Honoring the rice goddess occurs in many ways, but one important way is through both sex and sound to encourage the fertility of rice. Early reports of either actual or simulated sexual activity at the rice fields note the laws of contact between the fertility of humans and the growth of rice (Wessing 2020: 93). The clustering of bamboo around the edges of rice fields—and springs—also links that strong, flexible, water-based plant to local fertility cosmologies. G.A. Wilken noted in 1912 that the bamboo along the rice fields had holes drilled into them so that the resulting wind-generated music could entertain the rice goddess (cited in Wessing 1998: 52) and generate fertility. Similarly, the tuned bamboo rattles of Sundanese *angklung*, and their accompanying erotic and humorous songs, inspire Dewi Sri to bring fertility to the fields (Baier 1985: 9). Access to the erotic equals male access to power—both creative and political—in local mythology. The combination of the presence (and sounds) of the flexible bamboo and the human voice, the fertility of rice and humans, and the magic of the liminal places is rich territory.

In Sundanese folklore, sexual encounters between gods and humans take place near water: in pools, springs, bamboo groves, and wet rice paddies (Wessing 2020: 83). This is the place where the connection between Dewi Sri and the sex workers of the twenty-first century comes into play. If historically the gods and kings who witnessed the widadari bathing in springs and pools were unable to resist them, the water is the place of liminal eroticism. The tembang song addressing Dewi Sri ("Mupu Kembang," "Picking Flowers [in preparation for marriage]") to the accompaniment of the bamboo flute and the (unclothed) kacapi zither enacts that erotic relationship and takes listeners to the waters.[11] It also focuses attention on the importance of weaving by literally naming the parts of the loom in one of the verses. Wim Van Zanten notes that before marriage, ". . . a girl should have learned to spin, weave, work in the (rice) fields, and prepare food (rice)" (Van Zanten 1984: 292). Singing "Mupu Kembang" is itself a form of preparation in its evocation of the goddess thinking of her physical and sexual connection to a mortal man. In remembering the words of my Sundanese teacher Euis Komariah, the sex workers of Lembang were at the edge of the underworld. By remaining close to the springs and the bamboo, the potentially erotic allure of the women was in a controlled but nonetheless dangerous location for men at a liminal connective point to the spirit world.

The Sirenas of the Andes

Given the exceptional reach of European colonialism during (and after) the Age of Exploration (fifteenth to seventeenth centuries), the presence of an alluring female figure associated with water, music, and danger wherever the Europeans went is not coincidental. In the Andes, Iberian connections to not just the sirens but to the stringed instrument called the *vihuela* were already being imported shortly after Pizarro's crews arrived in 1532 (Stobart 2006: 107). The *charango*, having developed locally from the vihuela, is irrevocably associated with the Peruvian *sirena*. In Brazil, the Iara figure of local mythology is a fish-woman. "With long black hair and brown eyes, the mermaid Iara emits a melody that attracts men, who are captivated and mesmerized by her singing and sweet voice."[12] In the Patagonian region of Southern Chile and Argentina, the *sirena* (of the lakes and rivers) and the *pincoya* (of the sea) have featured in local tales since at least the seventeenth century.

The *sirena* or *sirinu* of the Andes is a figure with or without a fishtail, connected with colonial Spanish mythologies, who has become interwoven with local Indigenous beliefs about music and seduction. "Accounts of sirens in the Andes, as elsewhere, highlight the beauty of their music and its ability to enrapture or seduce the listener, who is attracted irresistibly and sometimes fatally toward the source of the sound" (Stobart 2006: 116). While local variations about the specific powers and characteristics of the sirena exist, the figure itself appears in folklore and mythology all along the Andean range from Colombia to Chile; I heard people discuss it during my visit to Ecuador. The central importance of this figure in Andean agriculture and courtship cannot be overstated, and its connection to sound and water is widely understood.

Thomas Turino, who has worked extensively in the Peruvian Andes, drew from his work on the *charango* (a small, postcolonial Andean lute based on the Spanish guitar) and its cultural context to discuss the sirena (Turino 1983: 81–119). Because young men of the (highland) Cusco region use the charango as a central part of their courtship rituals, they learn to play it in order to locate and acquire a potential lover. They enlist the power of the sirena, a fishtail water nymph from whom magic can be drawn to imbue the *charanguista* with more allure in his search for a mate. In that particular area, where stringed instruments are strictly associated with colonial ventures, the colonial-era sirena is tied *only* to the charango and not to the Indigenous wind or percussion instruments.

The sirena lives in waterfalls, springs, lakes, and other natural sources of water, and is linked to the ability of music to draw (or ward off) rainfall (Solomon 1997: 249). As Turino points out, each town has its own sirena (living in water), and they are so profoundly tied to musical production that "if a certain town does not have a *sirena*, then there will be no music in that town" (Turino 1983: 96). To increase their chances of attracting young women with the charango, young men offer gifts to the sirena by placing the gifts near a spring and next to the charango at night. The sanctification ritual thereby links the instrument to the sirena and her water source. If the gifts have been accepted, the "voice" of the charango will be more compelling, the charango will be tuned, and the *charanguista* will have successfully drawn from the seductive power of the sirena in order to be successful in courting women. In general, it is the *men* who play all the stringed instruments (Stobart 2008: 72).

Similarly, in Bolivia, the *sirinu* figure is equally connected to Spanish colonial mythologies, but with a local emphasis on agriculture. In contrast to the association that Turino noted with the charango, the Bolivian people with whom Henry Stobart worked described the sirinu as connected to wind instruments such as the *sikura* panpipes and *pinkillu* flutes (Stobart 2006: 113). He points out that visiting the springs inhabited by a sirinu the evening prior to a feast—with the wind instruments—will bring the panpipes and flutes "in tune" for optimal performance. She herself does not sing, but the instruments "sing" as a result of contact with her. She enters the instrument at that point, ensuring that "the player will never run out of new tunes to play" (Solomon 1997: 237). As in Peru, the Bolivian sirinu lives not only in springs, rivers, and waterfalls, but also in rocks near water. Stobart notes the presence of celestial sirens on a number of Andean churches, where they are depicted playing stringed instruments against a backdrop of stars and clouds.

Bamboo grows in some areas of the Andes, and is used to create flutes and panpipes. It grows where there are sources of fresh water; that the sirenas are associated with fresh water enables us to recognize the importance of the laws of contact—as with the willow world of the geisha and the birch trees of the rusalki—and note that strength, flexibility, and moisture are important elements connected to this musical plant, just like the others. In the case of bamboo being used for a flute or panpipe, the sound of the flute is the *voice* of the flute (Jonathan Ritter, personal communication).

For the purposes of connecting the sirena (a European import) with the other powerful water nymphs of this chapter, let us note that drawing from her abilities to enhance musical skill—or lingering too long in the area where she dwells—might also potentially bring harm to the man who approaches her (Solomon 1997: 245). Henry Stobart points out some commonalities among the Andean sirenas: among other features, they can imbue musical instruments with fine "voices"; they can make a man irresistible to women when he plays such an instrument; they are a source of musical creativity and inspiration; they are dangerous; and they require a contractual relationship to bestow their gifts (Stobart 2006: 113–114). One can meet a sirena by stepping outside of one's *own* environment and approaching that liminal place; it is the dangerous allure of musical and sexual or charismatic power that draws people across those boundaries (Sáenz 2017: 446). In all cases, the sirena (or sirinu) is a known entity to local musicians and others; the figure's power and ambiguity—it could be evil and deadly, and it could bring blessings and luck in love or agriculture—is at the heart of its living, liminal identity. And it is always linked to water.

Mami Wata Across Sub-Saharan Africa

The hybridity of sacred female water figures connected to music is widely distributed across Africa and its diaspora in the Caribbean and South

America. Mami Wata, one of the generic names for many local female water goddesses (primarily in West Africa), blends layers of traditional belief, colonial imports, and local practices; her followers comprise an array of insiders and outsiders who respond to her with music and visual arts, among other creative works. While generally not a singer herself, she and her many manifestations convey musical gifts to those who serve her; compare her work with that of the Andean sirenas, above. The name—possibly (ambiguously) from Pidgin English, "Mother Water"—is used in many different regions within West Africa, but so are other names specific to individual locations; all of them have some connection to a female deity connected with water (even if that deity is not located precisely in or next to water).

The clear and obvious importance of the female water maiden to Europeans—the mermaid figurehead seen so often at the front of ships, for example—led to the syncretic blending of colonial models with local belief systems already in place. And yet, her own ambiguity is precisely who she is; she can inspire music or bestow material wealth or a longed-for pregnancy. She can also destroy a livelihood or take a life. She is sacred, alluring, and dangerous in every way. "In short, it is her hybridity, her trans-ness, that helps to explain her power and presence. She is compelling because she transgresses boundaries; she embodies the qualities of 'mixed origins'" (Drewal 2008: 2). Transgression is a path to power (see Chapter 6), and her very ambiguity highlights the erotic currency of the unknown. This ambiguity is never far from the minds of performers who seek her out as their muse.

Because she crosses so many religious, linguistic, and cultural divides in intensely local and regional Africa, a few practical standards appear in local practices. Among those standards are included the creation of altars with water themes and items of beauty—combs, mirrors, perfume—to make her feel welcome; playing music for her also serves as an act of propitiation (Drewal 2006: 300). Contemporary devotees sometimes discuss communicating with her "by telephone," which appears as a modern manifestation of older forms of "lines" of communication to the spirit world (Egonwa 2008: 225). Note the similarities in the use of music in West Java to please and welcome the rice goddess, earlier in the chapter. But music is not only an important way of pleasing the deity; it is also a means for communication with her. And the voice, so crucial in musical communication with the spirit world, is part of one's engagement.

Part of the danger of Mami Wata is her agency: she may choose whom she favors or destroys, and singers offer her praise in order to connect with her power. In one example, Michelle Kisliuk illustrated this tension through her translation and analysis of a hit song by Thiery Yezo of Centrafrique—the Central African Republic—titled "Mami Wata." In the song, the lyrics praise Mami Wata, and indicate that she is welcome to take the singer back (to the water) with her; if she doesn't, he will die. That the singer in this case *did* die after the release of the song added to the mystique surrounding his possible connection to Mami Wata (Kisliuk [Drewal] 2006: 310). It is the combination of danger and allure connected to Mami Wata that has caught the attention of various Christian churches within Africa who seek to suppress her appearance in local culture. "In both forest and urban settings, musicians, dancers, and healers negotiate a fine line so as to avoid censure by Christians" (Kisliuk 2008: 420). While the celebration of Mami Wata is an important element in developing one's own musical creativity, it is risky not only in regard to the church, but in regard to the agency of Mami Wata herself.

A regional variant of Mami Wata appears in East Africa, which highlights the importance of the female water deity as a healer. Kubandwa is a pan-East African women's system of religious beliefs and practices dispersed through the "interlacustrine" or interconnected lakes and waterways region around Lake Victoria, which intersects with Uganda, Kenya, and Tanzania. Frank Gunderson discusses this belief system in connection with practices that take people underwater to study healing. Referring to healer, dancer, and singer Kisunun'ha Nyumbani, Gunderson writes: "He was introduced to the healing arts by his grandmother, who in a classic shamanic scenario, took him to be schooled by his ancestors who live beneath a lake, probably Lake Victoria-Nyanza, for seven years sometime during or after World War II" (Gunderson 2010: 79). As someone whose outward appearance was somewhat genderfluid, Nyumbani may well have been recognized as akin to the women versed in the healing arts. When one comes to the water as a supplicant, one can undergo a powerful transformative experience. Mami Wata persists across different parts of Africa because she and the many other related female water spirits are among the driving liminal forces of musical creativity, danger, healing, and syncretic spiritual practices and beliefs.

Music and Erotics

In each case study in this chapter, one notes the power, tension, and instability of desire. The figures are "ambiguous and furtive, veiled but showy, performative, and meretricious" (Feldman and Gordon 2006: 3). In the case of the human courtesans, their very positionality draws on the capacity of their spiritual sisters to lure, challenge, and even kill their amorous pursuers. However, none of this is actually dependent on an outsider-imposed sense of simplistic opposition between male and female, because the erotic energy that animates each of these figures is not limited to just one side or another. It challenges existing power structures. It is, in fact, the *currency* of power in musical interactions, situated in a cultural context of erotic hyper-awareness. If, for example, we return to Japan for a minute, we know that the people playing geisha characters on the *kabuki* stage are men. They are no less sensual or erotic than the real-life geisha, and can be even more so, precisely because they know to tap into the culturally bound set of expectations around dangerous ambiguity, and so does their audience, in its recognition of their desire and desirability. To assume that the erotic is identical to the pornographic is to place a terribly limiting stricture on the power of human imagination, creativity, and desire.

Austern and Naroditskaya hold the key to a crucial element of our understanding here: "But an encounter with a siren is not always about sex. It may be about creativity, the dream, artistic transgression—or the nature of music itself" (2006: 9). And that reveals the folly of conflating the erotic and the pornographic. Audre Lorde has written and spoken at length about the power of the erotic, and that the suppression of the erotic, its exclusive restriction to mere sex, and its separation from *all* of our great passions serves only the patriarchy. "But the erotic offers a well of replenishing and provocative force to the woman who does not fear its revelation, nor succumb to the belief that sensation is enough" (Lorde 2006: 88). Because desire is often directly related to that which may be forbidden—by law or by local custom—it can exist in perpetuity, forever unanswered.

In each case study, it is the female-coded beings doing the luring, with little apparent interest by storytellers in these beings' *own* desires and their *own* opportunities for *jouissance* or effervescent pleasure. Instead, their very reason for existence would seem to be as the object of unattainable desire. Would the *sirena* of the Andes be equally needed by women who wished to become better musicians and agents in their courtship of men? Would the modern vestiges of the Sundanese *widadari*, now primarily serving as sex workers near hot springs, have a reason to hover near the water? It seems that rather than merely serving as objects for the male gaze, it is their above-mentioned disruption of the social order that serves the larger purpose here.

If erotics have to do with power and control, transgression and agency, then their employment through performance offers a measure of vulnerability as well. Some of the erotic draw of performers has to do with the possibility of access across boundaries; by gaining access, a spectator is engaging in a disruptive structure. It is, as Henry Spiller writes, "a case, then, where the particular protocols and frame of a performing arts tradition clearly both reveal durable structures that govern gender ideology and, at the same time, empower individuals to exercise their own agency to deform, and perhaps eventually alter, those structures" (Spiller 2014: 342). The desire for embodied access to other ways of knowing is strong enough to engage in transgression, to step outside of one's comfort zone, and ultimately to risk death and/or displacement.

I would like to point out that it is not the music alone—specific melodies or rhythms, for example—that is doing the job of erotic enticement. Notes and rhythms on their own, devoid of context, can have some impact, but that is not where the magic lies. The magic, instead, is in the mind: the combination of sound and lived experience and mythology and context. It affects human beings across the spectrum of sexualities and orientations rather than being confined to some idealized heteronormative standard. That combination, then, is fired into a crucible of erotic capital (Hakim 2010: 501) that leads to irresistibility. Without that high level of historical and cultural knowledge—about the culturally bound powers and limitations of engagement—the erotic capital of a nymph or a living human would see diminishment.

Some of the people in these case studies are living beings, while some are water nymphs or other mythological creatures. All of them, however, are representative of the ambiguous allure of the feminine principle (regardless of actual gender) in connection with water, whether in hot thermal springs or ice-cold high-elevation waterfalls. So much of their power depends on their ambiguity and instability; their very existence emphasizes liminal hybridity (Austern and Naroditskaya 2006: 7). While Kyōto's geisha may well be charged with eroticism, it is the fact that physical sex is no guarantee (and not even necessarily the point) that imbues them with power. Similarly, the rusalki in the Russian rivers aren't always ready to kill the men who wronged them, but they might. The apsaras and devadasis of India are threatening in their erotic power—to the ascetics who would challenge the spiritual strength of the god Indra and to the human men who would engage in sacred sexual intercourse—and must be controlled.

The dangerous allure of water, eroticism, and music all highlight the importance of ambiguity, and with that ambiguity the rigid conventions of sexual morality can waver. The widespread linkage between the singing voice and the spirit—to the point that the word of God arrives through the *voice* in several major religious practices—lends an air of spiritual power to the promising eroticism of the singing female body. In connecting these singing women to elements of nature—water, of course, but also the willow of Japan, the cane of the Andes, the bamboo of West Java, the śāla tree of India, and the birch of Russia—the fundamental essence of these figures is grounded in the chthonic forces of the earth. They are neither entirely of one side nor of the other, but have access to both.

5

The Presence of Absence

Toda saudade é a presença da ausência alguém. All of *saudade* is the presence of someone's absence. (Gilberto Gil, Brazil)

In the lyrics from "Stranger Blues"—a blues song that appears in *Our Singing Country* (John A. and Alan Lomax 1941)—the protagonist is left alone at a railroad station with a newly deceased mule, no place to go, and a sweetheart who has caught the "KT" (Missouri–Kansas–Texas train) and is waving goodbye:

I'm a stranger here
I'm a stranger everywhere
Yeah, I could go home
But I'm a stranger there.

The combination of someone caught at a liminal place (the train station), a liminal moment (separation from his sweetheart), and a liminal animal (a mule is a combination of a horse and a donkey) at the moment of its death could be more emphasized *only* through the addition of a sunset (neither day nor night) and alcohol (neither sick nor well). It seems like an appropriate way to begin a chapter about migration, music, food, longing, and home/not-home.

Migration is often experienced (and assumed) in the United States as an arrival from another country. Most of us who went through the public school system in the United States have photographic images of poor white European (*always* white European!) immigrants newly arrived at Ellis Island burned into our brains.[1] Even as the appallingly racist legacy of slavery worked its way into our national systems of education, politics, and social interactions, the Great Migration of Black people from the South to the North in the 1930s and 1940s looms large—because it rests so vividly in *living* memory—in the public imagination of a subset of American society. And lest we make

Music at the Threshold from The Sacred to the Dangerous. Sean Williams, Oxford University Press. © Oxford University Press 2026. DOI: 10.1093/9780197761762.003.0005

the mistake of assuming that Indigenous people "have always been here" in one place ("America"), keep in mind that the horror of boarding/residential schools, language loss, the Trail of Tears, the very existence of reservations, missing and murdered Indigenous women, and repeated exterminations continue to hover, large and loud, over Indian Country.

Beyond the arrival from another country, though, is the near-inevitable separation from place. Timothy Rice has explored the ways in which ethnomusicologists have worked to build awareness of immigrant challenges and discrimination. "Wars and other forms of conflict, as well as economic deprivation, often force people to migrate from their homelands to other parts of the world, where they not infrequently become unwelcome minorities within nation-states defined by nationalist ideology as coterminous with the majority nationality" (Rice 2014: 197). Moving from majority to minority, then, is more than leaving home; with that separation lies trauma, emotional displacement, and a damaged sense of longing—damaged because there were reasons to leave the previous home in the first place. For some contemporary refugees, the use of social media to broadcast music serves as a way of insisting on the legitimacy of their existence; it also allows them to hear the sounds of home in the absence of live music (Hebert and Williams 2020: 481). In his extraordinary work *The Uprooted*, Oscar Handlin keenly perceives that damage and the fact that immigrants were alienated from both *there* and *here*.

> The old folk knew then they would not come to belong, not through their own experience nor through their offspring. The only adjustment they had been able to make to life in the United States had been one that involved the separateness of their group, one that increased their awareness of the differences between themselves and the rest of the society. […] They had thus completed their alienation from the culture to which they had come, as from that which they had left. (Handlin 2002: 285)

Most first-generation migrants never fully assimilate, yet they often change so much that they are no longer fully able to feel welcome at home. With a foot in each place, they have access to both "homes," yet they are no longer fully *of* either place once they have departed. I offer the following quotation, from Season 3 of the early 1990s American television series *Northern Exposure*, to my students before I take them on study abroad to Ireland; it is from the African-American character Bernard Stevens (who has recently come to Alaska after three months in Africa).

> In a sense, it's the coming back, the return, which gives meaning to the going forth. We really don't know where we've been until we've come back to where we were. Only, where we were may not be as it was because of who we've become. Which is, after all, why we left.

Few people have the chance to return to what they left behind; when they do, they discover how different it is, at least partly because of how different *they* have become. The artist Bruno Catalano created a series of bronze sculptures titled *Les Voyageurs*; each one features a missing piece representing what they have left behind (Figure 5.1). The loss, though, is two-fold. They are neither here nor there, and their neither/nor status becomes part of who they are forever, poised at the edge of between. It is brought into deep, searing presence with the senses, particularly in two areas: music and food. And for some, especially a generation of two down the line, home is a place of pure idealized imagination so remote that one doesn't even have to visit it to recognize its calling. In my own work with Irish-American music and musicians, I often encounter people for whom Ireland is a dream-like location. Because I visit Ireland about once a year, I forget that for many, a visit to the "homeland" is out of the question. It is stronger in the imagination than in the reality.

Food and drink are crystal-clear signifiers of home and of distance from home. Because 30 million Europeans emigrated to North America in the latter part of the nineteenth century, they infused their new communities with attitudes, systems of food preparation, and often a sense-laden ability to evoke *place* through food. Historian Hasia Diner, whose *Hungering for America* focuses on the role of hunger in driving migration from one place to the next, regards food as often forming a central locus of identity.

> Migrants, when they settle down in new places, regardless of how long they plan to stay in their new homes, attempt to recreate familiar foods. They find ways to prepare them, cooperating with each other to make them available on a community basis. Their stores, bakeries, boarding houses, cafes, and restaurants all bear witness to the desire of the newcomers to relive the foodways of places left behind. (Diner 2001: 9)

Figure 5.1 "Le Grand Van Gogh," part of the series *Les Voyageurs* by Bruno Catalano (photo credit @ Robert Poulain). © 2026 Artists Rights Society (ARS), New York/ADAGP, Paris.

Food can serve as a deeply evocative taste of home in its connection to what feels right. It brings their families and their childhoods to the front of their minds and allows a somewhat idealistic sense of home to permeate the sensual experience of taste. As you read this chapter, I urge you to think about what food evokes the taste of home for you. It might surprise you. For me, it is the taste of Japanese miso soup that instantly returns me in my mind to my Berkeley upbringing, where I learned to use chopsticks as a young child. As an adult, now that I have actually lived in Japan, that feeling of deep security and safety triggered by the taste of miso has only been strengthened in my mind.

Whereas some European migrants celebrated food as the heart of who they were, others leaned harder on alcohol. Alcohol enhances the liminal state in that one is neither sick nor well; it can also render a person powerless and, sometimes, deep in addiction. The common stereotype of European—Bohemian, Irish, Russian, Norwegian, Czech, etc.—immigrants who spend their entire paychecks at the bar (pub, tavern, saloon, etc.) is an old one. The emphatically male culture of such places reinforced images of masculinity—in the context of the drinker's subaltern status as immigrants—and drinking together arose as a mark of male community-building.

> One's ability to drink hard demonstrated great powers of manliness, just as athletic prowess or expertise in storytelling did. The more an individual had proved his manliness, the greater his status within the group. Moreover, the ethic of hard drinking imposed minimal standards of hard drinking on all bachelor-group members. (Stivers 1976: 91)

In that the Irish were a significant immigrant group in the mid-nineteenth century, with several million arriving in North America during and after the Great Famine (1845–1850), their behaviors paved the way for other Europeans who followed. Irish-themed sheet music (and, later, recordings) that had been marketed to them—as one ethnic group—became marketed to others as well, and St. Patrick's Day grew into a general celebration of (white) ethnic heritage over time. Richard Stivers points out that the heavy drinking of the Irish immigrants, as an example to later European immigrants, came to serve as "a means of consuming one's ethnic identity and heritage" (Stivers 1976: 197). And because stereotypes are hard to break, older European immigrant men, in particular, face an array of assumptions about their use of alcohol to break down their longing for home.

Mark Slobin uses the term *superculture* to describe the existing dominant culture (Slobin 1993: 29); in a situation of migration, the migrant comes into a place and has a hard encounter with the superculture that does not always go well. In each community of migrants, however, the rush of feeling that surges through the system from hearing the music or experiencing the taste of home in the context of the superculture is repeatedly, heartbreakingly, temporary. The elusive power of taste, whether musical or culinary, is that it draws us in, again and again. And even though that ephemeral nature of *home* is part of our individual and collective identity, its temporary nature compels us to try to hover, right there, in between where we are and where we were, or who we are and who we were.

To Transplant in Alien Soil

Let us begin our exploration of this liminal moment with the example of the Great Migration from the Deep South of the United States to the Industrial North. Primarily between 1916 and 1930 (but really, all the way to the 1970s), more than six million African Americans left the rural South for the industrial North. During World War I, there were shortages of industrial workers, and the segregationist laws and policies of the South drove people north to the cities along rivers and railroad lines, where wages were nearly three times as high as they were in the South. Labor agents from the North signed up Black workers to serve as strike-breakers, leading to conflicts and race riots down the road; in the South, the labor supply began to dry up. Journalist Isabel Wilkerson refers to the Great Migration as a silent pilgrimage. "It crept along so many thousands of currents over so long a stretch of time as to be difficult for the press truly to capture while it was underway" (Wilkerson 2010: 9). Black artist Jacob Lawrence's *The Migration Series* comprises sixty extraordinary paintings that capture the urgency and chaos of the time.[2]

In his 1945 semi-autobiography *Black Boy*, Richard Wright points to his set of expectations about leaving the Jim Crow South and heading north to Chicago in the 1920s. His poem, "The Warmth of Other Suns" (Wright 1993: 496), reveals that he and other people migrating north were not leaving the South so much as bringing something green and alive north with them; something potentially fragile, but capable of growth.

> I was leaving the South
> To fling myself into the unknown . . .
> I was taking a part of the South
> To transplant in alien soil,
> To see if it could grow differently,
> If it could drink of new and cool rains,
> Bend in strange winds,
> Respond to the warmth of other suns
> And, perhaps, to bloom.

Musically speaking, one of the hallmarks of the Great Migration was the shift of the blues from a primarily solo, male, guitar- (and harmonica-) based genre of the Mississippi Delta region to a multi-person group that often included piano and amplification in the cities farther north such as St. Louis, Chicago, Detroit, and Pittsburgh. By the 1920s, female singers—and to a lesser extent, instrumentalists—were a key feature of the blues scene. Having left the South, usually for good, many of the key figures of the musical migration continued to perform the same songs they had performed at home. For those who flocked to the clubs to listen, the songs were a poignant reminder that home was not what it could have been: a place of ease and comfort and safety. Home was dangerous. So the migrants to the North were well aware of the fact that they had thrown in their lot with the increased opportunities and a different kind of racism in their new place, while missing a powerful image of what they had left behind and all of the missed potential for the thriving home it could have been, were it not for the bitter realities of enslavement and segregation.

The liminal "blue note" itself—neither a natural third nor a flatted third degree of the scale—is often highlighted as one of the most direct and obvious musical signifiers of the blues. Regardless of its origins (Is it a direct holdover from West African pentatonism? Is it something created in the Mississippi Delta?), it is the hallmark note of the blues, and therefore one of the primary ingredients in jazz. And as readers familiar with Ralph Ellison's *Invisible Man* will remember, there is a moment that the narrator perceives the scent of roasted yams being sold by a street seller and is overcome with memories of home. As he tastes the food of home, slathered with hot butter to the point that it drips down through his fingers, his revelation—that the yam is his birthmark that tells him who he is—becomes a catalyst in his rejection of the outwardly imposed shame about where he comes from (Ellison 1952: 266). The ache of sense-based memory is richly familiar to any migrant.

The Great Migration brought not only blues musicians from the Mississippi Delta, but jazz musicians from New Orleans. Those who migrated also included people who became the audience members for these musicians, and an African-American-centered music scene developed in the northern cities. As was the case with instrumental urban blues, standardization and amplification for singers became an aspect of jazz in northern big cities. Cities along the major transportation systems of the Mississippi and Missouri rivers, the railroads, and the seaports became centers for jazz. Kansas City, Memphis, and St. Louis are still well-known for their music scenes, but they might not have been so famous if it weren't for the important developments in transportation and technology such as the radio and recording industries.

The jazz singer Billie Holiday (1915–1959) continues to have a presence in the public eye of the twenty-first century for many reasons: her gifted voice, her extraordinary life, and her presence at some of the most important moments and places in African-American history. She was introduced to the song "Strange Fruit"—perhaps her signature song—by the club owner of New York's Café Society (the only integrated club in the area); he had been given the song the previous day by its author. Abel Meeropol was a Russian Jewish schoolteacher, songwriter, and poet from the Bronx; originally titled "Bitter Fruit," his song was an anti-lynching piece. She sang it night after night at the club, and it has been recorded and performed by many other singers; record producer Ahmet Ertegun calls the song "the beginning of the Civil Rights Movement."[3]

Southern trees bearing strange fruit
Blood on the leaves and blood at the roots
Black bodies swinging in the southern breeze
Strange fruit hanging from the poplar trees.

Pastoral scene of the gallant south
Them big bulging eyes and the twisted mouth
Scent of magnolia, clean and fresh
Then the sudden smell of burning flesh.

> Here is fruit for the crows to pluck
> For the rain to gather, for the wind to suck
> For the sun to rot, for the leaves to drop
> Here is a strange and bitter crop.

Though much has been written about the song, and Holiday's 1939 recording and subsequent performances of it,[4] take note of the song's extraordinary liminality. The lynched figures hover between earth and sky, connected by the blood on the leaves and roots. They are fruit, but they are not. They experience the moment of death in (literal) unspeakable suspension. The sun, wind, and rain—so life-giving under other circumstances—leach out the very essence of their vital humanity. Billie Holiday herself was liminal; she spent some of her early years in a brothel, was the first Black singer to perform in front of an all-white orchestra (Artie Shaw's band), was bisexual, and spent years of her life imprisoned by addictions (and literally imprisoned for drug charges). But her performances in clubs, on the road, and in the recording studio were all temporary gigs; like most musicians, she had no permanent place of employment. Part of her enduring appeal was her identity as simultaneously damaged and gifted; both elements have shown through in her singing. "She really was happy only when she sang," Ralph J. Gleason, the jazz critic, wrote. "The rest of the time she was a sort of living lyric to the song 'Strange Fruit,' hanging, not on a poplar tree, but on the limbs of life itself" (Margolick 2000: 22). Hovering between damaged and gifted, performing liminal songs for liminal people in liminal places, and the tragedy of dying too young (from cirrhosis) are all part of her continuing renown.

The eminent performing artist Lena Horne (1917–2010) is quoted as follows:

> For many years I was to be virtually rootless in the world—a stranger in the white world, of course, for color must keep you forever a stranger there—but also a stranger in the world which most Negroes inhabit and with which they are forced, from birth, to come to terms. Neither world was ever to be totally mine because I would never stay long enough in either of them to acquire that intimate, bred-in-the-bones knowledge of them that comes from having roots so deep you cannot see or even trace some of them. (Horne and Schickel 1966: 3)

Lena Horne's own ancestry (African-American, Native American, and European) kept her simultaneously from fitting in anywhere and from being entirely excluded; she was an insider, and an outsider, and a stranger everywhere.

Part of exploring the idea of migration, longing, and performance in African-American communities is recognizing the strong presence of specific southern customs that have persisted not just in the industrial North, but across the United States. Part of marking the change from one year to the next is preparing specific foods and following traditions to ensure that the next year begins well and invites prosperity. First, the main meal is Hoppin' John, the name of which may derive from Haitian Kreyòl *pois pigeon* ("pigeon peas" or black-eyed peas). This meal features highly symbolic features that signify wealth and progress, including peas (coins), pork (moving forward), collard greens (folded green bills), garlic, peppers, and other ingredients. The cornbread that it is served with is gold (money). Also on New Year's Eve the house must be swept and scrubbed to remove the bad energy, the windows left open to invite good fortune, and the invitation of a specific person (a child, a person of the desired sex, someone with money in their pocket, etc.) to cross the threshold into the home right at midnight.[5] The continuous liminal elements surrounding this transitional day fit right in with the idea of effecting change at the one truly transitional time of the year when it will be most beneficial.

We Don't Have a Word for This

> Rivers are the old roads, as are songs, to traverse memory.—Joy Harjo (Muscogee)

At the end of Chapter 3 the term *wa'as* came up as a Sundanese (Indonesian) exemplar of the liminal point between joy, bitterness, longing, sweetness, sadness, nostalgia, and other feelings. In connection with the migrant experience—regardless of whether one is going out, coming back, or moving on—this concept is paramount to not just the encapsulation of the experience, but the importance of the senses in both triggering it and responding to it. In brief, you once had it (whatever it was) but can't have it again; your memories are profoundly and simultaneously sweet and sad. As a reminder, wa'as connects the sounds—plucked strings, bamboo flute, low-pitched voice—that you hear in a Sundanese performance of *tembang Sunda* to the simple quiet home next to a rice field with the sun setting, the fireflies dancing, a volcano in the distance, and the one who used to love you sitting nearby.

One of my strongest memories of my two years of living in West Java, Indonesia (home of *wa'as*), was on Christmas Day of 1988. My brother and his husband were visiting, and we were invited to the home of my teachers, Euis Komariah (voice) and Gugum Gumbira (dance), for a small Christmas dinner. We were so very touched by their kind gesture; since they were Muslims without a prior encounter of the Christmas holiday, they guessed what we might like (songs and foods, of course). When they and their four teenaged daughters invited us to sing the special songs that go with the holiday, we complied even though neither my brother nor I were raised to be anything more than mildly culturally Christian, and my brother's Spanish husband is a confirmed atheist. They sang along with the melodies, and in a few cases the songs translated easily into Indonesian and they learned those quickly. I translated all of the songs that we sang, and then I came to the song "I'll Be Home for Christmas." I translated it, as I had the others, and was startled when the teen daughters began filling in all the categories. "You have special foods, right?" "And decorations!" "Is there snow?" "And the whole family gathers!" "And everyone shares all the good memories!" They leaned in with excitement. The song, representing the viewpoint of a World War II soldier who won't be home for Christmas because he is overseas (and likely to die in battle, after all), is a *devastating* tear-jerker. It was recorded in 1943 by Bing Crosby.

> I'll be home for Christmas
> You can count on me
> Please have snow and mistletoe
> And presents on the tree
> Christmas Eve will find me
> Where the lovelight gleams
> I'll be home for Christmas
> If only in my dreams.

When I reached the end of the song, I shakily translated the final line, suddenly realizing with horror that I was drastically altering the joyous mood and their excitement. There was a collective gasp. "WA'AAAS!!" "Aduuuuh, dalam mimpinya saja!" they said ("Oh noooooo, only in his dreams!"), and we all tried unsuccessfully to blink back our tears; for my brother and me, the image of our parents at home alone without us on Christmas Day loomed uncomfortably large in our minds. Then we ate grilled skewered chicken, rice, and other delicious local foods, ending with fresh mango slices and plenty of raucous laughter for dessert. Given that the local song tradition is famous for its many songs about heartache, and its sense of wa'as, it was all deeply satisfying from a local perspective. There is both beauty and pain in this image. Sundanese musical culture is not the only location for this sentiment, however; it appears all over the place. In Japanese, it's *natsukashii* (懐かしい); see also *hali'a aloha* (Hawaiian), *benkshaft* (Yiddish), *hiraeth* (Welsh), *añoranza* (Spanish), *hanin* (حنين—Arabic), *sehnsucht* (German), *cumha* (Irish), *toska* (Russian), and many others. Each one of these liminal terms has nuances specific to the local context, but there is very much a sense of profound personal memory— looking back— and engagement. How is it that this concept appears to be a normal word nearly everywhere but in English?

The Portuguese and the Brazilians (and Portuguese speakers, more broadly) use the term *saudade* in music, in poetry, in literature, and as an almost national ethos. With a contested etymology but possibly connected to the Arabic *sawdā* (melancholy mood), saudade appears in Portugal in the *fado* genre (and others), and in Brazil in the *bossa nova* genre (and others). The word's connection to music is so well-known in the United States that some jazz musicians who have played bossa nova—a pared-down version of samba rhythms for guitar used to accompany the voice—know and regularly use the word for the sense of melancholy for something that one can never truly possess . . . if one ever did. Brazil's long history of immigration— both voluntary and involuntary—and migration within the country itself indicates that the importation of saudade from its colonial source paved a pathway for it to thrive in the centuries that followed as its people were on the move.

With its beginnings in the early nineteenth century, the Portuguese song genre *fado*, "fate," is based on a much older sensibility, present in both Portugal and Brazil, that celebrates saudade. In its earliest form, fado performance comprised a song accompanied by a guitar. Fado was a working-class genre of the port cities early on; it spread to places such as Brazil with the migration of its working-class musicians. More recently fado came to be adopted as one of Portugal's traditions added to the UNESCO Intangible

Cultural Heritage list in 2011, with Amália Rodrigues as one of its primary artists. In contemporary Portugal, it can be accompanied by all kinds of instrumentation, including a full orchestra; its home is in cafes and clubs. In sharp contrast to the minimalist sound of bossa nova vocal style, fado singing uses a very pronounced vibrato, dramatic dynamic shifts, pauses, and a near-sobbing quality of expression.

Brazil was colonized by Portugal at the start of the sixteenth century, achieving its independence in 1822. The continuous interchange between the two countries included musical instruments of all kinds, and the sense of saudade. Two Brazilian bossa nova songs exemplify this idea of saudade: "A Felicidade" and "Chega de Saudade" (both by Antônio Carolos Jobim with lyrics by Vinícius de Moraes). In the first, it begins with the idea that sadness (*tristeza*) has no end, but happiness (*felicidade*) does. It notes the ephemeral nature of happiness—like the lift of a feather in a breeze, the joy of the poor during the experience of Carnaval, a dewdrop on the petal of a flower, or the happiness in a lover's eyes. These poetic images all illustrate the ways in which our moments of joy are fleeting . . . as are our lives. Written for the 1959 film *Orfeu Negro* (Black Orpheus), a French film setting of the story of Orpheus (the Greek god of music) during Carnaval in Rio de Janeiro, the song is a clear indication that saudade is the steady-state experience of being Brazilian.

In "Chega de Saudade" ("Enough of Longing"), the singer hopes that his lover will return and help him say farewell to saudade. Without her there is no beauty; only sadness and melancholy. But if she returned, it would be crazy with so many hugs and kisses. I don't want to live like this—without you—anymore. Both songs were popularized by the soft singing of João Gilberto, whose recording of "Chega de Saudade" was the first to popularize the sounds and rhythms of bossa nova. A key feature of this sound is the equal role of voice and guitar, with the voice held to an intimacy achievable only through the sense of being in the same room as the singer. Gilberto (and his then-wife Astrud) sang without vibrato in the early recordings, leading others to follow suit and serving to establish some of the standards of North American cool jazz as well. In his elegant obituary for João Gilberto—rich in liminal references—*Washington Post* writer Chris Richards described him as the mapmaker of bossa nova. "Every syllable that appeared on his lips carried an air of effortlessness, but Gilberto had worked hard to locate that sacred place where a human breath becomes music."[6]

Musically, the expression of saudade uses the guitar- and voice-based sounds of bossa nova in Brazil and fado in Portugal to create not just an intimate atmosphere of being among like-minded people. It also builds a sense of community and identity through its use of saudade to hold people at the edge of sadness and happiness. It is that off-balance feeling of ambiguity—the neither-here-nor-there sense—that is the pinnacle achievement of highlighting saudade. It indicates, as singer Gilberto Gil put it in the song "Toda Saudade," "*Toda saudade é a presença da ausência alguém*"; "All of saudade is the presence of someone's absence." More than 80 percent of Brazilians are urbanites, and a large proportion of those urbanites are in-migrants from rural areas. High rates of domestic migration—and separation from home within Brazil itself—contributes to that sense of saudade.

Longing for Home in North America

Anthropologist Arjun Appadurai (1990: 296) envisioned five dimensions of what he called global cultural flows: ethnoscapes (humans), technoscapes (technology), financescapes (money and business networks), mediascapes (cultural industry networks), and ideoscapes (ideas and images). In direct contrast to the binary ideas of (exclusively) here and (exclusively) there, the idea of cultural flows reflects a more realistic sense of a continuum that allows significant blending of cultures, class levels, and more in a deterritorialized context. In the United States, millions of people cross-cultural boundaries every day; for those members of immigrant communities, the cultural flows of which they are a part hold them continually bound to home and separated from it at the same time. The immigrant who wakes up in the morning in the midst of a non-English-speaking family, goes to work in a day job and speaks English all day, then comes home to pick up a musical instrument and go out to a wedding gig that night (where several languages are spoken and requests pour in for tunes from several related regions) is operating in their own personal cultural flow.

As part of embodying liminality through sound, two musical instruments have been a strong part of European immigrant life in the United States: the accordion and the violin. The accordion, which was created in the early nineteenth century, came to the North America with immigrants from Central Europe and found a home in so many local musics of immigrants: Mexican, Irish, Croatian, Italian, German, Basque, Scandinavian, Russian, and many more. It also long been established among Indigenous communities of the American Southwest and among Inuit communities of the far north. It is featured in African-American musics such as the blues and Cajun zydeco. With its clear, strong voice and ability to play rhythm as well as melody, the portable accordion is often regarded as the best and most flexible choice to accompany dances.[7] As an instrument that easily migrates from one genre to another, its liminality lies in its ability to be central to so many completely different types of music.

The violin/fiddle came to North American with the first colonizers and missionaries, and it belongs to people all over the continent from the Rarámuri (Tarahumara) people of Northern Mexico to the Mi'kmaq of Canada's First Nations (Moro 2019: 56–57), and so many others as well. As a solo or group instrument, it is performed at all the same events where one might find the accordion: weddings, parties, dances, and concerts. The unique feature of the violin, though, is its voice-like quality. Unlike the accordion, the violin does not have pre-determined pitches. This frees the player to adhere more closely to the just intonation of singers as well as to the fine gradations of pitch in Arabic, Turkish, and Indian musics, and to allow silences where breaths might occur. Whereas the accordion and violin both have plenty of opportunities to appear in public for celebratory events, the violin has an intimacy that connects with the human body in its voice and its ability to sound as if it is "breathing."

One feature of the waves of immigration that characterize the United States from the nineteenth century forward is that earlier immigrants often expressed disdain for later immigrants. That has been true for the Irish who came before the Famine, the German Jews who came before the Russian Jews, the Chicanos who established themselves before the more recent Mexican arrivals, and others. An element that characterizes immigrant communities to the United States is a sense of ambiguity about what constitutes home. Musical styles, too, have separated the layers of immigrants in ways that they might not have in their home countries. Music and food are obvious connections, as are films and tourist ventures that present an idealized version for twenty-first-century consumption; the Irish Tourist Board/ Bord Fáilte campaign for American tourists in the 1990s (part of a series called "Ireland: the ancient birthplace of good times") showed a number of rural images with the slogan, "It's like being in a nineteenth century romantic novel. With better food and a happier ending." The assumption is, of course, that one need only return to the Olde Country for all of one's nineteenth-century-rural fever dreams to come true. We know that can't happen, and so does the Irish Tourist Board, but the ephemeral moment of laughing at the conceit and heading straight for one's favorite travel booking site online is precarious.

Irish Americans

The defining impetus for Irish migration to North America was the Great Hunger of 1845–1850. In causing the Irish population to drop to less than half of what it was, the Famine changed everything about Irish and Irish-American ways of being in the world. Ireland had shifted from Irish-owned to English-owned (primarily through absentee landlords) in a relatively short time; farmers paid their rent with livestock and grains, subsisting on potatoes for themselves. When the potato blight arrived, the English refused to change their system of rent collection so that people could consume what they produced. Disease, death, and massive emigration for the survivors ensued, depopulating the countryside. The Famine was followed by the Devotional Revolution of 1850, a dramatic re-Catholicization of Ireland and a shift to deep conservatism. Though Ireland had a strong tradition of instrumental playing and singing, the villages are said to have fallen silent when people died, or fled the bleak conditions at home. The depopulation of Ireland's countryside has left stark reminders across the island in the form of ruined stone cottages, which—not coincidentally—became one of the most powerful images in the development of musical remembrances among Irish Americans.

One of the legacies of the Devotional Revolution was that it encouraged an overwhelming silence about what had happened during the Famine. The embarrassment and devastation of having to leave home in the midst of chaos served to disconnect the ties between Irish history and Irish-American memory, and led to a near-complete silence about what had happened. In addition, the Devotional Revolution supported a men's drinking culture to keep men and women separate; "public houses" were created where men could gather with each other to drink. Because so many Irish priests emigrated to North America in the years following the Famine, that kind of conservatism and need to separate men from women served as a foundational element of American Catholicism. Furthermore, many Irish people found work as urban laborers in the large east coast cities, living in crowded enclaves and connecting with each other through the church, the union, and the political wards.

While there was no settled sense of "what it means to be Irish" in Ireland of the nineteenth century, the sublimation of Ireland's diverse identities under an American "stage Irish" persona led to theatrical depictions of the Irish as clumsy, temperamental, drunken, and weepy. By the turn of the twentieth century, with the dramatic upswing of the sheet music industry, composers were cranking out songs about "dear old Ireland," the weeping mother left behind at the ruined cottage, the "sweet colleen," the friends and neighbors left behind, etc. The Catholic Church had almost no mention in these songs. The silence within Irish-American families about the Famine itself created a vacuum of information, and commercial stage images swept in to fill it. The emphatic denial of realities "at home" in Ireland meant Irish Americans were free to reinvent themselves as they chose. That included the use of corned beef and cabbage (emphatically Irish-American tenement fare, purchased from kosher butchers), selective personality types ("he's a rebel!" "she's got her grandmother's fiery red hair!"), and a dark undercurrent of silence about family difficulties, alcoholism, and body shame.

"Food lay on the margins of Irish culture as a problem, an absence, a void"; talking about food meant mentioning its existence (as fuel) rather than discussing whether it was tasty (Diner 2001: 84). There was almost no actual "Irish cuisine" to engage any sort of longing for Ireland; instead, corned beef, cabbage, green "Jello salad" (lime jello mixed with canned fruit and whipped cream) have stood in for Irish food for a century, even as Irish cuisine *in Ireland* has blossomed. The authenticity of Irishness sought by so many on St. Patrick's Day in America bears no relationship to what people do in Ireland; an Irish-American "typical Irish meal" is considered American food in Ireland.

Musically, the equivalent of corned beef and cabbage for "authentic Irish fare" is the early twentieth-century Irish-American hit parade of songs such as "When Irish Eyes Are Smiling," "Mother Machree," "My Wild Irish Rose," and of course, the ubiquitous "Danny Boy" (somewhat awkwardly of English origin).[8] These songs, and many others, have stood in for actual Irish songs for over a hundred years, and are fiercely defended as "authentic Irish songs because my granddaddy sang them to me" across North America. Singing "Danny Boy" (Figure 5.2) to a certain North American demographic ignites a painful sense of loss and longing coupled with the dreamy embedded memories of an Ireland that may or may not have ever existed.[9] As I have

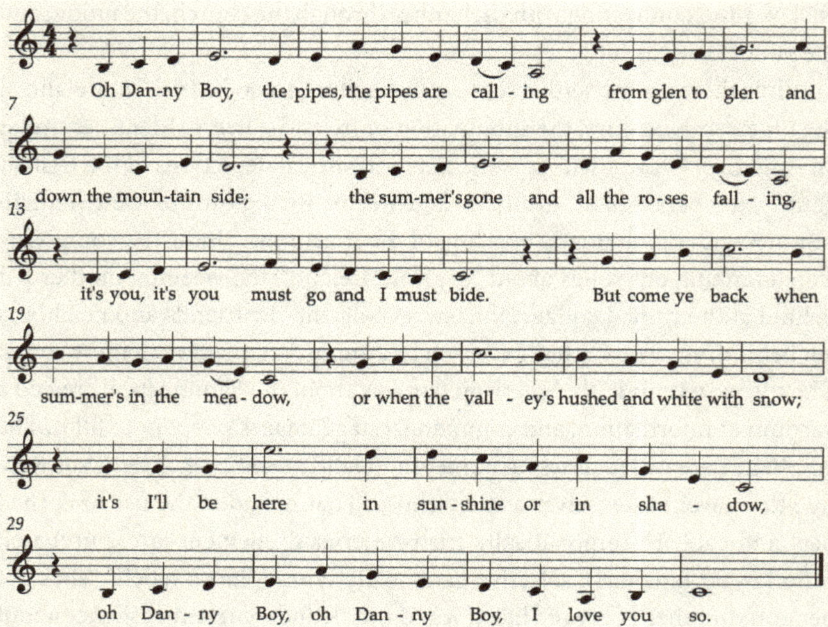

Figure 5.2 "Danny Boy" by Frederic Weatherly

discussed elsewhere (Williams 2015: 46–64), that strong desire to envision Ireland as they hope it used to be is clearly in contrast with contemporary Ireland, but the Irish Tourist Board (Bord Fáilte) walks a fine, liminal line between simultaneously promoting Ireland today and the unexamined Ireland of the imagined nineteenth century.[10]

> Oh, Danny Boy, the pipes, the pipes are calling
> From glen to glen and down the mountainside
> The summer's gone and all the roses falling
> It's you, it's you must go and I must bide.
> But come ye back when summer's in the meadow
> Or when the valley's hushed and white with snow
> And I'll be here in sunshine or in shadow
> Oh Danny Boy, oh Danny Boy, I love you so.

The presence of Irish instrumental music is significant in all the larger North American cities; there are regular instrumental playing sessions in which jigs and reels are strung out by fiddles, accordions, and other instruments. One tune stands out, however, for its ubiquitous presence in the sparse lists of tune requestions: "The Irish Washerwoman." The title of this tune is highly evocative of a standard late-nineteenth-century stereotype of a sweaty working Irish woman scrubbing someone else's clothes by hand in her own frumpy clothing. That it should stand in for *all* instrumental tunes is the result of its use in films, stage shows, and even classical compositions as a cultural shorthand. Irish people, to those who are not Irish, *are* "The Irish Washerwoman."[11]

What Irish and Irish-American music does to Irish-American (and, often, other American) audiences is two-fold. It reminds them of what they believe to be a happier time that can never be experienced again, and it also enables them to feel something that they don't normally feel in their everyday lives. The once-dominant position of the Catholic Church in Ireland has faded. The fact that Ireland has shifted to a much more tolerant set of attitudes regarding such political hot potatoes as marriage equality and various diversities means that Irish America and Ireland have grown farther apart in their collective worldviews. And whereas "Danny Boy," "The Irish Washerwoman," and the St. Patrick's Day meal of corned beef and cabbage are all firmly associated with Irish America and its longing for an Ireland of the rural past, such features are not necessarily connectable to Ireland of the twenty-first century. They have become their own type of authenticity.

Mexican Americans

It is far too easy for Anglo-Americans to imagine that Mexicans who live in the States are "foreigners." But they have forgotten their fairly recent history. Much of the American West *was* a major section of Mexico until 1848, when the Treaty of Guadalupe Hidalgo resulted in more than half a million square miles *of Mexico* being ceded to the United States. Mexico lost over half of its territory as a result of the treaty and the various local machinations that preceded it. This means the people who were once *home*, in those territories, are no longer "home," even though they live in the very place where generations of their families have lived. People who live in the American Southwest live in what was once Mexico, and of course all of it—including Mexico in its current formation—is on unceded Indigenous territory. This historical issue complicates what constitutes ideas of home, migration, and longing. Because one-fifth of the residents of contemporary Mexico make their home in Mexico City, the prevailing US image of Mexicans as uniformly rural migrant workers—based at least partly on the Mexican and US film industries—is wildly incorrect.[12] Other images are rampant; American popular songs, for example, have generally characterized Mexican women in much the same way that Hawaiian women have appeared in popular culture ("Mexicali Rose," "Down in Mexico," "Mexican Girl," and too many others). Never mind that Mexicans comprise all races, classes, genders, levels of education, wealth, and occupations; immigrant communities face unacceptable levels of stereotyping.

In exploring the relationship between Mexican Americans, music, and home, the first point to recognize is that Mexicans connect with place: the *land*.[13] One is connected to the land first, then the community, then the state, then the nation. So in bringing oneself closer to the land, one cooks and eats the food, listens to and sings the music of the place, and follows specific signifiers of what it means to belong. Whereas the descendants of Irish immigrants ended up developing their own removed and somewhat artificial sense of a post-Famine home in the absence of open conversation and continuous contact, people from Mexico thrive on their constant engagement with a living culture in the United States, whether it is in San Antonio or Los Angeles or Chicago.[14] Being away from home for generations can change a person, a family, and a community, but multiple layers of connection with home can be both revitalizing and recentering.

In deep connection with the land is what grows on the land. That food should loom so large in the popular imagination is a key feature of understanding how migrant communities—not just Mexicans—connect with the land. While Mexican restaurants in the United States tend to lean heavily on cheese, restaurants at home often use fresh local ingredients in endlessly creative ways. For example, in the state of Puebla, the dish *chiles en nogada* is a stuffed green poblano pepper in fresh walnut sauce, covered in pomegranate seeds. Said to have been created by nuns in 1821 for a visit by Mexican General Augustín de Iturbide, this dish evokes the colors of the Mexican flag and is sometimes served to celebrate Mexican Independence Day (September 16). The flavor of the land can manifest the flavor of the nation.

In its history, the sounds of home developed fully in the early- to mid-twentieth century through the radio, recording, and film industries. The work of professional songwriters—similar to those of Tin Pan Alley in regard to Irish Americans at the turn of the twentieth century—set up in their songs a series of images and a standard of values that idealized the national character of the Mexican: loyal to the land, the family, the parents, and the community. That industry's development then "contributed to the formation of solidarity and collective identity, predominantly within an expanding Mexican population" (Ragland 2009: 65). Regardless of one's actual origins, one could connect to the songs whether rural or urban. "Thus, a mutually reinforcing cycle arose, in which rural tastes influenced the popular media, and then in turn were influenced by popular creations appealing to those tastes" (Sheehy 1997: 141). Once the popular media was widespread in both Mexico and the United States, the music became both portable and easily accessible to anyone with a radio. Janet Sturman notes that the popularization of radio and recording technology led to the development of musical stars and the conformation of composers to fit the three-minute length of tracks; its "domestication" into radio-friendly formatting was part of its popularity (Sturman 2016: 211).

One of the features that serves to connect Mexicans in the States with the part of them that is still in place, at home, is the sense of the actual embodiment of that place. They cannot leave home behind if home comes with them. The acoustic sounds created through the blend of local melodies, harmony singing, the use of the Spanish language, instruments largely from Central Europe and Spain, the use of major modes, and various dance rhythms (polka, waltz, etc.) imported from Europe characterize that connection. Established as a liminal border sound—fully established in both northern Mexico and the southwestern United States—the sound is found wherever Mexicans live. It is primarily associated with the accordion, percussion, and bajo sexto or other bass-functioning instrument, but may also include one or more violins or other instruments. The diversity of the Mexican-American population in region, age, class, and other factors is reflected in the richness of musical styles in the States: *mariachi, conjunto, norteña, son jarocho, banda orquesta, grupo*, and others are broadly popular. Each genre has its own specific instrumentarium and popular repertoire; each one also carries class distinctions and embedded sonic symbols. The instrumentation serves to accompany the song or, in the case of instrumental tunes, the melody.

While *corridos*—narrative ballads that detail the stories of famous people, border crossings, fights, romances, and other events—are extremely popular, the lyric song expresses longing—*añoranza*—without a specific narrative. If there is one such classic song that causes community members to burst into full voice when it appears, it is the "Canción Mixteca" (Figure 5.3) from the state

Figure 5.3 "Canción Mixteca" ("Song of the Mixtec") by José López Alavez

of Oaxaca. Written by José López Alavez in 1915, the lyrics express his profound sense of añoranza—perpetual longing for home—after having moved to Mexico City. And when everyone sings along, swaying in unison and slowing way down at the precise moment before the final line ("I would like to cry, I would like to die of feeling"), the liminal sense of communitas is powerful.[15]

Qué lejos estoy del suelo donde he nacido
Inmensa nostalgia invade mi pensamiento
Al verme, tan solo y treste cual hoja al viento
¡Quisiera llorar—quisiera morir—de sentimiento!

Oh tierra del sol, suspiro por verte
Ahora que lejos yo vivo, sin luz, sin amor
Y, al verme tan solo y triste cual hoja al viento
¡Quisiera llorar—quisiera morir—de sentimiento!

How far I am from the soil where I was born
Immense nostalgia invades my thoughts
Seeing me so lonely and sad like a leaf on the wind
I would like to cry, I would like to die of feeling

Oh Land of the Sun! I sigh to see you
Now how far away I live without light, without love
And seeing me so lonely and sad like a leaf on the wind
I would like to cry, I would like to die of feeling.

It does not matter so much that this is a Oaxacan song; this is one of *the* songs of home among the many dozens of songs that bring people directly into contact with their living traditions in an urgent and vital way. The image of *cual hoja al viento* ("like a leaf on the wind") is every bit as powerful in representing añoranza as the line *de orvalho numa pétala de flor* ("a dewdrop on a flower petal") in Brazilian bossa nova is in representing saudade. But it is the sense of communitas brought on by that song and others that engages everyone in their collective ephemeral liminality of embodying home, together.

Arab Americans

Of the more than two million people of Arab descent in the United States, the American states with the highest number of Arab Americans include Michigan (especially the greater Detroit area), New Jersey, and Connecticut. Because the largest subset of Arab Americans are Lebanese Christians, most Arab Americans are Christian, with a smaller proportion in the United States following Islam. There is also a significant Arab Jewish population, with their own synagogues that include Arabic musical pieces translated into Hebrew. This demographic statistic runs in contrast to the fact that the majority of Arabs in the Middle East follow Islam, and that many other religious faiths exist in the twenty-two Arab states of the region. In addition, the musics of Turkish, Iranian, and Armenian immigrants to North America are in their own distinct categories, separate from the music of the Arab Americans.

The establishment of Arab communities in the United States began in the late nineteenth century as people escaped the chaotic occupation and challenging economic conditions of what was then the Ottoman province of greater Syria (which also included Jordan, Lebanon, and Palestine). Many of the first Arab immigrants found work as laborers. In 1924, the Johnson-Reed Immigration Act brought a halt to all immigration from Asia, which meant that the first immigrants from the Arab world were separated from a continuous infusion of new people from the old countries. Twenty-four years later, the revolutions of Iraq and Egypt, together with the Arab-Israeli War, led to a second wave of immigrants in 1948, many of whom belonged to the middle and upper classes. Later changes to the laws allowed a gradual influx of new immigrants; they have represented a diverse set of classes, nations, ethnicities, and interests. The different stages of immigration, however, have resulted in the formation of different subgroups within the communities.

In an article about the relative invisibility of Arab-Americans in the United States, Therese Saliba notes that contemporary pan-Arab nationalism tends to inform much of Arab American political activity today, compared to the first wave of immigrants who saw themselves primarily as being of a specific place of origin (Saliba 1999: 306). The exceptional diversity of Arab Americans is invisible to those outside the community but it is evident in the music and its American contexts: weddings, festivals, radio, recordings from different eras, and, currently, social media. Two main events form the semi-public centerpiece of the Arab-American musical experience: the *mahrajan* (festival, either indoor or outdoor) and the *haflah* (more general party associated with weddings, baptisms, fundraising, and other activities). These performance contexts create opportunities for community-building, and for fundraising to occur (Rasmussen 2000: 1032). They are also a place for young people to socialize (often in English) and for the elderly to reminisce. These have been important opportunities to enjoy music, dress up, see people, make matches, and experience some sense of home in a protected environment.

One of the other primary contexts for the performance of Arab music has been at nightclubs and cabarets that feature Arab music accompanying belly dancing. The golden age of this form extended across several decades, starting in the 1930s. While an apparent haven of orientalism, the sights and sounds of the nightclub were a once-removed version of the diverse contexts of home, with all the different elements of Middle Eastern performative culture re-shaped (and retuned) to fit a single exotic evening experience (Rasmussen 2000: 1033). Although the United States belly dance scene currently includes hundreds of variants, most of which feature non-Arab (usually white and Asian) American women, the cabaret performance circuit was—and still is, in some east coast cities—a thriving place for Arab music in the evenings.

The food and music of Americans of Arab descent at these events has been every bit as evocative of home as it is in other immigrant communities. "The combination of aromatic Syrian and Lebanese cuisine, the Arabic language, the sights and sounds of musical performance, and the movement of dance created an ambiance and experience of the homeland" (Rasmussen 1997: 76). But because the Arab World is so large, including the Maghreb (North Africa) and the Levant (Eastern Mediterranean), no one food says "home" to everyone in the Arab communities of the United States. However, the combination of *shawarma*—grilled flat strips of intensely marinated meat—and hummus or tahini and vegetables wrapped in pita is nearly unbeatable in appealing to the largest proportion of the Arab-American population.

Music of the Levant that came to the States is also strongly evocative of home *because* it cannot be transferred to standard fixed-pitch Western musical instruments; its lyrics, too, are in direct reference to home. The violin, with its ability to play in tune in any tuning system, is uniquely suited to cross over into the very specialized tunings of the *maqāmāt*—modes—of the Arab world. One of the classic sounds of Arab music, generally, is the large string orchestra playing melodies in unison behind a singer; another is the rich timbre of the heterophonic *takht* ensemble, comprising plucked and bowed stringed instruments, reed flute, and several percussion instruments. In both cases, the melody is the focus (whether in unison or heterophony), and the percussion gives shape, tempo, and accent to the meters of the individual melodies. Classic rhythmic modes are also important signifiers of (displaced) location for Arab-American listeners; at the moment when a musical performance shifts from a free-rhythm improvisation to a metered piece, the musicians have the full engagement of the audience.

The people of each of the subcultures in this chapter have in their hearts—and sometimes, in their language—the combined sense of longing, nostalgia, joy, and wistfulness. The special Arabic word to connect with that sense—out of many that convey a sense of longing—is *hanin* (pronounced "ha-*neen*") written in Arabic as حنين. The two singers best-known in the Arab world for evoking hanin are Umm Kulthūm of Egypt and Fairuz of Lebanon. As the majority of older Arab Americans are Lebanese Christian, Fairuz—another Lebanese Christian—is a musical spokeswoman for home, popularly said to embody the "soul of Lebanon." Her songs are ubiquitous, beloved, and highly evocative especially for the older generation of Arab Americans.

The song "Nassam Alayna El-Hawa" ("The Air Breezed upon Us") evokes the quality of hanin through its lyrics of the land, of love, and of separation (Figure 5.4).[16] Beyond the lyrics, however, the sounds of this song feature

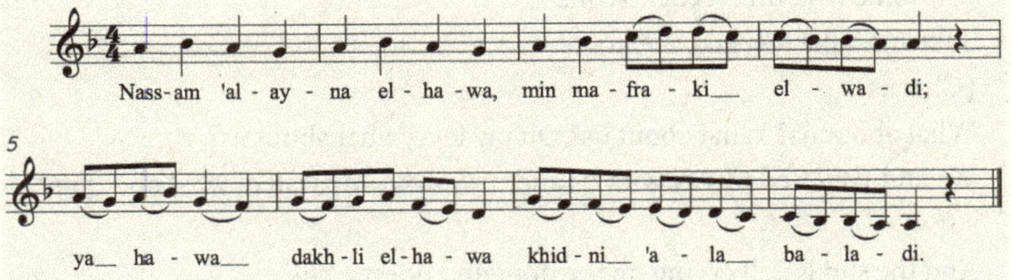

Figure 5.4 "Nassam Alayna El-Hawa" ("The Air Breezed Upon Us") by Assi and Mansour Rahbani

the sound of the Lebanese *buzuq*, a plucked metal-stringed instrument (in contrast to the oud with its mellower nylon strings). It also features a singable chorus and significant repetition between Fairuz and her male backup singers. Because most Arab radio stations play at least one song by Fairuz in the morning, hers is the voice to accompany the start of one's day.

Chorus: Nassam 'alayna el-hawa, min mafraki el-wadi
Ya hawa dakhli el-hawa khidni 'ala baladi (sung 3 times)

Ya hawa, ya hawa, yalli tayir fil-hawa
Fi mantoura ta'a w soura, khidni el-'andhoun ya hawa.

Fiz'ani ya albi tekbar bi ha l'ghirbé
W ma ta'rifni baladi khidni, khidni, w khidni 'ala baladi
(Chorus)
Chou bina? Chou bina? Ya habibi chou bina?
Kintou kina dalou 'andna w ftara'na chou bina? (sung twice)

Ou ba'dha echams batibki 'ala bab ou ma tahki
Ou yahki hawa baladi khidni, khidni, khidni 'ala baladi.

Chorus: The air breezed upon us from the pass leading into the valley
Oh breeze, for love's sake, take me home. (sung 3 times)

Oh love, oh love, that is flying in the breeze
There's a mantoura flower with energy and image
Take me to them, oh breeze.

I'm scared, my heart, to grow up in this foreign land
My home wouldn't recognize me
Take me, take me, take me home.
(Chorus)
What about us? What about us? Oh my love, what about us?
We and you used to stay with us and now we've separated, what about us?

And the sun is still crying on the door and doesn't talk
And the love of home is talking take me, take me, take me home.
(Chorus)

Individual musicians in the Arab-American community have agency and power in their ability to evoke the sense of home through taste or sound, but also to create that sense of displaced belonging so that those listening to the instruments, songs (in Arabic), melodies, and rhythms feel transported. As Anne Rasmussen points out, " . . . music has the power to move people to different times and places and is thus one of the most compelling agents in the definition of community and individual identity" (1997: 75). Through the nuance of flavor—of music, of food, of conversations, and of relatively intimate contexts where such musical experiences take place—the diverse Arab communities of the United States are, in fact, "at home."

Balkan Americans

In the two decades on either side of the turn of the twentieth century, millions of immigrants—some of whom had become stateless—arrived in the United States fleeing the political upheavals that were occurring in the region of southeast Europe. Those leaving their home regions included people from the Balkan region: what are now Slovenia, Croatia, Bosnia and Herzegovina, North Macedonia, Albania, Kosovo, Montenegro, Greece, Bulgaria, and Romania; the immigrants included Romani and Jewish people as well. The immigrants were primarily male; many of them came to the industrial towns of the east coast and upper Midwest. Depending on the numbers of immigrants prior to the Johnson-Reed Immigration Act in 1924, immigrants from the different locations of the Balkans were able to establish communities in the United States that enabled the development of musical groups and performance contexts such as taverns and nightclubs. As the immigrants started families and rounded out their communities, weddings, parties, and other contexts became the norm for musical performance. Later patterns of immigration took place related to World War II and following the collapse of the Soviet Union toward the end of the twentieth century.

The regions "at home" had experienced so much in the way of transfers of power, takeovers, rebellions, migrations, and dramatic political and religious shifts that the Balkan peninsula has had plenty of opportunities for cultural exchanges of all kinds. In the post-Soviet scene, the members of each nation have labored to create a national sense of identity, independence, and culture that extends to languages, foods, and musical traditions. Because of the many layers of cultures that have crossed the Balkan region, foods and musics have become adopted as "our own," including when "our own" means "across the region." For example, *banitsa* is breakfast. Layered with filo and a mixture of yogurt, eggs, and feta (or other) cheese, it can be sweet or savory, and is served with Turkish coffee. Associated with the *börek* of nomadic Turkic people of over a thousand years ago, this particular food made its way everywhere. Banitsa is common in Bulgaria, North Macedonia, Montenegro, Serbia, and elsewhere (with different names), both at home and as street food. At Christian holidays, it takes on special importance as a slice is set out for the Virgin Mary. But its importance across the region as the way to begin the day and as the food most closely associated with home has extended to the Balkan diaspora in North America. "Though it had found its way onto the table of khans and kings, it was—and would remain—a culinary witness to generations of migration, conquest, and displacement" (Lee 2019).

Similarly, the Turkish song "Kâtibim" (also known as "Üsküdar'a Gider Iken," "While Going to Üsküdar") is widespread across the Balkans with consistency in the melody, but differing lyrics according to which community performs it. In Turkish, it is about the love a woman has for her handsome clerk. The 2003 Bulgarian documentary *Whose Is This Song?* by Adela Peeva explores the many manifestations of the song in different countries and features the heated exchanges as one person after another (Bosnian, Serbian, Albanian, Bulgarian, etc.) insists that it is native to Bosnia, Serbia, Albania, Bulgaria, and so on. In most cases, it is the *melody* that made the rounds, established itself in a community with lyrics in that language, and eventually made its way to North America and the Caribbean.[17] The Turkish version (Figure 5.5) uses these words in translation, but the many other versions use different lyrics that are relevant to local sensibilities, needs, religious practices, and values.

Figure 5.5 "Üsküdar'a Gider Iken" ("While Going to Üsküdar")

Üsküdar'a gider iken aldı da bir yağmur
Kâtibimin setresi uzun, eteği çamur
Kâtip uykudan uyanmış, gözleri mahmur.

Kâtip benim, ben kâtibin, el ne karışir?
Kâtibime kolalı da gömlek ne güzel yaraşir!

Üsküdar'a gider iken bir mendil buldum
Mendilimin içine de lokum doldurdum
Kâtibimi ara iken yanımda buldum.

On the way to Üsküdar, rain poured down
My clerk's frock coat is long, with mud on the hem
The clerk just woke up, his eyes are sleepy.

The clerk belongs to me, I belong to the clerk, what is it to others?
How handsome my clerk looks with starched shirts!

On the way to Üsküdar, I found a handkerchief
I filled the handkerchief with Turkish delight
As I was looking for my clerk, I found him next to me.

The intense nationalistic pride associated with this song mirrors the pride associated with the regional variants of banitsa: each nation's version is superior to that of the others. Regardless of the language of its performance, this very catchy melody has people in each of the immigrant communities singing along, moving their bodies, and leaning forward with pleasure as it expresses a powerful sense of belonging for its listeners. That belonging signifies a kind of home-in-place, even though they may be not just far from their actual homeland, but far from the homeland of the past evoked by the music. The popularity of the song in North America has led to multiple recordings by performers as distant from the Balkans as Eartha Kitt (1953) and Pink Martini (2013).

One of the ways that the descendants of the immigrants from a century ago express their connection with home is through dance, and dancing occurs at festivals, clubs, camps, weddings, and other region-specific events. With special attention paid to regional clothing—not nearly as important in the other groups mentioned in this section—dances are quite specialized, often using combinations of rhythms that do not lend themselves to casual participation. Mark Levy notes, in reference to Macedonian communities in North America, "Costumed dance groups tend to perform choreographed versions of folk dances for a seated audience and are generally composed of elementary and high school children" (Levy 2000: 925). But this is just one performance context; Mirjana Laušević points to the large American community of people whose connection to the music and dance might be through just a single grandparent or friends. The level of engagement is very strong regardless of the specifics of their backgrounds.

> The Balkan scene is enacted on multiple fronts, including regular participatory music and dance classes and events, band rehearsals, public concerts and recording sessions, annual weeklong camps, weekend retreats, websites and chat rooms, newsletters and other publications, individual and group travel to the Balkans, concert promotion and sponsorship of touring Balkan musicians, and more cloistered activities such as practicing, listening to recordings, and collecting related memorabilia. (Laušević 2007: 18)

It is precisely the diffusion of roots in the Balkan-American communities that has led to the diffusion of cultural materials such as music and food. If banitsa is widespread, the melody for the song "Üsküdar'a Gider Iken," is widespread, and the costumes and dances switch from one ethnic group to another, it is a complication to locate *just one type of representation* that connects to home. And perhaps because of that complication, finding home is tricky and not something that is easily solved with the senses. Instead, Balkan Americans build an ephemeral home on sonic connections, imaginations, and emotions.

The profound emotions we feel are triggered by sound, scent, and taste. Why don't we have a word for it, beyond the rather bland and inadequate "bittersweet"? Shouldn't we have a word that encompasses the dear, sad joy and heartache that jolts through the body from hearing a piece of music, tasting a food, or noting a scent that takes you right back, instantly, across time and space? The inadequacy of English, which has been built from so many different languages, is obvious. Is it possible that American English speakers in all our racial diversity, with our political roots in thou-must-not-feel-anything Puritanism, couldn't fathom experiencing the simultaneous heights and depths? Perhaps it was considered better not to feel anything at all. Regardless, English doesn't do the job. These terms, and in particular the associated powerful feelings they convey about carrying home away from home in the body or in the spirit, are deeply connected to a sense of liminal identity. This is who we are.

The "Home" of Your Dreams

For each of the American immigrant examples detailed in this chapter, there is a shared experience of migration from what might be considered a homeland to a new territory. In each case there has been a reason for the departure—not necessarily shared among all the participants in that particular migration—along with very specific elements about the experience of being in the United States with other migrants that creates a sense of longing. With the migrants and their music now spread all over the country, other people can peripherally or temporarily join the group in its public celebrations of foods, festivals, and associated musics and dances. Between the Festival of American Folklife in Washington, DC, the series of popular ethnic festivals all summer long in Milwaukee (and elsewhere), and all the music camps for adults and children year-round, these opportunities for sharing, pride, and community create a sense of *imagined* community, as first discussed by Benedict Anderson. He writes, " . . . members [of such communities] will never know most of their fellow members, yet in the minds of each lives the image of their communion" (Anderson 1983: 6). Furthermore, once we have imagined such a community, we can just as easily imagine those who *do not belong* to that community. It is every bit as exclusive as it is inclusive, and is one of the root sources of nationalism.

We shift now to discuss a type of imagined community to round out the idea of the immigrant/migrant communities, mentioned earlier; it features mainland North Americans dreaming of Hawai'i (from their perspective on the mainland), and imagining it as a very specific type of nostalgia-laden home.[18] The creation of that sense of welcome, and that concurrent sense of deep longing and nostalgia, has been the twentieth- and twenty-first-century result of a very specific set of historical circumstances that made some mainlanders long to play the 'ukulele and dance the hula. Note that unlike the other examples, food and drink has had less of an impact on these migrants. As we consider why the scents of traditional Hawaiian food don't necessarily strike longing in the hearts of the *haoles* (non-Hawaiian people either in or longing for Hawai'i), note that these are *not* people whose early sense memories ring with the taste of *laulau* (pieces of meat wrapped and cooked in taro leaf); other factors have been at play.

Hawai'i has a history of being overrun by white people. Beginning in 1778 with the arrival of British Captain James Cook and his two ships, the following colonizers, whalers, entrepreneurs, and missionaries all disrupted the existing Hawaiian monarchy, culture, and system of governance. Prior to the illegal overthrow of the monarchy and its incorporation by the United States, Hawai'i had absorbed numerous musical, cultural, and linguistic influences from the people who visited (many of whom came to stay). Many Hawaiian men signed up to join whaling crews; although they worked for less pay, life on the ships was preferable to working in the sugar cane and pineapple fields of the islands (Carr 2014: 61). The musical standouts—'ukulele and steel guitar accompanying popular songs—and the hula dance became mainstays of twentieth-century Hawaiian tourism and beyond, and their promotion has been deliberate. But they have often been presented within the context of the white person's gaze.

The marketing of Hawai'i as an authentic and exotic home-away-from-home has been fully in place since before the twentieth century; in 1903, the Hawaii Promotion Committee (later the Hawaii Tourism Authority) was formed to present the islands as a tourist destination to mainlanders. In 1915, the Panama Pacific Exposition in San Francisco featured numerous musical acts and brought the islands to the attention of the more than seventeen million mainlanders who visited the exhibit. One particular musical element that appeared at the Exposition was the steel guitar. Invented by Hawaiian Joseph Kekuku[19] when he was a teenager and perfected over the next few years, the sound of the steel guitar—the *kīkā kila*—dominated the 78 rpm markets by 1916 (Troutman 2013: 32). Kekuku had begun touring the mainland by 1904, by which time Honolulu in particular was alive with the new sound. But Kekuku's departure from Hawai'i was connected to a larger exodus from the islands because of the illegal overthrow of the monarchy and the banning of surfing, hula, chant, and the use of the Hawaiian language; many musicians, singers, and dancers simply left the islands.[20] The guitar (lying flat on the lap, played with picks on the right hand and a piece of metal in the left to slide across the strings) was vividly influential in the hands of its experienced Hawaiian practitioners in exile, whose sounds came to find their way into the burgeoning blues and country sounds of the American Southeast and elsewhere.

Part of that overall marketing scheme, including musical sounds and images, reached a fevered pitch between the 1910s and the 1930s as "Hawaiian traditions were romanticized, eroticized, primitivized, and consumed as safe and soft savagery" (Diamond 2008: 26). From the postcards featuring alluring hula dancers (sometimes playing the ʻukulele) next to palm trees to the songs and films that sustained Hollywood for a time, both visual and sonic imagery have been important props in celebrating Hawaiʻi as simultaneously Other but close enough to the west coast for tourism.

Tourist-oriented performance practices became quite popular as part of the attempt to lure visitors (and more white settlers) to the islands. *Hapa-haole* ("half-white") songs featuring images that appeal to visitors—girls, ʻukulele, sand, surf, romance, flowers, and so on—surged in popularity after their initial development at the turn of the twentieth century. Rapidly becoming a hit-making sound among the songwriters of New York's Tin Pan Alley, the newfound approachable exoticism left by the annexation of the islands resulted in Hawaiian-themed songs emerging as immediate bestsellers. Recordings of these songs burst onto the scene at the same time as the emergence of "race records" (recordings intended to appeal to African Americans); they included all the same images that one might see on a postcard from the era. Lyrics that focused on the distance to Hawaiʻi and especially to a presumed sweetheart left behind ("I Left Her on the Beach in Honolulu," e.g., by Louis A. Hirsch and Gene Buck) amplified the importance of longing. Using big-band accompaniment, steel guitar (but not slack-key guitar), or ʻukulele alone, these songs have lured (and continue to lure) tourists to Hawaiʻi for over a hundred years. Whether written and performed by Hawaiians as part of their home traditions or by outsiders, hapa-haole songs remain embedded in the fabric of Hawaiian music.

Television commercials for C&H (California and Hawaiʻi) sugar were ubiquitous in the 1960s and 1970s, showing happy laughing and singing Hawaiian children out among the sugar canes, accompanied by the sounds of the ʻukulele and/or steel guitar. The Dole Hawaiian Pineapple Company interspersed its mention of the pineapple in its televised advertisements with vigorous clips of barely clad local men running with torches accompanied by high-speed pounding (ahem: Tahitian) drums; one of them places a pineapple on a pedestal and lifts the crown to reveal a can of Dole pineapple slices.[21] The irony of the plantations having taken Indigenous land from the very people featured in its advertisements is not lost on locals. Marketing

Hawai'i's authenticity is about marketing Hawaiian bodies and Hawaiian labor in the name of *aloha*.

Aloha has multiple implications, including hello, goodbye, welcome, love, kindness, reciprocation, joy, and grief. Like the other words in this chapter, it is complicated and has no equivalent in English. In its translation by missionaries, aloha came to be presented to outsiders as closer to the concept of Christian agape love rather than the warm reciprocity indicated by, for example, the less-known-to-outsiders word *'ohana* or family (Teves 2015: 707). It is used to represent the core of Hawaiian mutual respect and affection, and in 1986, the Aloha Spirit law was enacted, requiring that people be treated with aloha.[22] It was a codification of the principle that angry resistance to settler colonialism was against the ethos of aloha. By reframing various local materials for outsiders through translations and publications, such incursions over the twentieth century "drastically reduced the say that Hawaiians could exercise in print over their own traditions" (Bacchilega 2007: 85). The misappropriation of these materials and beliefs in government and tourist circles have, in essence, trapped locals into always providing but rarely receiving.

> The uncritical celebration of aloha affects all Pacific Islanders, for aloha's deployment in a number of discourses undergirds the ongoing military occupation of the Pacific, the cultural exploitation of our cultures, and attendant environmental degradation across our sea of islands. (Teves 2015: 706)

None of this contextual work diminishes Kānaka Maoli—Native Hawaiian—agency; nor does it negate the successful promotion or production of local musical and cultural materials. Hawaiian festivals, recording studios, hula *hālau* (traditional places for teaching and learning), performance opportunities, and island-specific musical communities can and do support local music-making and dance. Beyond the 'ukulele and the steel guitar, though, is the slack-key guitar (*kī hō 'alu*). It is a six-string acoustic guitar with one or more strings slackened to change the tuning into one of dozens of alternate tunings and altering the overall sound. The guitar was imported with Mexican cowboys in the late nineteenth century, so it was connected to Hawaiian ranching culture at first. Because the slack-key guitar was *not* something performed regularly for tourists until the 1970s, it bypassed the marketing machinations of the earlier decades and developed exclusively among the Hawaiians themselves, in private until the mid-1940s with the release of several recordings by Gabby Pahinui. Hawaiian musicians now perform the slack key guitar at festivals, weekly shows, and at restaurants and other gathering places. Because it is usually used to accompany the voice, it has provided rich soil for singer-songwriters performing largely in Hawaiian.

For *haole* visitors, upon whom many Hawaiians depend for much-needed financial sustenance, visiting anywhere in Hawai'i is a chance to live one's idealized best life and to assume an entitlement of aloha. With an economy built around the fantasy of authenticity and welcome, the aloha spirit embodied within the idea of Hawaiian culture is both pervasive and attractive. Visitors are surrounded by flowers, stunning views of mountains and ocean, and can sip their umbrella drinks while listening to gorgeous slack key guitar and wearing brand-new attractive (and comfortable) clothes that they can purchase at any one of hundreds of shops set up to serve them. Reader, I have absolutely done this multiple times. It is an intoxicating combination, and one that keeps locals continually financially beholden to the same violent system that compelled them to offer hospitality to the whalers and missionaries of the past (Teves 2015: 705). In building the aloha spirit to such sacred heights and creating an alluring sense of what outsiders might partake in upon their arrival, the colonial and postcolonial power brokers have built something that is nothing less than dangerous for the fragile Hawaiian ecosystem, humans included.

Home/Not-Home

What is home? According to Robert Frost in 1914 ("The Death of the Hired Man"), "Home is the place where, when you have to go there, they have to take you in." If that were really true, though, we might all think fondly of home, and be grateful for its unchanging nature. There would be no mixed feelings, no wariness about the way it (or we) change over time, no blend of laughter and tears, and especially no wa'as, saudade, cumha, hanin, or añora. There would be no collective memory of the horrific events leading to the creation and performance of songs such as "Strange Fruit," choking one's sense of the place. But home, and its artistically realized, idealized engagement in our hearts and minds, resists logic and convenience. If there is an emotional equivalent to the call of the siren in Chapter 4, it is the depth charge set off by the sensual *home* experiences that bypass all of one's contemporary filters.

The Kenneth Graham book that remains my favorite—*The Wind in the Willows*—includes a riveting passage in which Mole scents his own burrow for the first time in a long time as he and Rat rush home on a snowy evening. Rat "did not notice poor Mole when the summons reached him, and took him like an electric shock" (Graham 1908: 85).

"It was one of these mysterious fairy calls from out the void that suddenly reached Mole in the darkness, making him tingle through and through with its very familiar appeal, even while yet he could not clearly remember what it was. He stopped dead in his tracks, his nose searching hither and thither in its efforts to recapture the fine filament, the telegraphic current, that had so strongly moved him. A moment, and he had caught it again; and with it this time came recollection in fullest flood. Home!" (Graham 1908: 86).

The electric shock of recognition—which alerts every sense and yanks us out of whatever we were thinking about or doing at the moment—is triggered by seemingly small events: the taste of a particular food, a single melody or rhythm, or a scent. In Mole's case, the presence of the neighborhood (mouse) carolers, and the food and drink, made his reunion with his home complete. Whether it's the profound ache of tasting a specific flavor or detecting a scent in the air,[23] the wrenching sound of a song or a genre from home, long ago, the mixed feelings that arise are complicated and unlike any other. Unlike almost anywhere else in our contemporary lives, our sense of home recalls and refutes Gloria Steinem's dismissal of Oakland, CA ("There is no there, there") with the opposite: "There *is* a there, there." But you can't get there from here, ever again, no matter how much food or drink or music that you consume, and you know it.

6

Sounds like Transgression

Out beyond ideas of wrongdoing and rightdoing, there is a field. I'll meet you there. (Jalāl al-Dīn Muhammad Rūmī, Persia)

Transgression seems to be the one label constantly lobbed at people of color, disabled people, women, teens, and other marginalized people, including musicians. Those speaking the accusation of transgressiveness tend to inhabit positions of power in terms of race, class, gender, caste, and ability, and are ready to assign the adjective *dangerous* to anyone different from themselves. It is too easy to view the idea of transgression as somehow breaking the rules or acting in ways that are contrary to what mainstream society believes. Indeed, that *is* one of the ways to interpret it, and it certainly finds relevance in a discussion of the liminal. Transgression, however, is not necessarily what some people imagine it to be. Its literal meaning from Latin, "to step across," does not automatically mean to break all the rules. It really means moving outside of expectations (your own or someone else's) and to explore and experience another perspective—not a "wrong" one.[1] When something sounds like transgression, the fresh urgency of the musical experience is one of access and attention to other points of view, other grids, and perhaps even the warmth of other suns. Stepping across a perceived barrier of binarism—sacred *or* secular, gay *or* straight, male *or* female—and holding that ambiguity enables the subversion of the Eurocentric gaze, and the ability to stand directly in the center of the liminal space rather than being perpetually at the margins.

As an example, imagine the white middle-class suburban American teenager—neither child nor adult, neither urban nor rural, neither powerless nor powerful (though they are the target of endless marketing campaigns to wring potential teen dollars from their hands), and in possession of that most valuable of commodities: time. All the casual observer needs to complete this particular liminal picture is to imagine sex, drugs, and rock 'n' roll. Sex breaches the boundary between two humans; a person on drugs is neither

Music at the Threshold from the Sacred to the Dangerous. Sean Williams, Oxford University Press. © Oxford University Press 2026. DOI: 10.1093/9780197761762.003.0006

sick nor well; and rock 'n' roll facilitates the search for identity and the imagination of rebellion through identification. Cue the scolding adults: parents, teachers, politicians, and religious leaders, all raging about "these young people today."

Now let's transgress the surface of this rather simplistic scenario. By the end of the second decade of the twenty-first century, half of American teens are BIPOC (Black, Indigenous, People of Color). One-third of American teens live near, at, or below the poverty line. Twice as many American teens live in the suburbs as live in urban areas; twice as many American teens live in urban areas as live in rural areas. Marked differences in access to education, healthcare, safety, and other factors tend to fall along racial and ethnic lines.[2] As for having all that alleged free time, many teens hold down jobs, serve as caregivers for family members, or are otherwise in positions of obligation to an authority figure. Not surprisingly, music that engages various identities and values tends to loom large in teenage lives.[3] Because the eyes of corporate America have had a laser-like focus on white American teen music dollars for decades (Taylor 2012: 116–117), it is a fascinating conundrum to see the musicians that teenagers are said to admire be so celebrated—witness the fascination and stratospheric financial array connected to Beyoncé and Taylor Swift, for example—*and* reviled as corrupting the hearts and minds of American teens since the 1950s (Stephens 2016: 98).[4] American popular musicians (and their music) command top dollars in terms of ticket sales and corporate advertising, yet to serve as a professional musician outside of places such as Carnegie Hall is often to invoke scorn because of the automatic assumption of transgressive behaviors.

Alan Merriam, one of the early scholars of ethnomusicology and to whom many point for their earliest understanding of the field, had choice words to write about musicians as transgressors. Using an example of the Basongye people in what is now the Democratic Republic of the Congo, he discussed the local stereotypes of musicians as "lazy, heavy drinkers, and poor marriage risks." He also notes, however, that "without musicians a village is incomplete; people want to sing and dance, and a number of important village activities simply cannot be carried out without musicians" (Merriam 1964: 136). The importance of musicians is unquestioned; their status within society (whether as part of a village in the DRC or in New York City) can vary. Merriam's work on musicians as "low status, high importance" serves us well here because the very point of this chapter is to highlight the ways in which musicians' actions and values, along with those of their audience members—for better or worse—have led to significant societal delineations.

Similarly, Zoe Sherinian's work on the South Indian Dalit *parai* (frame drum) musicians of Tamil Nadu reveals the simultaneous necessity of the drummers to facilitate funeral and other life-cycle rituals, and the custom for high-caste people in positions of power to simultaneously exploit and revile those same drummers. The Dalit people—who are outsiders to the centuries-old caste system of India—are also of low status but high importance. Without *parai* drummers, the funeral rite is incomplete. Yet the drummers must sit and eat separately, and they have traditionally been compelled to perform on demand for uncertain pay (or none).[5] In her film—*This Is a Music: Reclaiming an Untouchable Drum*—Sherinian explores the ways in which the positionality of the Dalit villagers shifts as a result of a visit to a festival in which they are celebrated as performers, and what it means to bring this revelatory experience home only to face oppression again.[6] Elements of alleged transgression of local tradition—being celebrated onstage, accepting that what they do is worthy *beyond* what high-caste people have determined, and the potential reclamation of the name parai for the drum rather than the seemingly neutral "drumset"—point to the ways in which one group's transgression is another group's development. The fact that the *parai* is the root of the word "pariah" should come as no real surprise. We recognize that a pariah is a social outcaste—notice the inclusion of the word *caste* here—and make assumptions accordingly.

It is often those in power who are allowed to decide who will be an insider or an outsider; insiders to power make the choices to place people in the status of Other. "Social groups create deviance by making the rules whose infraction constitutes deviance, and by applying those rules to particular people and labeling them as outsiders" (Becker 1963: 9). In declaring someone to be an outsider, or an Other, those in positions of power can choose to create an insider understanding of conformity to and deviance from the norm, with severe consequences for those who live their lives according to their own truths. This chapter explores the culturally bound notions of transgression from the perspectives of those who are so labeled, whether they were connected to the secularization of medieval Europe, or are part of a larger scene that has featured people in the performance of maleness and femaleness in Indonesia and Japan. In the early 2020s, the performative successes of American artists Amythyst Kiah and Lil Nas X have wowed certain audiences and annoyed others for the playful transgressions and ease with which they engage. But why use this chapter for these particular choices?

Drawing from the roots of European medieval music may feel oddly transgressive on its own for a book by an ethnomusicologist, but the bilingual motet came at an important moment in European cultural history, as Europe lurched toward a more secular society in its long trajectory toward the Renaissance.[7] Examining some of the varied and nuanced contexts of people who perform ambiguity joins the larger issue of connecting that ambiguity with the sounds that support it. Finally, Lil Nas X and Amythyst Kiah belong here because they themselves are simultaneously changing and enacting changes *right now*. People who have been labeled as transgressive because of their boundary-pushing efforts in composition and performance have often ended up at the center. But is it actually transgression, or does it simply seem like it to people at the centers of power?

One thing that some—but not all—alleged transgressors share is two or more features of intersectionality. Kimberly Crenshaw's coinage of the word (1989: 139–167) was a way to get at the cross-sections of identity; we are never carrying *just* a race, a sex, a heritage, a language, a nationality, or some other identifier. That would render us all as one-dimensional. Intersectionality is not new; there have always been people who combined different identities. The key here is recognizing that certain identities run up against the power structures that guard against difference, and that separating race from sex from the many "othering" identifiers doesn't work. For example, Salif Keita, a singer-songwriter (and hereditary prince) from Mali, has albinism. The condition has generally signified a bad omen in West Africa, and he was shunned as a child; as an adult he has created a foundation to combat the stigma. Having albinism alone, however, is not a defining feature of intersectionality; it is *one* element of difference. He is also a musician; the combination of instability of occupation with a very visible physical sign that evokes fear led him to have to leave Mali for Europe, where his identity as an African man added another element of difference. For the American musicians Amythyst Kiah and Lil Nas X, who are simultaneously queer and Black, and who each play with the borders between musical genres, their intersectionality is not transitional; it is who they are.

Transgressors are not transgressive to themselves; in something of a nod to bell hooks, they are at the center, rather than at the margins (hooks 1984) of their respective selves. In her discussion of the extraordinary cultural circumstances of the late 2010s in the United States, Susan Thomas writes that "The ability for music and sound to cross, to permeate, and to trespass has made it a key tool for the rendering, identification, and navigation of the boundaries that have marked the past half-decade" (2020: vii). In using music to navigate and express their own boundaries and norms, rather than those of the mainstream, allegedly transgressive performers and their audience members experience a reclamation of territory and an establishment of individual and collective power. It is precisely this phenomenon that can lead to great societal transformations, regardless of the location or time—even in the thirteenth century, or the twenty-first century.

Bilingual Motets and the Secularization of Thirteenth-Century France

Medieval Europe underwent a dizzying series of changes from what came before, not the least of which was an economic boom that enabled travel and commerce to flourish in ways that had previously been more difficult; furthermore, the discovery of Aristotelian and Islamic science led to a heady clerical and scholarly immersion in the understanding of the natural world by the end of the twelfth century (Chenu 1997: 10). The creation of the mechanical clock, windmill, compass, and other developments in technology led to efficiencies in transportation and construction. Sudden access to this newly acquired knowledge lay against a backdrop of scholars who "lived in a world where everything, both divinely created and manmade, was interpreted as meaning more; as symbolizing some deeper, Christian truth" (Davies 2013: 16). In this segment, the extraordinary technical shifts in the musical compositions in northern France were grounded in the reverence for and symbolism embodied by a powerfully liminal figure: the Virgin Mary. Her liminality—as a virgin mother, teenager, both sacred and worldly, connected both to Christ's birth and death, and her presence at the cave-tomb entrance—has been engaged by artists (performing, media, visual) for centuries.

One of the biggest musical changes to take place in Western European music of the Catholic Church was the advent of polyphony in the context of monophony,[8] and it occurred at the then-center of the Western European musical power structure: the Cathédrale Notre-Dame de Paris. Anyone who has participated in a "Western Music History" class is familiar with this period. Beginning with the works of the French composers Léonin (b. @1150

CE) and Pérotin (b. @1200 CE), this form of polyphony—*organum*—featured the melodies of plainchant slowed way down and serving as a fundamental, slow-moving ground for an up-tempo upper voice in triple meter. In a context where the Holy Trinity reigned supreme, using triple meter was an obvious connection to Catholicism, particularly as the original text of the chant became largely subsumed under the dominating sound of organum itself: melody with no discernable lyrics. The *Magnus Liber* or "Great Book" of organum (1160–1170 CE) is said to have been created by Léonin himself with additions by his successors, including Pérotin; his codification of short, repeated rhythmic patterns in church composition—*musica mensurabilis*—remains a significant achievement (Waite 1954: 29–39).[9]

In addition to more accurately notating rhythm, other innovations at the time included prioritizing collection and archiving of chants by getting them onto parchment, and the development of the idea that some chants, such as those written by Léonin and Pérotin, had actual named composers. During this period of *ars antiqua* ("ancient art"), 1170–1310 CE, the treatises and compositions are entirely of the Catholic Church; secular Western European music was proceeding apace outside the realm of the sacred. The liminal moment of transgression, in which the two sounds connect, occurred in the thirteenth century. Here is how it happened, using a single plainchant to illustrate the first steps.

In the original plainchant of "Viderunt Omnes," the following verse appears:

> *Viderunt omnes fines terrae salutare Dei nostri*
> *Jubilate Deo, omnis terra*
> *Notum fecit Dominus salutare suum*
> *Ante conspectum gentium revelavit justitiam suam.*
> > All the ends of the earth have seen the salvation of our God
> > Rejoice in the Lord, all lands
> > The Lord has made known his salvation;
> > In the sight of the people he has revealed his righteousness.

Both Léonin and Pérotin created polyphonic organum set to this text. In the original plainchant melody, there is significant melisma across most of the work (Figure 6.1).

First Léonin, then Pérotin, set this text polyphonically, respectively. Léonin included a single voice above the chant (which functioned as a drone), and

Figure 6.1 Plainchant "Viderunt Omnes" ("They All Saw")

Pérotin includes three separate polyphonic voices above the drone. To perform just the first *two words* of Léonin's "Viderunt Omnes" takes approximately 1:30; for Pérotin's, 3:30.[10] It should be clear that the development of
organum was a radical shift from the monophonic chant that characterized
the previous centuries. Both composers took liberties with the original plainchant melodies by creating *clausulae*, small newly composed melismatic
sections sung to a single syllable that were inserted into the existing organum.
Those clausulae later grew in importance as more composers adopted them
and became foundational in the shift from organum to motet.

The motet today is best known as a sacred polyphonic work in Latin, in
contrast to the secular polyphonic madrigal in vernacular languages; that
separation was established by the time of the Renaissance. In the thirteenth
century, however, the development of the motet began with the clausulae
of organum being troped: re-set with new text.[11] The plainchant original
functioned as the underlying melody—the *tenor*—as the foundation for the
piece. In addition to the tenor line, two voices at two different pitch levels—
duplum and *triplum*—and *two different sets of* lyrics in Latin formed the basic
shape of the early motet. Having two sets of lyrics meant that their meaning
was discernable only to those informed audience members who knew the
motets; because any lyrics attached to a plainchant tenor would be a trope on
the original lyrics, the general idea of all three lines was related. The largest
collection of motets is in the *Montpellier Codex* (ca. 1300 CE), which features
several hundred motets in Latin and French written by both anonymous and
named composers and from which these (anonymous) examples are drawn.

All of the early Latin double motets (double—two voices above the tenor)
were focused on sacred themes at the beginning, especially themes dedicated

to the liminal Virgin Mary; after all, Notre-Dame was and is dedicated to her, so musical compositions written onsite would logically connect as well. Yet, until the early medieval period, references to her were oblique. "In the Gospels her appearances are rare, shadowy, and inauspicious; she is arguably just a historical footnote to the life of Christ" (Davies 2013: 3). By the thirteenth century, however, things had changed dramatically. The motets that celebrate her life and venerate her liminal position between humans and the divine dominate the output of the Notre-Dame (and other) composers.

In the all-sacred, all-Latin motet "In Mari Miserere/Gemma Pudicicie/Manere" ("In the Turmoil of the Sea"), the plainchant is only the word *manere*, "stay." The duplum line is *Gemma pudicicie, laude plena, ex te sol* ("Jewel of chastity, full of praise, the sun comes of Thee"). The triplum refers to Mary as the "Star of the Sea"; in an allegorical sense, the Virgin Mary serves as a kind of star that guides followers to Christ. Since the medieval era, the image of Mary as the star of the sea has appeared in statues, grottoes, and paintings, and often appears in shrines at the threshold between land and sea: the pier. This sacred double motet, then, is fully dedicated to the Virgin Mary.

> *In mari miserie, Maris Stella,*
> *Errantes cotidie a procella*
> *Defende nos et precare Dominum pie*
> *Ut ad portas glorie nos trahat per hoc mare.*
>> In the turmoil of the sea, O Star of the Sea
>> Daily tossed about by the storm
>> Defend us and pray devoutly to the Lord
>> That to the gates of glory he may lift us.

Several major changes signal the shift away from the sacred in the liminal place toward the secularization of sacred music. First, the performance of the (originally plainchant) tenor line was performed on a musical instrument rather than a human voice; this meant that the original plainchant text, as well as its sacred meaning, was lost or only vaguely implied. Second, the inclusion of French lyrics on the upper voice meant the introduction of the vernacular to a formerly sacred genre. The use of French and Latin simultaneously in the same motet—the bilingual motet—meant that a form that had been used strictly within the boundaries of the Catholic Church was now at the borders of the secular world; it was precisely in between. Lastly, because the tenor line was played by an instrument rather than being sung, *any* melody could now serve as the tenor.

In the bilingual motet "O Mitissima Virgo Maria/Virgo Virginum/Haec Dies" ("Oh Most Gentle Virgin Mary"), the tenor line uses only *haec dies*, "this is the day," from the Easter plainchant Haec Dies: *Haec dies quam fecit Dominus; exultemus et laetemur in ea* (This is the day which the Lord hath made; we will rejoice and be glad in it). The duplum is a fully sacred supplication to the Virgin Mary, entirely in Latin:

Virgo virginum, lumen luminum, reformatrix hominum, que portasti
   Dominum
Per te, Maria, Detur venia, angelo nunciante
Virgo es post et ante.
>   O Virgin of virgins, light of lights, remaker of men, who has borne
>   the Lord
>   Through Thee, O Mary, may forgiveness be granted as the angel
>   announced:
>   Virgin before and after.

The triplum, however, has two parts: first in Latin, then in French.

[Latin] *O mitissima Virgo Maria, Posce tuum, filium, ut nobis auxilium*
Det et remedium contra demonum fallibiles astucias et horum nequicias.
[French] *Quant voi revenir d'esté la saison*
Que le bois font retentire tuit cil oisillon
Adonc pleur et soupir pour le grant desir
Qu'ai de la belle Marion, qui mon cuer a en prison.
>   [Latin] O most gentle Virgin Mary, ask Thy Son to give us help
>   And a remedy against the demons, their deceitful wiles and their
>   wickedness.
>   [French] When I notice the summer returning
>   When the woods resound with blithe birdsong
>   Then I weep and sigh in deep yearning
>   For lovely Marion, who has enslaved my heart.

It should be clear that with two lines being sung simultaneously—the sacred duplum and the bilingual triplum—the image of a lovesick priest swooning over his maid Marion can be deftly tucked into an overall sacred setting without much appreciable loss of the dedication to the Virgin, particularly since she shares a name with the earthly lover. It was just a short period of time that the sacred, Latin elements of the motet were abandoned in musical composition and the secular, French elements became celebrated, completing the shift of the thirteenth-century motet from entirely sacred to (mostly) secular by the end of the century. For example, the *ars nova* ("new art") motet "Quant je le voi/Bon vin doit/Cis chans" with the (French) tenor line *cis chans veult boire* ("this song requires a drink") is entirely secular; it is one of twenty-six such motets with French tenor lines (Everist 2007: 372). Over time, the term "motet" shifted back to its original sacred context, but it was only with the Renaissance and all its concurrent compositional innovations that it came to refer to exclusively sacred polyphonic song once more.

Mary has served as a prime intermediary between believers and the divine from the medieval period to the present; she appears in song, in visual representation, and in folklore throughout the Catholic world. From her manifestation as the Candomblé deity Yemanjá in Brazil to her ubiquitous presence in "Mary gardens"[12] and sites of healing, and dominance in processions and shrines in southern Europe (Breuner 1992: 66), Mary (rather than Jesus) is the enduring focus of the average layperson's attention. In mainland Europe, her importance and large-scale presence in both visual and musical arts was explosive in the medieval era. Mary is the one who appears in visions; to whom hospitals, gardens, and lives are dedicated; and to whom the bulk of the *Montpelier Codex* is dedicated. As a central figure in Catholicism, she serves effectively as a liminal focus of attention in *both* the sacred and secular lives of her adherents.

It is worth noting that while the dramatic upswing in Marian veneration was taking place both inside and outside the Catholic Church walls in the thirteenth century, another drama was taking place in connection to worship: the removal of ecstatic dance from inside the churches to the streets outside. The open plan inside the churches—and the lack of pews for sitting—enabled people to stand, move, and dance. While churches had been a place for dancing one's Catholicism with physical/kinetic leadership from the priests themselves, the thirteenth century in particular saw specific changes made to the rules, primarily aimed at women. Barbara Ehrenreich, in *Dancing in the Streets, a History of Collective Joy*, points out that "it was women's dancing that brought down some of the angriest condemnations" (Ehrenreich 2007: 80).

Upon great feasts and wake-days, choruses of women invaded with wanton *cantica* and *ballationes* the precincts of the churches and even the sacred buildings themselves, a desecration against which generation after generation of ecclesiastical authorities was fain to protest. (Chambers 1903: 161)

At least partly because of women's participation in ecstatic dance within the church walls, the leadership moved dance outside and away from the centers of worship, instituting a more solemn experience within. The institutionalization of confession in the Lateran Council of 1215 cited dancing as one of the sins to confess, but only if it occurred within the boundaries of church properties (Ehrenreich 2007: 81). If parishioners could access the divine through ecstatic dance with or without the leadership of a priest, what need was there for them to pay tithes and conduct the entirety of their spiritual lives within the confines of the church? The Catholic Church chose to emphatically regulate that connection, and did so through the allowance of dance celebrations on feast days and other times coincident with the sacred calendar.

If religious dancing became ecstatic dancing—and the stories of dancers being "possessed" by the devil suggest that it sometimes may have—then ordinary people might get the idea that they could approach the deity on their own (as did, for example, the ancient worshippers of Dionysus) without the mediation of Catholic officialdom. (Ehrenreich 2007: 84)

The actual "transgressions," in relation to the development of the bilingual motet, include the engagement of the trope as a means by which secular ideas could permeate sacred texts and the hyper-veneration of the Virgin Mary *above Christ* in the lyrics of the motets and in widespread folk practices of festivals, processions, and Mary gardens. In his article about double motets, Gordon A. Anderson writes that, "In fact, the reintroduction of Latin for motet texts was an unsuccessful attempt to stem the flood of secular influences, and was by its very nature a rear-guard action against the growing secularization of liturgical music" (Anderson 1971: 36). In connection to dance, the thirteenth-century shift of ecstatic dance from indoor religious ritual to outdoor festival life brought the connection to the divine across the church threshold into the public square, infusing the sacred with the secular. Once certain artistic and cultural features of secular French medieval society were in place, together with many other societal changes, there was no stopping the inexorable march toward the Renaissance in France and elsewhere.

Performing Ambiguity in Indonesia and Japan

Ethnomusicology and heteronormativity have been enmeshed for decades; the chapters of 2020's *Queering the Field: Sounding Out Ethnomusicology* comprise a major step in breaking that hold, as multiple approaches to understanding the connections between music and sexuality have emerged. While the sibling disciplines of anthropology, musicology, folklore, history, and others have been ahead of ethnomusicology in their published engagement with queerness (Barz 2020: 11), a number of queer ethnomusicologists are, in fact, *central* to their home discipline of ethnomusicology in their groundbreaking work. The malleability of the term and its broad application in understanding intersectionality, creative work, and human connections across differences can lead to effectively recontextualizing known musical scenes and their major players.

Making generalizations is always a problem; sometimes it helps to tell a story for clarification. Zoe Sherinian argues that ethnomusicologists need to free their culturally bound ideologies of sex, gender, and sexuality from their fieldwork, pointing out that such limitations distort our sense of the local just as much as trying to apply Western music theoretical concepts to world musics (Sherinian 2020: 33). As I read her words, I was suddenly yanked back several decades to my doctoral research in Bandung, West Java. Not having had the opportunity or funding to visit Indonesia prior to committing myself to spending two years there without my then-husband (who at the time was continually on tour as a bass player), I took a leap of faith, applied for and was awarded a Fulbright-Hays doctoral fellowship, and went off to study the *kacapi indung*, a large boat-shaped Sundanese zither that was used to accompany sung poetry. Many surprises awaited me, of course, but I learned right away that this type of zither is gendered female, and that my also being female posed a problem.[13] In fact, I was married-but-solo, already in my late twenties without having borne any children, highly educated, rode a motorcycle, and operated well outside the local norms simply by having the expectation that I could study a musical instrument rather than the publicly acceptable subjects (for women) of vocal music or dance. "Men play; women sing or dance" was the refrain. I was perceived as unacceptably transgressive and needed to be brought under control. Worse, my white skin, blue eyes, and reddish hair pegged me as 100 percent Dutch—no Dutch ancestry in real life, though—so I was forever a walking representation of 350 years of oppressive and violent Dutch colonialism.

Within a week of my arrival I was studying singing with Euis Komariah, and within the first month I was dancing *jaipongan*, a staged social dance that I studied with (her husband) choreographer Gugum Gumbira and their eldest daughter Mira Tirasonjaya.[14] Prior to my arrival in Bandung, I had participated in an Indonesian language intensive course in Malang, East Java, where I also studied *tari ngremo*, a kind of cross-gender dance local to the area (Sunardi 2015: 20). In Bandung I began to take kacapi lessons "on the side" as well, but it was widely perceived as being *demi penelitian*—in the name of research—to better inform my understanding of *tembang Sunda*, the all-important sung poetry that the kacapi is used to accompany. Within a few months Rukruk Rukmana, my kacapi teacher, decided that further conformation to local gender norms was necessary. He arranged for a ceremony in which my sex would change from (straight and cisgender) female to an indeterminant status that would enable me to play the kacapi without disrupting the status quo of "men play; women sing and dance."

In a *tawajuh* ritual described at length in my first book (Williams 2001: 213–216) and first mentioned in Chapter 3, I was asked to wear a specific dress I owned that had African wild animals printed on it (to connect me with "an older way of being"), collect ritual items (coffee, rice, water, and more) from the four directions, and prepare in other ways. My teacher arranged for a local *dukun* (spiritual intermediary) to perform the ritual, and as part of the ritual (normally used to elevate an apprentice musician to player status or to enable one to engage in a spiritual transformation before Allah), the *dukun* made a formal request to the ancestors to enact a change in me so that I could "safely" play the kacapi without disturbing them.

After the ritual was complete, the sense of ease among my Sundanese friends about my practicing kacapi (and even performing it publicly, once I had some skills) was palpable. It was a shift from my binary self to a liminal self; although I couldn't be a man, according to the *dukun* the ancestors had accepted that I was now allowed to play the kacapi. Though I was still impossibly (locally) transgressive in other ways, at least things were clear between me, the local musicians, and the ancestors with regard to musical practice. My participation in the ritual allowed me to move past my *own* American constructs of sex, gender, and sexuality and step into one that was local; my experience was localized and queered for me, whether I realized it at the time or not.[15] As a liminal person in terms of my now-ambiguous gender, my status as a resident/foreigner, and other transgressions, I was fortunate to work creatively and intensively with other people at the margins.

In the twenty-first century, the act of exploring queerness and queer theory moves us far beyond the simple (outsider) assumption that queer *must* equal exclusively homosexual. Instead, it explores the idea that thriving in queerness represents a disruption of multiple systems of oppression. And does performing across local gender roles indicate that the performers are transgender themselves? It does not. Tes Slominski defines queerness as "the condition of finding—or placing—oneself outside the symbolic order of everyday life, yet still needing to function within the institutions and practices structured by that symbolic order" (Slominski 2020: 221). It is political, and politicized, and directly focused on those who have historically been outside the mainstream. People choose what to call themselves, of course, and any generic labeling from outside tends to reflect the viewpoint of the outsider, not the insider. This section of the chapter deals with some of the subtleties and complications that arise from exploring the rich territory of Indonesian and Japanese performers whose work is fused to their performance of ambiguity.[16]

Across parts of Asia localized understandings of sex, gender, and sexuality do not depend on Western colonial or contemporary ideas. Being a performer who crosses the fuzzy lines of gender is not particularly unusual; men perform masculinity and femininity, and women perform masculinity and femininity. Similarly, dancers at various institutes develop an understanding of locally perceived masculinity and femininity rather than simply learning to move like a man or a woman (Fukuoka 2014: 24). It is not a dichotomy of "the West/the rest" (with Asia somehow standing in for the rest of the world); again, it is the *local*, in local context, without binary orientation or reaction to it. In many places in Indonesia, for example, it is common to see people of the same sex holding hands or lounging in each other's arms who have zero sexual interest in each other, and whose behavior does not imply *anything*.

In the performing arts of music, dance, and theater, people across the spectrum perform roles that might be strictly gendered male or female in parts of Europe or North America. Chinese *jīngjù* theater, Japanese *kabuki* theater, Indonesian *topeng* dance, and several North Indian dramatic forms—to mention just a few of the best-known Asian genres—all include men dressing as and performing as women. Some genres include women dressing as and performing as men. In reference to male performances of female dance roles during the colonial period in North India, Kathryn Hansen writes that "For both men and women, performances of feminine identity opened up an arena in which gender norms could be articulated and debated" (Hansen 1999: 128). Specifically, in a number of these theatrical productions there was, and is, a staged presentation of what it has meant to be most effectively female or male in that place and time. Gillian Rodger (2018) has written extensively about male and female impersonators in the United States (see, for example, *Just One of the Boys: Female-to-Male Cross-Dressing on the American Variety Stage*). The relationship between the performer's body and the gender being performed is not a separation; it is a liminal meeting place of profound creative energy and potential.

Indonesia's rich array of hundreds of performing arts traditions include puppet theater (shadow puppets and rod puppets, among others); they often perform selections from one of the two great Hindu epics from India: the *Rāmāyaṇa* or the *Mahābhārata*. In one of the Sundanese tales featuring Abhimanyu (a character from the *Mahābhārata*), he is in the middle of a battle with an ogre, who appears loud, angry, chaotic, and unfocused. At the height of the battle, Abhimanyu ceases to fight and holds his position in deep focus while the ogre flails, yells, and collapses in defeat. Abhimanyu, son of Arjuna, has invisible armor (a gift from his father). But he also has *sakti*, personal power, that enhances his focus and enables him to fight off an out-of-control enemy by turning away. From a Western perspective, he appears gentle, quiet, slender, modest, and almost feminine looking. How is it possible that someone so allegedly feminine could defeat a giant ogre? Simple: What mainstream Americans (for example) understand about sex, gender, and sexuality is *irrelevant* when considering the expressive culture of another place. Abhimanyu's power in battle does not come from the size of his body or the loudness of his voice, and he isn't "feminine." Any assumptions about the necessity of performing masculinity by being large and loud to win a battle are those of an outsider.

Christina Sunardi, in her work on dance traditions of East Java, points out the importance of leaning on the local in understanding gender and the performing arts.

While gendered dance styles characterize east Javanese dance, most artists in Malang [East Java] recognized that a person's ability to perform a particular gendered style did not necessarily map to his or her biological sex. Most recognized that male style dance was not necessarily best when performed by a male, and female style dance was not necessarily best when performed by a female. (Sunardi 2015: 14)

To perform across the local social construct of gender is emphatically not transgressive as a way of simply breaking a social rule in East Javanese society; instead, it is transgressive—crossing over—in the sense of *going beyond* one's own biology as a means of understanding and presenting the narrative beauty of both femaleness and maleness.

In Japan, over hundreds of years, this exact scenario has played out in both older (*kabuki*) and newer (Takarazuka Revue) theater forms, which intersect at the start of the Meiji Era (1868). Kabuki (comprising three words meaning sing, dance, and skill) dates from the early seventeenth century in Kyōto. Whereas the original use of the word itself implies deviation from the norm (*kabuku,* "to act in a unique or peculiar manner"), contemporary practices lean on the authority of "tradition" to enforce its normativity (Isaka 2016: 27). Kabuki's fame rests on its extraordinary combination of dance, theater, music, costuming, makeup, and stagecraft. The stories tend to feature the conflict between duty and desire, and highlights include outsized emotions, strong morals, and dazzling visual effects.

The audience members for kabuki crowded right up against and even onto the stage, creating a liminal sense of intimacy and immediacy between the actors and the observers rather than any strict separation of one from the other. Indeed, the *hanamichi* raised walkway—which allows the actor to process right through the audience—that is so integral to kabuki stage design and promotes the custom of vocal interjections, celebratory gestures, and general cheering on (by name) of the actors by the audience. Because the actors are known not just by the name of the character, but by their own name, when an audience member calls out a name, it is of the actor, not the character.[17]

Because the Tōkugawa Shōgunate (1600–1867) had forbidden women from performing onstage by the early seventeenth century, the custom of men dressing as women became normalized over time. Stage performance had not previously been limited to either men or women, but part of the growing expectation surrounding kabuki theater was that it was a locus of vice; banning women from the stage was intended to curtail their availability as sex workers. The initial ban of 1629 was also connected to overarching shogunate efforts to shift the nation to a more Confucian—hierarchical, among other things—structure, which would place women in a highly controlled position. As a result of the ban, young men—*wakashū*—took on the roles of women until they, too, were suspected of prostitution. At that point, adult males began to specialize in the portrayal of women onstage. Their roles, called *onnagata* ("women's manner") developed over time to exemplify what Maki Isaka calls "artistic-artificial femininity" (Isaka 2016: 17). The homoerotic undertones of the young male wakashū remained in the character of the older onnagata, even though the law had changed specifically to forbid either women or young men from the stage.

Because the men could not disguise—and did not actually *need* to disguise—their own maleness, they leaned on more subtle gestures. "Thus they singled out the most essential traits of a woman's gestures and speech and gave to these a special emphasis in much the same way that puppets exaggerate human gestures to appear alive" (Brandon, et al. 1978: 40). The artifice of male actors in performing femaleness featured attention to appearing demure, kind, reticent, and loyal; all of these were features of Tōkugawa-era Japanese ideals for women, and these ideals were upheld as the gender-hierarchical standards to which women should aspire. The liminal act of crossing over from male body to locally relevant feminine sensibility is part of the magic inherent in being onnagata.

The near-ubiquitous presence of men as onnagata on the big stages does not negate the simultaneous presence of *female* onnagata: women who performed as men performing femaleness. When the ban on women performing onstage was lifted during the Meiji Era (1868–1912), one female performer spanned both the period when proscription against performing onstage was in place and another after it ended: Ichikawa Kumehachi I (1846–1913).[18] By making adjustments to her costuming and voice to appear more "male" in performance, she represents a number of women who began performing as onnagata toward the end of the nineteenth century (Isaka 2016: 21).

Kabuki is a form of musical theater, and musical theater depends at least partly on the human voice in speech and song. The Japanese language is gendered, dividing into "rough" and "soft" patterns (*danseigo* and *joseigo*, respectively) associated with maleness and femaleness. Because the onnagata uses the soft, polite form of spoken Japanese, it is a signifier of performative gender. Whether the actor is biologically one way or another, the language in speech and song will convey volumes of information to the audience about who is being represented. Yet representation is not merely a one-way affair of men representing women, who cannot effectively represent themselves. Instead, and looking at onnagata from a level of remove that emphasizes the separability of sex and gender, it is not women that onnagata and their songs represent; it is femaleness, to which any actor may have access.

A direct counterpart to kabuki is the Takarazuka Revue, founded in the city of Takarazuka (near Kōbe and Ōsaka) in 1913 by railway industrialist Ichizō Kobayashi. It was conceived as a reaction to the all-male performances of kabuki in the post-Meiji Era,[19] and as an attraction to bring more visitors to the town and its hot springs via train. It has always featured an all-female troupe, regardless of whether the characters depicted are perceived of as female (*musumeyaku*) or male (*otokoyaku*).[20] The town included department stores, beauty salons, souvenir shops, and many other features that he thought would attract women, thus blending spectacle with consumerism. Kobayashi, the creator of the Revue, envisioned it as a counterpart to theater that he regarded as old-fashioned (i.e., kabuki); he "hoped to develop a mass theater that would facilitate the shaping of girls and women into seasoned consumers" (Robertson 1998: 153).

Because the Revue was created after Japan had begun to westernize, the repertoire includes stories drawn from both inside and outside of Japan. At the time of this writing, the Takarazuka Revue featured *The Rose of Versailles*, an adaptation of a manga series (written by Riyoko Ikeda) set in Revolutionary France. The majority of the shows are, in fact, written by Japanese composers,[21] but adaptations of popular American musicals (*The Sound of Music, Singing in the Rain*), Shakespearean plays (*Twelfth Night, The Winter's Tale*), novels (*Wuthering Heights, Zorro*), and other foreign works are common.

The vocal style of the Revue features the vibrato common to *bel canto* style and Western musical theater more generally. Whereas kabuki and other older musical theater forms in Japan use strong variation in how vibrato is engaged in singing (Kojima et al. 2004), the twentieth-century creation of the Revue connects it more directly to an outward-facing phenomenon (see also the genres of *enka*, J-pop, and other popular Japanese genres across several generations). Just as the kabuki onnagata use the "soft" voice in their songs and speech onstage to perform femaleness, the Takarazuka Revue otokoyaku and musumeyaku performers use the voices that correspond to the sex of their character types, signaling to their listeners an emphasis on those categories. The femaleness of the musumeyaku characters is in service to the otokoyaku characters; the performers are said to "help the masculine traits stand out more by emphazing their own femininity."[22] The Revue is currently divided into multiple troupes of female actors; the management and most of the musicians are male.

Any study that features the widespread connection between cross-dressing and gender in the theater must take into account the presence of

LGBTQ+ performers and audience members. And just as the sexual identity of any individual tends to lie somewhere on a spectrum, the sexual identities of performers and audience members do as well. To reinforce the idea that local fluid modalities are most important here, "sexual practices have not presumed a specific sexual orientation or identity" (Robertson 1998: 174). As has been the case with kabuki onnagata, performers in the Takarazuka Revue have elicited administrative concern about having relationships with female fans; as of the latter half of the twentieth century, 90 percent of their fans are female. By strictly monitoring the behavior and relationships of the performers, the Takarazuka Revue management has added barriers between performers and their audience members. Those barriers, however, have not stopped the Revue's millions of fans from creating fanfiction, magazines, clubs, and websites.

A Western lens might automatically render the performers of all-male kabuki and all-female Takarazuka Revue, particularly in regard to the potential androgyny and/or homoeroticism of the roles of onnagata and otokoyaku, as transgressive. However, that lens would ignore local cultural practices within the context of larger political issues in Japan. In both cases, the female characters strongly reflect the Japanese gender hierarchy initially codified by the Tōkugawa shōgunate and maintained through the rigorous training of the Revue performers in, as the "Takarazuka Revue: History" video explains, "modesty, fairness, and grace."[23] Fortunately, the presence of multivocal theatrical genres engages a variety of Japanese citizens of fluid orientations, generations, and identities; one need not look exclusively at kabuki *or* the Takarazuka Revue and ask for whom in Japan the theater speaks (or sings).

It would be almost comically simplistic to call out the degree of academic hand-wringing in the West about gender issues in Japanese theater, if there weren't reasons to do so. From the obsessive focus on the *onnagata* (female characters played by men since the seventeenth century) in kabuki theater to the uneasy recognition of the star power of the all-female Takarazuka Revue since its founding in 1913, people who write about gender in Japanese theater have sometimes allowed their own concerns and biases about gender to creep into their writing (Episale 2012: 93). Rather like the above example of Abhimanyu in Indonesian puppet theater, referring to a character as "feminine" or "masculine" can reveal one's profound cultural boundaries and biases without regard to the insider's view(s).

If, as Ruxandra Marginean has pointed out, "Japanese theatre exists 'in the world' not only in and of itself, but also through its scholarly interpretations," then what follows is yet another scholarly interpretation of what transgression might mean in a Japanese context (Marginean 2001: 133). I might have been raised near San Francisco as someone with a great love for Japanese traditional culture and music—as interpreted by my parents—and who studied Japanese theater with William P. Malm and his own scholarly interpretations; I even lived in Kōbe for part of a year. However, my own emphatically outsider status means that whatever I have said here should cause you to be *hanshin-hangi de kiku*—half in doubt of what you listen to.

One of the great advantages of shifting performance practices through fluid gender identity is the exploration of power and essence: the power and essence of femaleness, and the power and essence of maleness in the androgynous performance of what Jennifer Robertson—in her work on the Takarazuka Revue—refers to as "strategic ambivalence" (Robertson 1998: 21). To quote Judith Butler on drag performance, "As much as drag creates a unified picture of 'woman' (what its critics often oppose), it also reveals the distinctness of those aspects of gendered experience which are falsely naturalized as a unity through the regulatory fiction of heterosexual coherence. In imitating gender, drag implicitly reveals the imitative structure of gender itself—as well as its contingency" (Butler 1990: 137). Each performer destabilizes normative identity by moving forward, across, in ways that people less attuned to the moment might regard as rule-breaking. It is the very centrality of occupying this beautiful ambiguity, however, that places these performers at the center of their craft rather than at the margins.

Lil Nas X and Amythyst Kiah, Right Now

In North America and Europe, by the latter part of the twentieth century a number of stars in popular music were known for, and celebrated for, the ways that they played with the fluidity of gender and sexuality. David Bowie, Elton John, and Boy George were hailed as trailblazers in that regard; they work makeup, earrings, skintight clothing, and high platform shoes onstage and off. But they had a predecessor in Elvis Presley; his liminal work as a white performer of rhythm and blues and use of hip movements, makeup, and bright clothing led simultaneously to his celebration and condemnation as an Other. He walked the fine line of several mid-twentieth-century -isms. It is also noteworthy that he routinely played along the boundaries of sacred and secular. His background in Pentecostalism, which he shared with other performers such as Little Richard, Johnny Cash, James Brown, and Jerry Lee Lewis, came to the fore in the full-body ecstatic worship exhibited by his (and the other performers') fans. Furthermore, his home at Graceland in Memphis, Tennessee, is not just the site of his (and his family members') interment but continues to serve as a locus of pilgrimage and candlelit vigils.[24]

Michael Jackson, mentioned in Chapter 1, also focused attention on the liminal positionality of someone neither boy nor man, neither male nor female, neither Black nor white, and so on as part of his performative (and lived) identity. His predecessors in (comedic) film and television included Jack Lemmon and Tony Curtis in 1959's *Some Like it Hot*, and the character of Max Klinger in *M*A*S*H*; all were emphatically straight men, cross-dressing for a specific reason. In the twenty-first century, such public personalities as Billy Porter and RuPaul are celebrated, reviled, and never far from the public eye. Each of these performers are, however, men, and the comic examples not only mock transgender and gay lives but straight women as well, ending up potentially reinforcing heteronormativity.

For this final section, I have chosen two intersectional artists whose significance marks a turning point in American music; both are queer, and both are Black. Lil Nas X, the cross-genre performer whose social media-friendly country-trap hit "Old Town Road" was controversially placed on Billboard's Hot Rap Songs chart after having been unceremoniously yanked from the Hot Country Songs list, is one of two performers under consideration. The other is Amythyst Kiah, a singer-songwriter who has performed as part of the group Our Native Daughters—four banjo-playing singer-songwriting Black women—and first performed on the Grand Ole Opry in 2021. The two performers are strongly positioned to confidently break boundaries that have been set for them by the overwhelmingly white (and male) music industry. It might be argued that their very intersectionality is protective, in a sense, because they defy the popular boxes that music industry norms assign in order to achieve a profit. As Susan Thomas writes about Lil Nas X, "Lil Nas X's joyous gallop across and through genre divides wasn't about transgression [. . .]. Rather, it merely wiped those genre boundaries clean off the map, offering a sonic glimpse into a country/pop/urban music soundscape that had always been there but had been carved up by ideas of song, genre, and audience" (Thomas 2020: viii–ix). The interrogation of transgression, and who decides what, exactly, is transgression, is the heart of this chapter.

Popular musicians such as Boy George, Prince, David Bowie, Michael Jackson, and others have obviously broken boundaries before; however, their work was fully in place prior to the rise of social media giants such as Facebook (and its dozens of holdings, including Instagram) or TikTok. The ability of an artist to connect directly with audience members via social media is still surprising to those of us who came of age when the massive record companies held their artists at bay from audience members (Hebert and Williams 2020: 480). The collapse of that gate-keeping function has enabled an unprecedented level of participation by fans; for example, TikTok users created short-form videos of themselves magically shifting into Western wear that have appeared in versions of "Old Town Road." Similarly, Scotsman Nathan Evans' solo recording of the sea shanty "Wellerman" early in 2021 spawned hundreds of TikTok videos (including those in different languages and musical genres) that allowed people to participate in the song.[25]

Country trap is a combination of trap—an Atlanta-based, synthesized-drum-based sound connected to southern hip hop[26]—and contemporary country, with its guitar-centered, melody-based sound. One of the first country trap songs was hip hop artist Nelly's "Over and Over," released in 2004, featuring country singer Tim McGraw. Nelly already brought a southern sound to his rapping; his first album was *Country Grammar* (2005) in southern hip hop style. As a liminal song (the video of which features such elements as waking up, cars, telephoning, and airplanes), "Over and Over" is a not-quite country song with trap beats and a trap song with a not-quite country melody. The fact that Nelly and Tim McGraw were already firmly established artists in their own genres before doing this song lent credibility to them both stepping out of their own lanes.

"Old Town Road," also in the country trap genre, was Billboard's longest-running #1 hit (at 19 weeks on the "Hot 100"). With an original groove by Nine Inch Nails, beats by Dutch beatmaker Young Kio, and the words by Lil Nas X himself, the song's success was fueled by his relentless placement of lyrics, videos, memes, and cuts from the track online; after people began posting videos of themselves dancing to it on TikTok, its viral status was complete. He invited country singer Billy Ray Cyrus to join him, and the resulting collaboration was explosively popular. The controversy surrounding Billboard's choices to shift it to their hip hop category—noting that it wasn't country enough—may also have supported its continuing popularity.[27] By the time Lil Nas X came out publicly as gay at the end of Pride month in 2019, his multiple successes propelled him right past his critics. And he was just getting started.

Each new elaborately produced and costumed video since "Old Town Road"—including "Montero (Call Me By Your Name)" and "Industry Baby"—has featured Nas X in transgressive situations. In "Montero," he is seen in various sexual poses with Lilith in Eden (as a human-serpent hybrid with Nas X's own face), then the Devil, after sliding down a long pole into Hell. Throughout the video, Montero itself (which happens to be Lil Nas X's given name) is presented as a place where hiding one's true self is sinful. *Billboard*—which previously had added to his fame with its controversial genre switch—referred to Lil Nas X as having "made waves yet again" with "Montero." He is quoted as deliberately trying to normalize queer lust, and that "he wants to show the industry that this kind of queer narrative can exist in popular music."[28] The giddy comments of historians in response to "Montero" were featured in an article in *Time*, which celebrated the video's multilayered references to historical persecution in ancient Greece and Rome. With quotations in Greek ("After the division the two parts of man, each desiring his other half") and Latin ("They condemn what they do not understand"), the video is more about historical expressions of queer love than a paean to Devil worship, as a number of right-wing pundits have claimed.[29]

In his "Industry Baby," Lil Nas X sets the work in "Montero Prison," with naked Black men dancing in a group shower and multiple sexual references. In a very playful move aimed at his critics, the "uncensored" version of the music video has the video appear to stall right at the shower scene and remain "stalled" through the rest of the video while the track continuous. It also contains lyrics that directly address his critics:

> Get your soldiers, tell 'em I ain't laying low
> You was never really rootin' for me anyway

He also states plainly in the lyrics that he is queer and doesn't have sex with women. Part of the track includes a rap section performed by (white) artist Jack Harlow, in which he is physically engaging with a woman while all the other performers are men with men. Critics were quick to focus on the discrepancy, to which Nas X wrote that he is gay and that Harlow is straight, period. In a post on Twitter in late July of 2021, Nas X pointed out to his critics that "y'all be silent as hell when n***s dedicate their entire catalogue to rapping about sleeping with multiple women. but when I do anything remotely sexual i'm being 'sexually irresponsible' & 'causing more men to die from aids' y'all hate gay people and don't hide it."[30] It should be clear that the immediate access between audience members and performers afforded by social media is a two-edged sword: laypeople—not professional critics—can ask him questions (or publicly state their own misconceptions), and he can correct them in a heartbeat.

As someone whose songwriting and performance skills have taken her from an all-white subdivision of Chattanooga to the stage of the Grand Ole Opry, England, and more, Black queer artist Amythyst Kiah experienced an epiphany when she realized that the allegedly all-white genres of old-time and Appalachian folk music contained songs and tunes that were part of Black local heritage too. She learned about the Carolina Chocolate Drops (an old-time string band comprising Black multi-instrumentalists and singers) and later became a part of Our Native Daughters (Kiah along with Rhiannon Giddens, Leyla McCalla, and Allison Russell). The success of their 2019 CD *Our Native Daughters* led to a tour and a documentary (*Reclaiming History: Our Native Daughters*), and to Kiah's song "Black Myself" being nominated for a Grammy award in 2019. In the same way that Lil Nas X obliterates genre boundaries, Ms. Kiah works with rock, blues, old-time, and other blended influences according to her current interests.

In her Grammy-nominated song, "Black Myself," Ms. Kiah offers a set of seemingly problematic behaviors and situations, from being a Black woman who plays the banjo to being someone whose skin is darker than a brown paper bag. Complete lyrics to this song (and multiple performances of it) are available online; this is the first verse.[31]

> I wanna jump the fence and wash my face in the creek, but I'm Black myself
> I wanna sweep that gal right off of her feet, but I'm Black myself
> I'm tired of walkin' 'round with no shoes on, 'cause I'm Black myself
> And your precious god ain't gonna bless me, 'cause I'm Black myself.

By the end of the song, she focuses on the changes in society and in her own life. The hard-hitting first chorus includes references to both religion and slavery:

> Is you washed in the blood of your chattel? 'Cause the lamb's rotted away
> When they stopped shipping work horses they bred they own anyway.

In contrast, the final chorus is celebratory but cautionary as well:

> I've washed away my blood and tears, I've been born brand new
> There's no more work horses, but still some work to do.

In an interview with Kiah for the *Country Queer* website, she describes discovering other cool, nerdy Black kids only by the time she reached high school, and that her parents' well-rounded musical tastes were part of her decision to enter the Bluegrass, Old-Time, and Country Music Studies program at East Tennessee State University.[32] And in an interview with National Public Radio she notes, "Because I know what it's like to be othered and alienated and feel in-between, I wanted to write songs in a way where anybody can put themselves into the song."[33] That extends to the song "Wild Turkey," about her mother's suicide, "Hangover Blues," about struggling with addiction, and "Ballad of Lost," about a breakup with a woman.

How does Amythyst Kiah look back in the process of moving forward? She draws from acoustic string-band traditions—blues and old-time—and recognizes their roots in West Africa. She writes about her own history and her own truths as a queer Black singer-songwriter. She is open about who she has learned from and what she wants to explore more deeply. She says, "Every time I've opened up about something, whether it be my sexuality or my social or political leanings, anytime I opened up about that, for any person that I might have lost, I've gained so much more."[34] These are not the words of someone whose alleged transgressions are inhibiting her career or presenting roadblocks to her advancement. She started out Black and publicly queer from when she first began touring, so her identity is no surprise.

From her interview with *Country Queer*, she notes that the music she plays is between West African and Celtic influences, and she herself is between white and Black:

> Southern music is a mix of West African and British Isles—Celtic—musical influences; a big chunk of it is those two cultural folk traditions. [. . .] So the West African element really comes in with the clawhammer banjo. It's something that stems from West African culture. And mixing that with the Celtic culture of fiddling, created something unique and wonderful. [. . .] I grew up in a conservative, white, Bible belt, middle-class, suburban area, and then when I was around Black people, being accused of trying to be

white, because of the way that I spoke or the way that I carried myself. So there was a sense of in-betweenness within both groups.

To have two popular queer Black artists be clear about who they are onstage, on social media, in song lyrics, and in interviews, even as they obliterate genre boundaries, is what sets them apart from so many others. Neither of these intersectional artists apologizes, and both artists are upfront about what makes them who they are. This is not just about representation; it is about the systemic homophobia and racism that would keep intersectional artists held back. In other words, it isn't that they are Black or that they are queer; it is that they are Black, queer, genre-bending, and *popular* that defies the usual attempts to suppress them in the name of keeping the systems of power in place.

A proverb about the importance of looking back is connected to the Akan (Ghanaian) word *sankofa*: *Se wo were fi na wosankofa a yenkyi* ("It is not wrong to go back for that which you have forgotten"). It is about returning to one's sources and "fetching" knowledge from them. The Sankofa bird is a Ghanaian image of a bird looking back over its shoulder, usually to an egg on its back. Part of a group of Adinkra symbols (symbols used by Ghanaians to represent idioms or concepts), the Sankofa bird reminds us to focus attention on the past while facing forward. No new creative work, no matter how extraordinary, is without precedent.

In each case in this chapter, the people doing the alleged transgressing are achieving something extraordinary not because they abandoned a root source, but because they doubled down on it to create something new. The motet composers of the thirteenth century used plainchant as a springboard for (ultimately, Renaissance-bound) polyphony, while performers of Indonesia and Japan who engage the *local* essence of maleness and femaleness create new pathways through older techniques. For Lil Nas X and Amythyst Kiah, the choice to expand through hip hop, rock, old-time, and other genres has included direct nods to those musical styles in the development of their own specific sound. The liminality of each stage of their respective journeys marks a moment of ambiguity, change, and creative engagement in their respective societies.

7

Shifting Sands of Power, Identity, and Resistance

Nana korobi ya oki. Fall down seven times, get up eight. (Japan)

One of the great challenges in developing my own understanding of liminality and sound has been the temptation to be fixed on a central idea, rather than exploring something more ambiguous. Some of my own publications focus on specific genres and facts, or on a specific person. However, in this book, I have offered less about the hard facts—such as the notes and rhythms of music or thick description of a genre in all of its contextual complexity— and more about the musical *processes* that humans undergo in their efforts to grow, transition, and engage major issues in their lives. In this final chapter, I focus on the dangerous but effective practices of creative resistance through reliance on liminal places, people, events, and genres; those form the backbone of strength against hegemonic power. Their employment in reclaiming power and identity after colonization and other traumas, for example, are the equivalent of falling down seven times but getting up eight.

As part of this exploration, this chapter features several rich cultural experiences that include pathways to understanding power and identity through local forms of both existence and resistance in the context of people who have had their ways of life severely suppressed. The annual Tribal Canoe Journey of the Pacific Northwest (in the United States) and the quadrennial Festival of Pacific Arts (in Oceania) are events that feature Indigenous people traveling by canoe across saltwater to a location where they are welcomed by hosts with song and musical instruments at the shore. They present similarly rich musical and artistic approaches to a liminal experience of resisting settler interference and the powerful assertion of identity. During the Harlem Renaissance in the early twentieth century, those who were simultaneously queer and Black found in some ways a safe home and

Music at the Threshold from the Sacred to the Dangerous. Sean Williams, Oxford University Press. © Oxford University Press 2026. DOI: 10.1093/9780197761762.003.0007

place to connect with others in a hothouse of musical and artistic creativity. Through living out loud as LGBTQ+ people in Harlem, this public milieu of queer poets, musicians, dancers, and artists thrived during a precarious time. Lastly, the simultaneous advantages and challenges of being bilingual and singing in an endangered language has enabled countless people whose language and culture have been overwhelmed by a majority to maintain and celebrate their identity through subtle means. The emergence of local hip hop among minority language speakers represents a forthright challenge to linguistic and cultural hegemony. In each of these three cases, it is precisely the liminality of that experience that foregrounds both the challenges and the danger inherent in simply existing in a world driven by power and domination. It is also a community-driven development of a place of relative safety, healing, and resistance.

Pacific Rim Canoe Journeys

Canoe Nations are places where canoes that cross saltwater have historically served as the primary instrument of transportation, communication, and identity. Saltwater canoes are carefully built and utilized in two sections of the Pacific Rim: the Pacific Northwest coast of the United States and Canada, and the many islands of Oceania. A canoe journey involves a significant gathering of tribal (in the Northwest) or island (in Oceania) community members at a host location, to which some participants have traveled from home (sometimes over great distances) via canoes. The larger point of a canoe journey is to build a strong sense of unity and healing (from the violence of colonialism and its long aftermath) among participants, and to reaffirm the right to express the unique elements that mark their tribal or island identity. To quote Lului Whitebear, in her article about the Hawaiian activist and poet Haunani-Kay Trask, "The stir of the currents through our canoe paddles awakens our links to ancestors and our cross-Pacific connections" (Whitebear 2023: 116).

This segment of the chapter examines canoe journeys located in two parts of the Pacific, noting the importance of songs and percussion in support of the experience. In particular, the performances and celebrations at the places of departure from home and arrival at the host locations serve as a simultaneously liminal point of power, communal identity, and resistance to/recovery from decades of settler oppression and colonization of marine (and terrestrial) spaces that started centuries before with European settlement, backed up by legal statutes, unequal treaties, and downright theft.

> While the mobilization of law was a fundamental component of colonization and the extension of colonial authority of Indigenous lands and bodies, it was only one element of the multifaceted structures of oppression and dispossession that facilitated European colonization. (Wilson 2021: 391)

The Pacific Ocean is the obvious joining point between the Canoe Nations. Brian Diettrich, in his article titled "A Sea of Voices: Performance, Relations, and Belonging in Saltwater Places," connects the saltwater communities through the ocean itself. "Across Oceania and the globe, Indigenous communities maintain legacies of music and dance that embody close relationships to the ocean and its inhabitants: the animal and the spiritual life of the sea. These performance repertories hold significant implications for place-making in and connections to the sea environment" (Diettrich 2018: 46). In so many ways, the ocean is simultaneously the liminal place and the center. It is liminal because it is the active place of crossing, and it is the center because coastal community lives are deeply tied to it on multiple levels. The ocean is bound to local communities through local spiritual belief systems, and because of the importance of fish as a primary food source and as the means by which people communicate and trade, it is inescapably essential. Its constant shifts in the currents and tides, and its long history of taking lives and boats renders it worthy of both concern and respect. In that way, it has its own local connections to the sacred, alluring, and dangerous points referred to elsewhere in this work.

In the Pacific Northwest, United States federal law had placed old-growth cedar trees—the key material for canoes—under protection; it was not until the American Indian Religious Freedom Act was passed in 1978[1] that tribal communities gained permission for periodic harvests of trees in keeping with traditional ritual customs. Section 35 of Canada's Constitution Act (1982)[2] affirms the legality of traditional practices among Canadian First Nations. Cedar canoes comprised the heart of a community, facilitating communication, trade, hunting, fishing, and much more. Severely restricting their construction, use, and presence in local cultural expression was part of a long-term effort of restriction and suppression in settler culture in the region.

Similarly, in Oceania, European settlers—who showed up in the area over several hundred years—forbade the use of canoes as a means by which islanders could be restricted in their movements. In Fiji, for example, the Deed of Cession in 1874 "transferred sovereignty and ownership over all of Fiji to the British Crown" (Wilson 2021: 399), and what followed was control over what could be referred to as local customs and practices as well. Major colonial powers in the region included several European nations, Americans, British, Japanese, and others. Those disruptions, along with the arrival of missionaries, meant the profound erosion of local belief systems, internal hierarchies, and ways of understanding the world. Restrictions on trade meant that the normal practices of using canoes to transport goods and people fell out of use.[3] Epeli Hauʻofa also emphasizes the importance of being aware of the persistent impact of pernicious colonial viewpoints: "The wholesale condemnation by Christian missionaries of Oceanic cultures as savage, lascivious and barbaric has had a lasting effect on people's views of their histories and traditions. In a number of Pacific societies people still divide their history into two parts: the era of darkness associated with savagery and barbarism; and the era of light and civilization, ushered in by Christianity" (Hauʻofa 1993: 3). Indeed, the marginalization of the island communities is at least partly because of the colonial idea that the ocean cannot be the center (Roburn 2013: 107). The ocean, however, *is* the center. Because of the uneven and ambiguous application of the law over many decades, even in places where canoe usage is "legal" it has not necessarily been a welcome part of settler/colonial culture (Wilson 2021: 390). The concurrent position of legal/not legal and continuing presumption of non-Indigenous rights has served as a hindrance to the free and open expression of local identities, with or without canoes.

As part of a canoe journey, regardless of where it is held, months of preparation and practice—physical, spiritual, musical—help the participants to bond in the service of the event. Working with canoes, including making them and decorating them, is just one aspect. Learning to pull a canoe through the water, learning the songs and movements necessary for a successful trip, and bonding tightly as a crew are all key elements to the process. Learning the songs and dances, along with important tribal protocols, is crucial to the success of the event. Serving as host to the event is a significant responsibility, requiring hundreds of people to assist along with significant financial resources. Because some canoes can take weeks to arrive at the host location, careful planning ensures a timely arrival that follows local protocols.

One of the primary sonic indicators of celebratory arrival at the liminal site of the beach is drumming, singing, and the blowing of a large conch shell, either from the shore or from an arriving canoe. The shell itself (*Charonia tritonis* or alternately *Cassis cornuta*) has a wide opening that helps to focus and amplify the sound; it thrives only in water that is less than a hundred feet deep, so it is tied to the shore regions. It has different names in different Oceanic regions. Because the sound of the shell carries easily across water, it can be heard from a long distance away. Shells of this type have a long history of human usage that dates from the 3rd millennium BCE and are used in many places for sonic purification and clearing the air, metaphorically. In addition to their use as signaling devices, these shells serve as an important intermediary feature of ceremonies and specific rituals by helping tribal and island participants to connect with the spirit world.

These canoe journeys have been held annually or every few years, depending on local conditions, at a different location each year. What these two canoe journeys have in common is not just the rich cultural exchange that occurs when a different tribe or island hosts visitors, but the empowering reinforcement of local protocols and reclamation of pride and healing that happens when people unite in solidarity. In the first chapter of this book, the word *communitas* was used to describe the feeling of deep solidarity when a group of people undergo a liminal experience with others. By sharing the intensity of a threshold experience—such as traveling some distance to gather at the shores of a host nation—the participants connect to each other and any differences in their respective status become lessened. Canoe journeys build communitas, not just among the ones pulling the canoe through the water but among the thousands of participants on the shore as well.

Tribal Canoe Journeys of the Pacific Northwest

In the Pacific Northwest of the United States and Canada, the Tribal Canoe Journey celebrates the strength and identity of Indigenous communities through regular shoreline gatherings that feature songs, dances, and drumming. It has been held most years since 1989, initially held as part of Washington State's centennial celebrations. During the organization of the Washington State Centennial festivities in the 1980s, Emmet

Oliver—member and teacher of the Quinault Nation—suggested that Washington's Indigenous people participate through a gathering of canoes in what was called "The Paddle to Seattle." At that time no one had carved a canoe for decades. The Washington state governor at the time, Booth Gardner, commissioned the construction of eight cedar canoes. Fifteen tribal nations were represented that year and forty traditional canoes crossed the water to Seattle. Emmet Oliver is honored each year for his role in reviving not just the canoe journey and ceremonies, but for reigniting Indigenous pride in local traditions. The event was such a success and brought so much awareness of canoe traditions not just to the settler communities but to the tribal members themselves that it has been re-enacted ever since as a family-friendly, drug- and alcohol-free celebration of belonging.

At the end of the first event—the "Paddle to Seattle"—the members of the Heiltsuk Nation, led by Frank Brown, invited those present to come to Bella Bella, located on the central coast of British Columbia, in 1993 (Neel 1995: 3). In 2016, Frank Brown and others created a 48-minute film that covers elements of history and suppression by colonial powers, with the emergence of a new optimism connected to the *glwa*—the ocean-going canoe—and the way it has drawn tribal members and families together.[4] It features interviews, archival photographs and footage, drumming, dancing, and songs, and is a fascinating piece with which to compare footage of its equivalent at the Festival of Pacific Arts in Oceania, featured below.

Julian Brave Noisecat—member of the Canim Lake Band Tsq'secen of the Shuswap Nation in British Columbia—is the son of family members who were incarcerated in residential schools in Canada. In his description of the cultural resurgence that has occurred since the Tribal Canoe Journeys began, he notes the following:

In the Pacific Northwest, the canoe is central to this resurgence. It brings communities together to paddle ancestral waterways. It challenges elders and youth to revive old songs and dances and compose new ones so they can paddle onto their neighbours' shores, proudly singing-in the spirits of our ancestors. In an age of digital relationships, it brings families together to celebrate and work through troubles. It reintroduces people to water in an elemental way, reminding us that water sustains life.[5]

In what is now the annual Tribal Canoe Journey, Pacific Northwest tribal members journey by canoe from their homes in Alaska, British Columbia,

Washington, and elsewhere with crews and family members traveling by road. Pictures, videos, and calls of support and encouragement appear on social media for weeks in advance, stepping up as the time draws closer to the main event; search on *any* of them for the term "Paddle to . . ." the year's destination, and hundreds of photos will appear. In 2024, the "Paddle to Puyallup" theme was the celebration of tribal youth, so many of the canoe families featured younger members of their tribes. In Figure 7.1, you can see the younger age of many of the pullers, the use of feathers and canoe decoration with cedar, and someone playing the conch shell in the right side of the picture.

As part of the normal protocols, canoes with eight to ten pullers travel from home to the host's location, where they formally ask permission to land. Participants sing in the canoes and sing out the canoes when they arrive and when they depart. The protocols take many hours and usually include identifying the canoe's home; stating that they come in peace; speaking their own language; and that they wish to share songs and dances (*Tribal Journeys*

Figure 7.1 Members of the Quileute Canoe Family arrive at the shore in 2024 as part of the Paddle to Puyallup Youth Canoe Journey (photo credit @ Zoltán Grossman)

Handbook and Study Guide, p. 10). It is normal that the ones who travel from farthest away are the first to perform. The greetings and welcome include a multi-day celebration modeled after the traditional potlatch. The potlatch ceremony—banned in the Pacific Northwest since the 1880s but lifted in the 1930s—features generous hosting with food, distribution of gifts, songs, dances, speech-making, validation of social status, and reinforcement of Indigenous ties between tribal communities.

In 2025, when the Lower Elwha Klallam Nation hosted the Pacific Northwest canoe families, local community members were invited to help create gifts for the potlatch and to donate practical items such as new first-aid kits, batteries, and ponchos.[6] Songs, which usually feature a single melody, use non-lexical vocables as opposed to event-specific lyrics. Note that the songs themselves are crucial gifts (Olsen: 1999:107–108) offered to the members of the gathering: they are often accompanied by frame drums and other percussion. These drums—and the regalia of those who play, sing, and dance—are often decorated with images of liminal creatures such as whales and/or birds, and many of the participants wear feathers. Chapter 2 had as its focus the centrality of liminal sea and sky beings in connecting with ancestors and the spirit world, and this event is a strong visual and sonic reinforcement of that powerful role. The closing ceremony includes the invitation to the following year's celebration by the future hosting community, and may include the hosts offering a significant gift such as a carved pole, oars, or other culturally meaningful items.

Each Pacific Northwest canoe is shaped from old-growth cedar; it is felled, burned along the center, and then hollowed out with an adze in a lengthy communal effort. Cedar itself is used as a liminal portal, offering protection, support, and purification. The word *puller* is used for one who works with the others in the canoe to pull it forward through the water. Canoe pullers sometimes hear the command "Paddles up!" from the skipper; everyone points the ends of their paddles to the sky. According to the Jamestown S'Klallam tribe, the moment of holding paddles upright is how each canoe announces its arrival at the host's location: "telling the identity of the arriving tribe was done with songs, dances, traditional greetings, and asking for permission to come into another's tribal territory before landing."[7] It also serves to allow the pullers to rest, or to honor the presence of the canoe family's wild relations such as orcas and eagles.[8]

Drumming styles, shapes, and rhythms vary from place to place, but they are widely perceived to be the heartbeat of each community; at some canoe gatherings in the Pacific Northwest, the drums play duple rhythms with every second beat played slightly louder than the first, like a heart pumping. At other gatherings—easily located on social media—a strong pattern of rapid single beats accompanies dancers making low (two-footed) hops with both feet, followed by a rotation and forward movement in a large counterclockwise loop.

The Ten Rules of the Canoe Journey appear on many Pacific Northwest Tribal websites; they are quoted here from the Snoqualmie Tribe website in Washington State.[9]

1. Every stroke we take is one less we have to make.
2. There is to be no abuse of self or others.
3. Be flexible.
4. The gift of each enriches all.
5. We all pull and support each other.
6. A hungry person has no charity.
7. Experiences are not enhanced by criticism.
8. The journey is what we enjoy.
9. A good teacher allows the student to learn.
10. When given any choice at all, be a work bee—make honey!

Sound facilitates the actual pulling, the bonding between pullers and between the pullers and the community, and the crucial welcoming protocols between hosts and guests. In the Makah Nation—on the coast in the far northwest corner of Washington State—tribal members have been teaching the Makah language and songs in the local public schools since the 1960s (Goodman and Swan 1999: 101). Some of the songs are canoe songs that do not necessarily belong to a particular family and can be sung with dancing by anyone. The public teaching of singing and dancing at Makah is just one example of how tribal members weave in some non-tribal members of local communities too. Of the twenty-nine federally recognized tribes in Washington State, most of the coastal tribes (which includes those who live on the coast of the inland Salish Sea) participate in the Tribal Canoe Journey.

The Festival of Pacific Arts in Oceania

The island region of the southern Pacific Ocean can be roughly divided into three main areas: Polynesia, Micronesia, and Melanesia. Within those areas, the islands can be divided by sub-areas such as Western Polynesia (Tonga, Samoa, and others) or Eastern Melanesia (Fiji, Vanuatu, and others). Some are nations, and some are territories. While some of the Pacific islands are separated by just a few miles, the entirety of the Pacific Island region covers over 300,000 square miles, and it can take weeks to travel from one island to another. The span of ocean and islands across the area is so broad that diversity among the many island groupings has to be assumed even though interisland canoe travel, trade, and communication has been firmly in place for several thousand years. The distance coupled with so much diversity makes the prospect of a contemporary festival celebrating Pacific Island cultures and continuities a significant undertaking.

> Native Hawaiians, like other Pacific Islanders, view the ancestral Pacific as the repository of their history, including genealogies of fearless navigators who made their journeys from island to island and hemisphere to hemisphere with nothing but the stars to guide them. (Trask 1999: 53)

The Festival of Pacific Arts,[10] held frequently since 1972 on different islands within Oceania, bears a marked similarity to the Tribal Canoe Journeys of the Pacific Northwest. The Pacific Community—an organization of twenty-two Pacific Island countries and territories that was created in 1947 and is located on the island of New Caledonia—developed the idea to secure and encourage existing Pacific traditions; since then, the festival has expanded to welcome the inclusion of Pacific contemporary musical and artistic work. Part of the reason for that welcome is the rejection of the colonial idea that indigeneity is something frozen in time; instead, "Pacific-ness manifests as cultural process through embodied activities—the music, dance, and other interactions that people recognize as '*lokal*/local' or 'island style'" (Diettrich et al. 2011: 4). Previously the festival has been held in Palau, Rarotonga, New Caledonia, Western Samoa, Guam, Tahiti, and elsewhere. The next one is scheduled for New Caledonia in 2028. The intentions of the Festival are as follows:

1. Preserving and revival of traditional arts and cultures of the Pacific
2. Exploring new forms of cultural activities suited to the needs of the Pacific
3. Creating greater awareness of the cultural richness of the Pacific throughout the world
4. Fostering a greater sense of unity throughout the Pacific to promote excellence in arts
5. Promoting the development and use of ethnic [Indigenous] languages[11]

Unlike the cedar canoe in the Pacific Northwest, the canoe in the southern Pacific was traditionally created from wood local to each island; for example, builders used to use koa in Hawai'i, breadfruit in Guam, coconut in Kiribati, and mangrove in the Solomon Islands. Material selection used to depend on availability and local customs, but current conditions have dictated sourcing wood according to local needs. In each case, the tree is felled according to local ritual, treated with respect, and shaped into a canoe with the proper local protocols specific to each island. The traditional adze, which now includes metal but would have previously featured a strong, sharp shell, continues to be used in canoe shaping. While not every Pacific Island canoe is constructed in the same way, 50′–75′-long outrigger canoes made with panels rather than a single hollowed log serve to cover long distances in the water (Lewis 1972: 254). UNESCO (the United Nations Educational, Scientific, and Cultural Organization) designated traditional canoe building on Carolina Island in the Federated States of Micronesia as an Intangible Cultural Heritage.

The entire community participates in the construction of the canoe, which begins with the selection and felling of a tree and involves a detailed measurement system based on an indigenous mathematical tradition that is both accurate and verifiable. The carving is done almost exclusively with the indigenous adze. The asymmetrical design supports high-speed sailing and allows access to shallow water.[12]

Whereas the canoe songs of the Pacific Northwest use vocables that nonetheless have cultural meaning, songs in the island regions of Oceania are very dependent on lexical poetry with nuanced layers of meaning and interpretation. "The notion behind such poetry is that anyone can relate facts; real skill involves making the story less transparent and encourages listeners to search for additional 'readings' that require in-depth cultural knowledge, understanding of poetic conventions, and, in some cases, personal familiarity with the place and people involved" (Diettrich et al. 2011: 11). The use of lexical canoe songs—or indeed, any Pacific Island songs—allows people to engage meaningfully at the level at which they are best able. Furthermore, the musical coordination of action is key. "The task of paddling together on a canoe is often used metaphorically in Hawaiian to express unity of mind and body" (Keola Donaghy, personal communication).

At the most recent Festival of Pacific Arts—in Hawai'i in 2024—the arrival of the canoes launched the event. Referred to in Hawai'i as *wa'a* (pronounced "va'a," both for canoes and for the event),[13] the canoe arrival featured drumming, singing, movement, and conch shell blowing. A conference/symposium was held at the same time, including workshops on dance and song, athletic games, discussions of technology, speeches, and moments for island elders to share stories and ideas about (for example) climate change and ancestral knowledge.[14] The Festival, and others like it in the region, builds island unity and fosters pride in what it means to be from one of the islands. It also gives individual island communities the opportunity to showcase elements of Tahitian, or Chuukese, or Tokelauan identity, language, songs, and dances. Groups compete to be selected for performance and the representation of their home islands in the Festival.

Canoes gather at dawn—neither day nor night—and the hosts wait for them at the shore. Participants wear what is locally appropriate for important ceremonies: feathers, shells, flowers or headbands made of leaves, and often locally made cloth. They play conch shells, bamboo trumpets, local drums, and other percussion, and perform a welcoming chant for each arriving canoe and nation. Gifts, including songs, abound from both the hosts and guests. Liko Hoe, Hawaiian language lecturer, quoted a canoe member from Papeete (Tahiti): "We come together like this . . . it helps us to kind of fill out our perspectives. Each of the nations, we all kind of bring a little bit different perspective of who we are as a collective. But when we have events like this, we really get to reflect amongst each other."[15]

The people of the southern Pacific Islands are renowned as skilled navigators, relying on star constellations, tides, and winds for guidance. They are also known for referring to some of the constellations as "sky canoes"; for example, the constellation referred to as the Southern Cross is the anchor of a great sky canoe for the Tainui Māori, while Orion's belt represents a sky canoe for the people of Tonga.[16] The Māori *iwi* or major kinship group connects with specific *waka* (canoes), signifying their arrival in New Zealand from Hawaiki, the mythical homeland. In the case of the Māori, Tainui is the name of both the kinship group and the canoe itself. The spiritual connections of canoe culture are a shared element among Pacific Islanders, and the sky canoes connect navigators with their ancestral ocean paths. In fact, when islanders encounter floating logs, local lore considers them "canoes of the spirits" (Diettrich 2018: 59).

One of the issues facing all Indigenous peoples is that colonial boundaries rarely coincide with Indigenous ones. In both the Pacific Northwest (between Canada and the United States) and Oceania (among many nations), contemporary international boundaries run the risk of obscuring older pathways of community connection and lock local communities into awkward loyalties that may not have been their own. As historian David Wilson points out, "the existence of multilateral overlapping jurisdictions across local, national, and international scales means that the rights of Indigenous peoples and local communities are being both recognized and contested across all levels at all times" (Wilson 2021: 407). Complicating the issue in the twenty-first century is that *any* festival, when projected on television and advertised in mainstream media, might draw so many outsiders as to overwhelm both the participants and the point of the gathering in the first place.

The legacy of a gathering such as the Tribal Canoe Journey or the Festival of Pacific Arts is its ability to perpetuate family and tribal traditions, respect community elders, encourage the youth, strengthen intertribal or inter-island identity in the aftermath of lengthy and brutal settler suppression of customs and oral histories, and to engage in renewal each year. Victor Turner's assertion was that *communitas* occurs through a shared liminal experience. The experience described here features one liminal event after another: the annual repetition of preparation of gifts, songs, and bodies; the reception at the shifting sands of the shore with songs; local language use, drumming, and dancing; and ritualized protocols for arrival and departure. There is a direct acknowledgment that these ceremonies are simultaneously resisting the prohibitions of the past and the assimilationist encroachment of contemporary settler influences all while celebrating identity and community.

Acknowledging the connective power of the ocean is precisely one of the shifts in worldview that these events celebrate. Whereas colonial and settler societies worked assiduously to convince tribal and island people of their irrelevance, the oral traditions of both regions envisioned an all-encompassing world of expansion and cooperation. "Their universe comprised not only land surfaces, but the surrounding ocean as far as they could traverse and exploit it, the underworld with its fire-controlling and earth-shaking denizens, and the heavens above with their hierarchies of powerful gods and named stars and constellations that people could count on the guide their ways across the seas. Their world was anything but tiny" (Hauʻofa 1993: 7).

In each case—with both the Tribal Canoe Journey and the Festival of Pacific Arts—the participating canoe families are pulling their communities on a journey of healing and recovery from lifetimes of colonial practices attempting to force assimilation and ignore centuries of Indigenous networks. The recovery occurs, over time and through many repetitions, precisely through this powerful act of physical and sonic resistance at the liminal site of the shore. Between the use of drumming, singing, playing the conch shell, gathering at the shore (often at dawn), wearing regalia featuring liminal animals and birds, and emphatically stating their identities and their right to gather, these two sets of Indigenous peoples refuse to go down silently. In her poem "It's Raining in Honolulu," Joy Harjo (Muskogee [Creek]) says "We will plant songs where there were curses" (Harjo 2015: 108).

All Roads Led to Harlem

The Harlem Renaissance—in the United States, in upper Manhattan (New York City), in the first part of the twentieth century—was a time and place of exceptional creativity and freedom for LGBTQ+, Black, and foreign artists to be at the center of the scene; what transpired was a unique moment of liminal fluidity. As part of a literal rebirth of African American culture in the aftermath of enslavement and the retrenchment of racist attitudes and laws after Reconstruction, marginalized people found an in-between place to engage in deeply transgressive acts of creativity—in music, fashion, literature, visual art, and more. That in-between place was Harlem, where many of these marginalized people were doubly marginal as recent arrivals from the South and the Caribbean; the area between Manhattan's 125th and 145th streets, north of Central Park, was the center of nightclubs, places for artists to gather, and the 135th Street branch of the New York Public Library, which served as a gathering place for artists, writers, and thinkers.[17] At a time of great economic uncertainty—between the 1918 influenza pandemic, the 1921 Tulsa race massacre, and World War II—the Harlem Renaissance was tied into the instability of both the Jazz Age and the Depression. As a welcoming home for newcomers of various class levels, the establishment of thriving Black-owned businesses led to the district's emergence as a destination forging its own identity.

Prior to the era of the Harlem Renaissance, there were few safe urban spaces for people to gather who fell between categories. In *Gay Voices of the Harlem Renaissance*, A.B. Christa Schwarz points out that "These interzones, ranging from cafes and black-and-tans—racially mixed clubs—to speakeasies provided spaces for marginalized men and women, some of whom desired members of their own sex" (Schwarz 2003: 11). There were specific political, cultural, and economic events that built up to the emergence of Harlem as *the* place to be a marginalized artist at the center during a certain time.

As part of the Great Migration (discussed in Chapter 5), those who had come to the industrial North were instrumental in the establishment of new cultural centers in the form of clubs and dance halls, not to mention churches, where musicians and audience members could spend their time in community. First called "The New Negro Movement," after the book *The New Negro* by philosopher Alain Locke, the Harlem Renaissance flourished between 1919 and 1935.[18] This extraordinary scene, which featured such luminaries as Locke, Langston Hughes, Zora Neale Hurston, Jacob Lawrence, and Countée Cullen, spawned an outpouring of artwork, poetry, music, and literature. Because all the thinkers, artists, writers, and musicians at the apex of the movement had either lived through the violence of the post-Reconstruction era or had immediate relatives with first-hand experiences, the injustices of that period loomed large during an exceptionally creative time. The visual artist Aaron Douglas, whose works illustrated the covers of both *Fire!!* and *Crisis* (two literary magazines of the time and place), wrote the following to Langston Hughes on December 21, 1925:

Let's bare our arms and plunge them deep through laughter, through pain, through sorrow, through hope, through disappointment, into the very depths of the souls of our people and drag forth material crude, rough, neglected. Then let's sing it, dance it, write it, paint it. Let's do the impossible. Let's create something transcendentally material, mystically object, earthy. Spiritually earthy. Dynamic. (Griffin 2008: 46)

Musically speaking, the Great Migration brought not only blues musicians and their audiences from the Mississippi Delta but jazz musicians and audiences from New Orleans and elsewhere. Standardization of musical genres (such as the establishment of the 12-bar blues) and amplification for singers became an aspect of performance practice in the big northern cities. Places along the major transportation systems of the Mississippi and Missouri rivers, the railroads, and the seaports became centers for jazz, thanks to developments in technology such as the radio and recording industries. In addition to the basic trio of piano, bass, and drums, the larger clubs featured big bands with a rhythm section, horns, and woodwinds playing arrangements of compositions. The big bands were often featured on the radio and in popular dance films from the 1930s to the 1950s such as *Swing Time* (1936) and *Hellzapoppin'* (1941), extending their popularity beyond the largest urban centers. Famous bandleaders of the period include Louis Armstrong, Count Basie, Duke Ellington, Cab Calloway, and Fletcher Henderson; they played big band jazz at venues such as the Plantation Club, the Cotton Club, the Exclusive Club, and other popular gathering sites.

Even as the public face of the Harlem Renaissance was a locus of culture and entertainment, it was also a safe(r) space for members of the LGBTQ+ communities. In addition to the best-known performers, some of whom were straight, many of the local composers, singers, dancers, instrumentalists, club owners, producers, and audience members were not (entirely) straight. The Jimmie Daniels supper club (114 West 116th Street), for example, was run by Jimmie Daniels himself, a prominent cabaret singer with performance connections across North America and Europe. The club hosted a diverse clientele of various races, classes, nationalities, and orientations. It was also the hottest new party location for LGBTQ+ British people who wanted to visit, according to Michael Adams of *The Guardian*.

> Few noticed overcrowding and poverty, or appreciated that the parents and grandparents of its residents had often been slaves. Rather, among the British who visited a fashionable notion prevailed: that Negros held an unspoiled vitality. By this mojo alone, some thought, the spent-force of white humanity might be saved from itself.[19]

Part of a vague notion among some white people of New York that Harlem was the place to be "free" of (white) societal constraints was the sense that connecting oneself to the jazz scene or imitating Black fashions would lead to that elusive sense of freedom (devoid of irony). It would not be the first (or last) time that white people muscled into a Black musical space or took over some aspect of Black expressive culture, but visits to Harlem from "respectable" Midtown Manhattan and elsewhere were perceived as explicitly transgressive. To "slum," a word dating from the 1860s, was specifically in reference to visiting an area for the purpose of engaging in vice. It also meant that white people could perform their own type of voyeurism of coolness that they hoped might somehow adhere to them as well.

Henry Louis Gates, Jr., pointed out in an interview that there is a belief that "the Harlem Renaissance was as gay as it was black" (Rowell

1991: 453). While the most famous literary people of the scene were gay men—Langston Hughes, James Baldwin, Claude McKay, Countée Cullen, Richard Bruce Nugent, and others—the often-bisexual female vocalists of the era were a major part of the draw to LGBTQ+ Harlem. Singer Bessie Smith (1894–1937) was also connected to both men and women. Gladys Bentley (1907–1960) played the piano and sang at speakeasies in Harlem while wearing suits and ties. Her taboo-breaking performances, which included singing and speaking about her relationships with women, drew the attention of police and caused her to leave Harlem for California. The tragic life of Billie Holiday (1915–1959) sometimes overshadows her musicianship; she was openly bisexual. Ma Rainey (1886–1939), celebrated in Langston Hughes' 1932 poem "Ma Rainey," was the subject of August Wilson's play *Ma Rainey's Black Bottom* (1982), which was released as a film in 2020. She was known for her relationships with men and women; her song "Prove It On Me" referred specifically to one of her lesbian relationships.

> Went out last night, had a great big fight
> Everything seemed to go on wrong
> I looked up, to my surprise
> The gal I was with was gone.
>
> They say I do it, ain't nobody caught me
> Sure got to prove it on me;
> Went out last night with a crowd of my friends
> They must've been women, 'cause I don't like no men.

Being able to openly claim and represent their sexuality onstage was an exceptional point of freedom for men and women in Harlem, and part of its draw for people from outside the scene. But they also often resisted the exclusivity implied by being gay or lesbian, continually living in between binary definitions. Thinking of "queer" as more of a general term than a must-be, must-do definition leaves room for the creative sexual fluidity that characterizes the period. "Its ['queer's'] brilliance as a naming strategy lies in combining resistance on the broad social terrain of the normal with more specific resistance on the terrains of phobia and queer-bashing, on one hand, or of pleasure on the other" (Warner 1991: 16). In the kind of space that Harlem offered at the time, being queer was multiply resistant.

The "A" train (established in 1936) crossed from Brooklyn through lower Manhattan in New York City, making its way as an express line to upper Manhattan. In taking the A train to Harlem, a kind of transformation occurred that brought all kinds of people into an inner circle of musicians, poets, scholars, dancers, artists, playwrights, and others. In some ways, the train facilitated the exchange not just of the arts among artists but the transformation of—for example—an otherwise heteronormative white man into a gay man, for an evening.[20] The A train was the channel of transgressive transformation: leave Midtown Manhattan as a married straight man and arrive in Harlem as a single gay man. After living one's true self for a time, in a safe and welcoming space, one could take the A train back through Manhattan and assume the mantle and privilege of a straight white man again. And while white men were doing the transforming in that context, Black men in Harlem "suddenly had the freedom to have white sex partners," according to Richard Bruce Nugent, one of the major artist/writers of the scene (Schwarz 2003: 10). To deny the multifaceted sexual desires of the scene (and to focus exclusively on musical sound, devoid of context) does violence to the agency of the people both within it and entering from outside it. The musical sounds were deeply in the mix, but they were never *all* there was to experience. Even the line "Listen to those rails a-hummin'" implies not just the idea of the listener humming with excitement to get to Harlem but also the idea that the train itself, which has a sense of agency on its own, is singing you there.

"Take the 'A' Train," composed in 1939 by Billy Strayhorn (and the signature song of the Duke Ellington Orchestra), started out as an instrumental swing band composition. Joya Sherrill created the lyrics in 1944. Note that Billy Strayhorn (1915–1967)—composer, lyricist, arranger, and pianist—was openly gay and a frequent collaborator with Duke Ellington.

> You must take the A train
> To go to Sugar Hill way up in Harlem
> If you miss the A train
> You'll find you missed the quickest way to Harlem
>
> Hurry, get on, now it's coming
> Listen to those rails a-humming
> All aboard, get on the A train
> Soon you will be on Sugar Hill in Harlem.

Big band jazz groups played jazz standards; they form the central musical repertoire drawn from jazz compositions and recordings of the 1930s through the 1950s and are common to all jazz players. The writers of these jazz standards—part of the canon of what is now referred to as the Great American Songbook—were largely Jews. Jewish composers of standards included Irving Berlin, Richard Rogers, George and Ira Gershwin, Harold Arlen, Jerome Kern, and others; some were gay, and some were straight. Others were bisexual. Cole Porter was gay, but not Jewish. As immigrants themselves or the children of recent immigrants, the marginal status of Jewish citizens of New York simultaneously enabled the composers to work professionally in a musical system that supported them, and to engage with Black composers and performers of the scene. The producers and managers who presented jazz to the public were almost disproportionately Jewish, compared to the general non-Jewish population; they worked in radio, recording studios, publishers, and newspapers.

The in-between place that Jews held in the early twentieth century kept them simultaneously in the majority—because of their whiteness—and the minority—because of their Jewishness (Hersch 2017: 3). The earlier participation of Jews in blackface performance—as represented by Al Jolson in *The Jazz Singer*, for example—was one way in which Jews (and earlier Irish blackface minstrelsy performers) had been able to physically remove their "color" at the end of a performance, emphasizing their white identity if they wished (Roediger 1991: 104). But Jews themselves were simultaneously white/not white; the privileges which pertained to their relative whiteness were not—in the mainstream—extended to the Black musicians who played their compositions. They could, however, hire Black musicians when other white bandleaders did not. As Charles Hersch put it in reference to the activities of bandleader and clarinetist Benny Goodman, "Encompassing Jewish ethnic identity, mainstream American culture, African American musicians, and hybrid musical forms [jazz], no simple narrative will suffice" (Hersch 2017: 2). For those who were also gay, the intersectionality of being both gay and Jewish was just as potentially problematic as being gay and Black; that the two New York subcultures coincided in the Harlem Renaissance was no coincidence after all.

A key point of the Harlem Renaissance—perhaps a desired outcome— was the rejection of a world in which, to paraphrase W.E.B. DuBois, Black people forever were seeing themselves through the eyes of white men (Higgins 2007: 245). To wrest the gaze from white people—who may well have been expecting, patronizing, and encouraging an updated blackface minstrel show—and place it squarely with members of the community would require a powerful combination of words, sounds, and actions, but it succeeded.

At the height of the scene, queer artists and writers in other countries were paying attention. Those who could visit made the pilgrimage. The Spanish poet and playwright Federico García Lorca (1898–1936) was part of the *Generatión del 27*: a group of progressive Madrileño poets. His early poetry reflected both the currents of the avant-garde and his depression and anxiety concerning his sexuality. Leaving Spain in the late 1920s, he attended Columbia University in New York, within easy walking distance to Harlem. He witnessed the stock market crash of 1929 and noted its immediate impact on the Black community. But his long fascination with music and folklore (represented by the fact that he often wrote literary pieces inspired by musical compositions) carried him well into the Harlem scene. "What marvelous songs," he said. "Only our Andalusian *cante jondo* could be compared to them" (Gibson 1989: 255). Lorca was simultaneously a successful writer in public and, in many ways, a tortured individual in private. Yet it was in Harlem that he was, at least temporarily, free to be his authentic self. Lorca's *Poet in New York* detailed his sense that the people he met in Harlem were primed for an uprising. His assassination in 1936 by right-wing gunmen marked him as just one more of Spain's most promising transgressive artists silenced during the following decades through exile or death because of fascism.

Even closer to home, however, were the connections between the artists of Harlem and those of Haiti. As the site of a successful rebellion against colonialism in 1804, Haiti's majority-Black population and culture was a firm draw for Harlem Renaissance artists interested in a connection to a different kind of Black identity than what they had experienced in the States. Zora Neale Hurston, Langston Hughes, and Jacob Lawrence were among those who visited the region for research and inspiration. In turn, a number of Caribbean artists found a home in Harlem, to the point that a quarter of Harlem's residents during this time were born outside the United States.

> The West Indian presence in Harlem made itself felt not only in radical and literary circles, it brought to African American intellectual thought a postcolonial perspective that shaped the ideology of the Harlem Renaissance in fundamental ways. (Philipson 2006: 146)

As part of the local presence of Caribbean artists and writers came the sense that Harlem presented them with a mouthpiece; their ideas and perspectives brought an infusion of inspiration (and sometimes, intellectual conflict) to those who lived there, and they were able to publicly proclaim their ideas about a new way of understanding what it meant to be part of the African diaspora—as artists—and to form a new kind of Black identity to a ready audience. And, as Nathan Higgins notes, the writing of artists such as Claude McKay and Langston Hughes had a significant impact on African intellectuals as rejecting "the natural supremacy of European civilization and [championing] the superior humanity of African culture" (Higgins 2007: 188).

The intensely creative poets, writers, composers, artists, and musicians of the Harlem Renaissance built their work from the artistry of their own roots in the South, the Caribbean, and right there in Harlem itself to place themselves as marginalized people at the center, released from the perpetual white gaze. Jamaican-born Stuart Hall (1932–2014) wrote about cultural identity specifically in the context of the Afro-Caribbean diaspora, emphasizing the importance of an ever-evolving positioning process on both sides of the colonial effort.

> Identity is not as transparent or unproblematic as we think. Perhaps instead of thinking of identity as an already accomplished fact, which the new cultural practices then represent, we should think, instead, of identity as a "production" which is never complete, always in process, and always constituted within, not outside, representation. (Hall 1990: 392)

It is precisely the *resistance* against clear-cut, binary, straight-or-gay, mainstream-or-marginal identity labels that makes the Harlem Renaissance and its musical figures so interesting. The financial significance of Black-owned and Black-run businesses (sometimes with white patronage), the involvement of (often gay) Jewish composers who themselves were both minority and majority, the significant presence of foreign (Caribbean) Black artists, the relative safety of expression for LGBTQ+ sensibilities, and the embodiment of resistance through the public performance of improvisatory-but-arranged jazz compositions at the height of the inter-war years was a heady combination. Such a dazzling blend of these exact liminal elements is rare, and the artistic, musical, philosophical, and literary output of the time continues to have an impact on contemporary culture bearers.

Engaging Hip Hop with an Endangered Language

By focusing on issues of power, identity, and resistance in this chapter, I can think of no better way to close off the book than by offering a glimpse into the transformative power of hip hop, one of the most important developments in popular music of the past fifty years. As the collective term for rappers, artists, DJs, and dancers, hip hop has been centered in Black culture in the United States since the 1970s with antecedents in the musical cultures of West Africa, the Caribbean, and the southeastern United States. With the basic concept of a rapper performing rhythmic speech over specific beats, hip hop highlights the words rather than the melody and can bring an air of competition to musical performance. The content of the lyrics often features an attitude of rebellion or resistance, affirming the right to exist, and railing against injustice.

When hip hop expanded beyond the United States, which it did fairly quickly, it became common to hear it in other languages such as Spanish, Portuguese, French, German, and Russian. It had expanded into Asia and the Middle East by the 1980s, with artists performing in Japanese, Arabic, Mandarin, Korean, Persian, Thai, Indonesian, and other major languages of the Eurasian continent; a quick YouTube search for "Arabic rap," for example, will yield hundreds of results. This section, however, focuses on the possibilities offered by performance in a minority or endangered language. Most of the mainstream languages mentioned above are in a dominant position over regional languages and dialects—in some cases, over hundreds of local languages. It is one thing to listen to Hindi or Portuguese hip hop for the first time. It is another to imagine what hip hop could be in the hands of a gifted artist and speaker of an endangered language such as Hmong (Tou SaiKo Lee), Tlingit (Arias Hoyle), Sámi (Mihkku Laiti), Basque (La Basu), or Khoisan (Zothiemind); and it is worth doing searches for those exact people, because they exist and deserve to be heard. As Liz Przybylski points out, "In addition to lyrical topicality, choosing or integrating rappers' own First Languages is connected to sovereign articulations" (Przybylski 2023: 25). Hip hop artists who work in minority or endangered languages have reasons to do what they do, and this section uses several examples to explore the liminal use of these languages in hip hop. Note that they all speak the mainstream language, but their choice for performance is generally not.

One of the first things that migrants, colonized people, and marginalized people learn is to modify their language to avoid being targeted. So many people in the world have developed a kind of blended language over time to try to function that rich linguistic regionalisms have developed virtually everywhere, again and again. For the descendants of the colonized, marginalized, and displaced people, the system of receptive bilingualism (understanding a second language without necessarily speaking it) can result in the insertion of words, phrases, or grammatical structures from a second language. For example, speakers of Pennsylvania Dutch (Deutsch) in the United States might append a German suffix to an imperative command: "Outen the lights." In Irish-Gaelic, responding to a question in the positive or negative requires the inclusion of the verb because there is no way of saying simply "yes" or "no" in that language. "Have you been to the shop?" "I have." A speaker of Spanglish in Mexico might use *librería* rather than *biblioteca*, or insert whole phrases of one language into a sentence based primarily on a second language. Haitian Kreyòl (spoken by at least ten million people), while based firmly in eighteenth-century French, is so richly infused with several West African languages, other European languages, and one of the local Indigenous languages, Taino, that no contemporary French speaker would be able to understand it beyond the basic words and phrases such as *orevwa* (*au revoir*).

In North America, the number of languages outside of English that are spoken daily number in the hundreds. English, however, dominates the airwaves, academia, and much of popular culture with Spanish reaching a close second in the southwestern United States, and French in eastern Canada. As of this writing, English has been designated the United States' official language since it was passed by executive order (03/01/2025), but it has not gone through official channels in Congress; in Canada, English and French have both been official languages since 1969. But what about places in which speaking a language other than the main one puts a person at risk of punishment or worse? This high-risk activity and dire consequences of it has happened multiple times in history, and is happening right now. Speaking a minority language can be challenging to the ruling power, whether one's language is one of the more than 3,000 languages listed as endangered, or whether that language is considered an affront to those in charge. The employment of a language in a famously rebellious genre can speak out loud as an affirmation of power and identity.

Carrie Louise Sheffield writes that "Globally, hip hop has been an instrumental vehicle for the articulation of resistance and nationalism in the face of oppressive regimes" (Sheffield 2011: 99). That essential draw toward hip hop as a mode of expressing resistance is enhanced by using a specific tool: not just one's own language of identity, but all that it can express in its unique epistemology. For example, some languages such as Finnish, Hebrew, and Gaelic do not feature the verb "to have"; rather than being able to express ownership, they express relationship. Some languages—majority or minority—feature words and concepts that do not appear in English, such as *hygge* (Danish), *wabi-sabi* (Japanese), *saudade* (Portuguese), *schadenfreude* (German), or *dharma* (Sanskrit). Developing hip hop that centers itself on concepts other than those "normally" found within a majority language allows for extraordinary creative play. In addition to the textual possibilities afforded by minority languages in publicly staking a claim for the right to exist, hip hop artists sometimes choose to infuse their work with sounds, clothing, and concepts from both their own language and their own cultural context.

North America's Indigenous populations have been subject to violent erasure, conversion, displacement, and destruction for hundreds of years, but colonization was *not* the beginning of their existence in spite of what some settler texts might have schoolchildren believe. Among other acts that forced Native assimilation, the placement of Native children in residential schools, where they were punished for speaking or singing their own languages, severely damaged connections between traditional ways and settler ways. Meanwhile, settler children have been taught for decades to think of Native Americans in the past tense only; it is just one more step in colonial erasure, and the idea that speakers of minority or endangered languages are (and should be) relegated to the past is a common thread in the rest of the world. Although many tribal people live on reservations (in the United States) or reserves (Canada), most Native North Americans today are urbanites.

A number of Indigenous artists in the United States and Canada were already participants in hip hop from its beginnings, including Melle Mel (Melvin Gibson, Cherokee), the lead singer of Grandmaster Flash and the Furious Five. A Tribe Called Red (Cayuga and Mohawk), Drezus (Plains Cree), Litefoot (Cherokee), Snotty Nose Rez Kids (Haisla), DJ Tall Paul (Leech Lake Band of Ojibwe), and many others connect their work with the array of liminal experiences of being simultaneously Native and urban. DJ Tall Paul's recording "Prayers in a Song" features lyrics in both English and Anishinaabemowin about the powerful links between language re-learning and identity, and the struggles he experienced growing up as an urbanite without a direct language connection to his own heritage. The video includes images of scrappy graffiti of bison and wild horses, and weavings attached to a chain link fence.

> I feel the latent effects of assimilation
> Inner city Native raised by bright lights, skyscrapers
> Born with dim prospects, little peace in living as a child
> Hot-headed at the fact I wasn't wild, like they called my ancestors
> Imagined what it'd be to live nomadic off the land and free
> Instead I was full of heat like a furnace 'cause I wasn't furnished
> With the language and traditional ways of my peeps.[21]

The Apsáalooke (Crow) rapper Supaman (birth name Christian Parrish Takes the Gun) from Crow Agency, Montana raps in both English and Crow. He also wears tribal dance regalia, incorporates historical Native recordings and instruments in his performances, and creates videos that feature elements from both traditional culture and modern technology (see, for example, his "Prayer Loop Song" video). Some are playful, such as his performance of "Alright," in which he uses the modified time-traveling DeLorean from the film *Back to the Future* to connect with (and speak with) Apsáalooke speakers prior to contact with settlers. The video intersperses footage of his contemporary performances with his fancy dancing at the edge of a cliff in full regalia, break dancing, rapping in English and Crow, and ends with him setting his next destination on the car to 1491—prior to the arrival of Christopher Columbus.[22]

The far northern island of Hokkaido in Japan and Sakhalin Island of Eastern Russia are home to the Ainu, Indigenous animists numbering at least 13,000 people. Part of Salmon Nation (the North Pacific Rim wild Pacific salmon territory, which includes the eastern part of Russia, the Bering Island Strait, Alaska, British Columbia, Washington, and Oregon), the Ainu have regarded the salmon as their staple food and part of what makes them Ainu. The Ainu language is distinct from that of the area's colonizers, the Japanese, and is a language family isolate, meaning it has no discernable connection to other languages.

A history of Japanese forced assimilation of the Ainu included prohibitions against speaking their language, wearing tattoos, and harvesting their staple food of salmon. The initial goal of colonization, by the Tōkugawa shōgunate (1603–1868), was to create a barrier to Russian expansion from the north; the Ainu were declared citizens of Japan in 1854. As part of the Meiji Restoration

Era (1868–1912), The Hokkaido Former Natives Protection Act of 1899 erased their indigenous status, declared them to be "former aborigines," and sent Ainu children to Japanese-language schools. Forced marriages between Ainu women and Japanese men were part of a longer project of ethnic erasure.[23] The violent relocation from their accustomed territories to small poor-quality land plots, along with the official suppression of language and culture by the Japanese, led to the number of native speakers being reduced to just over a hundred elderly Ainu people by the early twenty-first century. The language has become critically endangered, though there are current efforts to foster interest in it among young people.

> Ainu today are the fortunate inheritors not only of beautiful traditions of weaving, embroidery, wood carving and other arts, but also of a magnificent repertoire of oral literature, including heroic and historical epics, folk tales, cradle songs and long chanted songs about the gods—*kamuy yukar*. Committed to memory by talented orators, these songs were sung on special occasions. (Kayano 1998: 29)[24]

Shigeru Kayano led the revival of interest in Ainu language and culture, and in 1997 the Act on the Promotion of Ainu Culture and the Dissemination and Enlightenment of Knowledge about Ainu Tradition was passed. In 2009, UNESCO declared a number of Ainu dances as "Intangible Cultural Heritage." All Ainu people speak Japanese, and—like so many other speakers of minority and/or critically endangered languages—are still experiencing significant externally imposed shame that leads to discrimination in employment, housing, and marriage opportunities (see also Przybylski 2023: 49). In 2019, the Ainu Promotion Act was an attempt to address this systematic discrimination by officially recognizing their status as Indigenous; it included the repeal of The Hokkaido Former Natives Protection Act (1899).[25] Each legislative step represents a long history of Ainu resistance to erasure (Cotterill 2011).

Hip hop came to Japan at about the same time it came to the rest of the world beyond the Bronx: the 1970s and 1980s. Regarding Ainu hip hop in particular, keep in mind that Ainu culture is flexible and hybrid after centuries of pressure, shaming, and forced intermixing with Japanese people and culture. The hybrid nature of hip hop contributes to Ainu hybridity in that most major Ainu performers are both Ainu and Japanese by heritage; they all speak Japanese, and they all have experienced the challenges that come from being Ainu—looking different, experiencing marginalization, and struggling to learn their own heritage language. These also apply to Ainu in diasporic locations such as Hawai'i, California, and elsewhere.

The Ainu Rebels are a group of hip hop artists from the region; comprising the Sakai siblings and Okitsu (half-Ainu and half-Japanese), they were active between 2006 and 2010. Sakai Mina mentioned her inspiration from seeing the pride of Indigenous people in Canada, and how she wanted to inspire Ainu youth to feel proud of who they are as well.[26] They spent time learning traditional songs and dances, and incorporate the language, dances, clothing, and musical instruments such as the *mukkuri* (bamboo mouth harp) into their hip hop performances. During performances, they would speak in Japanese and English to their audience, speaking to them about Ainu culture and playing several genres of music, especially rock, folk, and hip hop. The liminal nature of so many Ainu musicians includes the fact that they freely cross over into Japanese and Western genres; that crossing over does not make them any less of who they are than the speaker of any endangered language who also speaks the majority language.

The Andes Mountains, which stretch from Colombia through Ecuador, Peru, Bolivia, and Chile, have a long history of colonization by the Spanish. Prior to colonization, the Incan Empire had become a significant local power by the twelfth century; it was centered in Cusco, Peru. Because of the Incan Empire's record-keeping and building acumen, there are records of taxation, population numbers, military matters, complex stoneworks, and roads. When the Spanish arrived with invasions and executions in 1528 in search of gold and silver, Catholicism arrived as well. Initial policies of assimilation of local beliefs and musical sounds became a part of the new power structure, and the use of Quechua—even by the Spanish and by the Catholic Church— was normalized. It was not until the Indigenous rebellion in Peru led by Tupac Amáru II in the 1780s that Quechua was severely discouraged and banned outright in public by the Spanish (Adelaar 2004: 168). The Spanish use of forced labor, missionization, and the chaos engendered by internal power dynamics meant that Peru's postcolonial challenges continued long after its independence in 1809.

Local languages in Peru and Bolivia such as Quechua (ten million speakers) and Aymara (three million speakers) are spoken alongside Spanish, and because of the dispersal of the population in both the highlands and lowlands (and coast), Quechua and Aymara are spoken everywhere. In spite of the presence of contemporary national boundaries, people in the

Andes tend to prioritize the local before the national, and vocal music tends to be more important in the north. Centuries-long resistance to Spanish domination has been ongoing in the form of continuing to speak Quechua, engaging in armed rebellion, performing local music, and creating literature particularly since the 1940s-era *Indigenismo* movement began (Saldaña-Portillo 2015: 37–44).

In highland Peru and other places in the region where Quechua is spoken alongside Spanish, a localized system of organization called the *ayllu* functions outside of mainstream political boundaries. The ayllu is a small village basic social unit of the highlands, comprising an extended family network relying on mutual ties of reciprocity and cooperation.[27] It connects people in the urban areas as well, but its origins are in the highland precolonial villages. Placed in the context of hip hop, which relies simultaneously on social/familial ties and technological prowess, the ayllu still serves as a safe space for self-expression, resistance, and the healthy reinforcement of regional identity.

As was the case in many other places, hip hop entered Peru by the 1980s. In Peru, however, the upheaval caused by political change, internal conflict, and economic policies that disproportionately affected the poor opened up severe income disparities (Jones 2014: 7). Significant migration from the highlands into the cities—particularly of children—has led to a long-standing sense of ambiguity for migrated lowland dwellers in the city. "Not feeling, or not allowed to feel, a part of 'old Lima' or criollo society, and not being from or knowing the highlands themselves, they are caught somewhere in between" (Turino 1993: 178). Such migration of young people has led to the rapid spread and communication of musical sounds, dances, tagging (graffiti) styles, clothing, and much more even as it contributes to the liminal sense of perpetual displacement.

The engagement of Quechua artists as rappers, dancers, artists, DJs, and more has dramatically heightened the visibility of contemporary Quechua performance, even as the region's Indigenous languages "have often been dismissed as the speech of poor farmers and relegated to nostalgic cultural spaces, including festivals and museums. The message conveyed to Quechua speakers is that their identities are part of the region's past" (Turkewitz 2020). Language activist and hip hop artist Liberato Kani (Ricardo Flores Carrasco), whose stage name means "I am a liberated man," was raised in Lima, Peru until his mother's death, at which point—between the ages of 9 and 13—he lived with his grandmother in Apurimac in Peru's highlands, where he became fluent in Quechua. He states upfront on his website[28] the words "Quechua in Resistence" [*sic*]. He writes, "Kunanpachakuna Qichwasimipi takiyqa, kallpawan kutiparikuspa runasimi rimayta rikurichiymi" ("Making contemporary music in Quechua is a contestatory act that places this language on the current musical scene"). He knows exactly what he is doing, and his website is in Quechua and *English* rather than Spanish, bypassing the majority language of Peru. When faced with criticism about fusing Andean instruments and rhythms with hip hop, reggaetón, and other genres, Kani says that "if they're criticizing, it means they're listening" (Turkewitz 2020).

In the song "Yakuchallay" ("Don't Abandon Us, Water"), Liberato Kani raps about dire conditions facing highland communities because of the theft of water (and lack of rain because of climate change), encroachment on local territories by mining companies, and the imperative need of reconnecting with the water, land, and deities. He names such important local icons as condors, corn, slingshots, and *apus* (mountain deities), and directly addresses the water by asking it not to abandon the communities. As he raps, he stands at the liminal site of the riverbank; at the end of the video one can hear the high-pitched women's voices singing *harawis*, which is sung in south-central Peru for bringing in healthy water/rains (Holly Wissler, personal communication). At the end of the video, the following phrase appears: "Yakumama en Resistencia! Fuente de vida que debemos defender. Si no es ahora, CUANDO?" ("Mother of the Waters! Source of life that we must defend! If not now, WHEN?") Yakumama is a giant mythological water serpent, "Mother of the Waters." That urban/rural Liberato Kani should call on the water spirit Yakumama while standing at the edge of a highland river, using the verse-and-chorus structure of Western pop while rapping in Quechua interspersed with a few words of Spanish and English, reveals a deep level of understanding and playing with his own liminal position.

Ireland, with its native language of Irish-Gaelic (referred to here as "Irish"), was colonized by the English starting in 1169 with the Anglo-Norman invasion. As a result of that early colonization and its lengthy aftermath, the English language remains the primary mode of communication nearly everywhere in the Republic. The Irish language along with almost every expression of traditional Irish culture, including its liminal blend of local beliefs and Catholicism, was forbidden by law. By the time of the Great Hunger of 1845 to 1850, in which more than half the population of Ireland emigrated or died of starvation and disease, the proportion of Irish speakers declined sharply. This happened not just because hunger, disease, and emigration killed so many native speakers but because the Irish learned to associate a cultural cluster of language, songs, instrumental music, and dance with the bad old days of poverty and powerlessness (Ó Ceallaigh and Ní Dhonnabháin 2015: 181). Associating the English language with modernity, power, and money was a further consequence of its use in the new national school system, at which point the teaching of the Irish language was outlawed, and any children who spoke it were physically punished at school and home.

Ireland's partition into the Republic of Ireland and Northern Ireland—the latter of which is still part of the United Kingdom—has, for historical reasons, meant that Irish speakers in Northern Ireland have not had state (or social) support for the transmission and expression of the language. Indeed, to speak Irish in the North has almost automatically associated the speaker with one of the paramilitary groups—the Irish Republican Army and its splinter groups—attempting to achieve a united Ireland by whatever means necessary. By the time hip hop had become part of Irish musical expression in the 1980s, Northern Ireland had undergone a harrowing period of Protestant/Catholic violence and power struggles known as The Troubles, in which over 3,500 people were killed across two decades—1969 to 1988.

The best-known performers of Irish-language hip hop, among many others, are the three men of the group Kneecap, which formed in 2017 in East Belfast. Their name is simultaneously from "kneecap him," which is to shoot someone in the knees (a form of punishment by the I.R.A.) or from the Irish *ní cheapaim* (pronounced "kneecap 'im"), meaning "I don't think so." Playing with words is part of what they do, but they are steadfast in their insistence on performing in both Irish and English—though mainly Irish—as it reflects their bilingual upbringing and political choice to speak and perform in Irish as a matter of asserting their identity. They cite influences from two seemingly different genres: Irish rebel songs and hip hop. Of the two genres, though, both carry a strong current of resistance. Kneecap's first hit was 2017's "C.E.A.R.T.A.," meaning "Rights."[29] Northern Irish radio banned the song for its references to drugs and use of swear words, and it is well known among language activists. Since then, their popularity as a group that embodies Irish resistance to both English linguistic and cultural hegemony has grown, with the development of an award-winning 2024 semi-fictional film named for them, about them, and starring them.[30] Much of their work appears chaotic and irreverent, but they are committed to both protesting and normalizing the use of Irish. A music video of one of their songs, "Amach

Anocht" (Out Tonight), features them being warmly affectionate with older Irish men and women at a bingo game and in a taxi, interspersed with swearing and rapping about sex and drugs.[31]

"Kneecap's approach is almost old-fashioned, reneging on the borderless lyrical collage some contemporary rappers lean into, and instead rooting lyrics in storytelling, specificity, slang, geography, territory, representation and identity" (Mullally 2019). Kneecap criticizes British and Irish anti-immigrant rioters who attack the police; while they themselves use anti-British government symbolism and words, they recognize the difference between working-class English people and the British government. Their lyrics celebrate drug use and sex. They are against Hamas while being outspoken in support of Palestine and what they see as its parallels with Irish colonization. Their onstage calls for Irish-Palestinian solidarity have earned the anger of members of the British government and led to calls for censorship.

The band's members have no illusions that their audience can understand everything they say, and that is part of the point. By singing in Ireland's original language (which few people speak) rather than restricting themselves to English, they are playing with the power of symbolism: Irish is being spoken today, new words (including slang) are being added to it all the time, it belongs in the present and future, and it fits a very attractive and still-current pattern of Irish rebellion that dates back centuries. It is, in fact, the perfect combination of factors that builds support for greater interest in the language by Irish youth, and its use in fusion—such as with the Irish-speaking fusion group Kila and the Ainu performer Oki Kano (see "Ní Liom Féin")—is a gesture of minority language solidarity. Kneecap's liminality emerges from everything they do: Their entire context growing up was The Troubles, though they were all born *after* the Good Friday Agreement of 1998 (hence their references to being "Cease-Fire babies"). They move between Irish and English languages. They are residents of Northern Ireland and therefore British citizens. One is a native Irish speaker while the others learned it as children. Their primary influences are American hip hop and Irish rebel songs. For all their rebelliousness, one of them started out as a schoolteacher. Their biopic film is both real and fictional. They sing some of the oldest Irish-language folksongs and they rap. That sort of liminality is all in a day's performance for them.

In each case, the performers' chosen language is the one that colonizing forces forbade, sometimes under pain of death. It is an exceptional act of defiance that those raised in their national system with the national language should lean on their once-forbidden "home" language as a way to stress their right to exist as bicultural, bilingual, liminal people. Liz Przybylski—author of *Sonic Sovereignty: Hip Hop, Indigeneity, and Shifting Popular Music Mainstreams*—focuses attention on the enormous potential of Indigenous hip hop to reshape relationships, musical agency, and Indigenous land rights. "Music that circulates sonic sovereignty demands changing ways of being, moving, and sounding in the world: a shift from paternalist regulations and destructive assimilationist policies toward a strategy of copresence" (Przybylski 2023: 175).

The Spanish philosopher José Ortega y Gasset has stated that "language cannot be understood unless we begin by observing that speech consists above all in silences. [. . .] Translation is a matter of saying in a language precisely what that language tends to pass over in silence" (cited in Becker 1995: 6). We cannot convey everything through our translation of the intentions and deeper meanings of what others have said, but it is worth trying. The places where we find "silences," according to Ortega, are often the most fraught with creative tension and meaning; in this case, it is the linguistic silences themselves that we should be paying attention to. Przybylski adds that "silence is critical to (sonic) sovereignty and self-determination" (Przybylski 2023: 3). Those silences, and their underlying meaning, are buoyed and reinforced by sound. Consider also, however, that it is the points of pause *between* activities, ideas, sounds, and identities that allow for some of the greatest, deepest transformations, along with the choice not to perform in the majority language. For artists whose people have been silenced, and in a genre that engages so much with beats and rhythms, it is often what is not stated out loud that shouts the loudest.

Conclusion

In moving across, or transgressing, so many binaries in this book, I have attempted to keep ambiguity, flexibility, and potential at the center rather than at the periphery. By turning the specific theoretical lens of liminality on so many different cultural and musical phenomena, it should be apparent that an understanding of liminality offers a type of clarity in the midst of seeming ambiguity. In the *sacred* nature of musical communication with the otherworld through the sea and sky creatures and in the musical joining of multiple faith traditions, the fragile nature of belief and faith is central to liminality. In the *alluring*, erotic and sometimes deadly longing that song engenders, along with the painfully poignant immigrant feeling of being caught between two worlds upon hearing a song, the liminal place of never quite being able to reach one's deepest desires hovers between pain and pleasure. On the *dangerous* road of sacred and secular, gender and racial play, and reclamation of power and identity in the face of colonial and other hegemonies, music appears again and again to focus our attention on what is important in the ambiguous—the *threshold*—moments of our lives.

Notes

Chapter 1

1. The historical catastrophe of settler colonialism envisioned the frontier as the edge, too; if the frontier represented the point of contact at the edge of settlement, it served as a moveable barrier between what white people perceived as the "known" and the "unknown." What it really did, of course, was facilitate voracious and locally devastating expansionism.
2. Regional folklore and local stories about mistletoe are widely available online; naturally, customs about its properties and uses vary from place to place.
3. Many years ago I gave a guest lecture on liminality at a nearby (American) college to about four hundred students. I foolishly assumed that at least some of them would have heard of the mistletoe custom, but it turned out that no one had (or perhaps no one would admit to having heard of it).
4. To explore the bardo more deeply, the *Bardo Thödrol* ("Liberation through Hearing in the Intermediate State," popularly referred to in the West as the *Tibetan Book of the Dead*) is a major resource.
5. Turner's book focuses specifically on a deep dive into the lives and rituals of the Ndembu people of northwestern Zambia.
6. Being a member of a newly hired cohort at a university or business may also connect people through the initial transitory state; as part of the incoming cohort of new professors at The Evergreen State College in 1991, I am still close to the remaining members of my cohort. Our shared experiences over several decades have built that sense of communitas.
7. On a personal level, as a beneficiary of the either–or tenure system, teaching at an accredited state university, I have jumped through all the necessary hoops of tests, written works, and achievements. My personal and academic goal, however, has always been to disrupt the system from within; it places me in an ambiguous position as well, because the system I work within could use some significant changes.
8. Where I teach—The Evergreen State College in Olympia, Washington—is a queer-majority institution, and represents in some ways the movement "from margin to center," to quote bell hooks (1984).
9. In the spring and summer of 2002, I served as an exchange faculty member at Hyōgō University in Kōbe, Japan. My colleagues repeatedly mentioned the connection of cherry blossom viewing to Japanese identity, and the parks were filled with families, friends, and couples doing just that. The larger point was the fact that every cherry blossom reminded participants that life was temporary, and the use of song, sake, and togetherness placed everyone in a liminal state at once.
10. The environmental park called Northwest Trek is in Washington State. Visiting there enables one to see bison, eagles, foxes, mountain goats, and other regional wild animals in an expansive, natural park with forest and grasslands. It is popular with locals. Upon taking seventeen Southeast Asian visitors there, however, I learned that it was "a waste of time" and that there was "nothing to see." I found out that they had hoped to watch animals fighting, get on amusement park rides, and experience lots of people-watching of overweight white tourists. I had told them in advance what we would see, but it had no allure or excitement because their sense of attraction was tightly bound by their own cultural expectations.
11. I wrote a short article about how music is not an international language; the article is filled with hyperlinks to musical examples: https://conceptionsreview.com/music-as-an-international-language-think-again/ [accessed 03/29/2024].

12. Being approached by the Devil at a crossroads is in reference to the alleged experience of the famous early bluesman, Robert Johnson (Schroeder 2004: 27–33).

13. A "mode" allows musicians to organize pitches in relation to each other. Selecting certain pitches out of every possible pitch gives you a palette of notes from which to draw. If you have a keyboard, playing all the white keys from middle C to the next highest C gives you a "major" scale. In the case of the example, Aeolian mode can be heard by playing the white notes from low A to high A, and Mixolydian mode from G to G.

14. The author William Least-Heat Moon publicized the idea of the "deep map" in 1991's *PrairyErth* as a focused psycho-geography of a place.

15. https://policyviz.com/2018/01/19/remake-alabama-slavery-map/ [accessed 03/28/2024].

16. https://aiatsis.gov.au/explore/marlaloo-songline [accessed 03/28/2024].

Chapter 2

1. The renowned Irish poet Seamus Heaney wrote "The Given Note" about this tune. To hear a recording of Cillian Vallely playing the tune on the uilleann pipes, visit https://www.youtube.com/watch?v=TEWFwBpMH38&ab_channel=67Music.

2. I do not use the English form of this Indigenous word because of the way it has been so consistently commodified, overused, and misused in inappropriate contexts.

3. In 2020, in the midst of the COVID pandemic, I was driving my mother home from a doctor appointment when we were struck by a young man texting in his pickup truck. As the months of physical recovery (surgeries, physical therapy, etc.) went by, I explored counseling to help me with the ensuing severe PTSD. My counselor, Dr. Leticia Nieto (author of *Beyond Inclusion, Beyond Empowerment: A Developmental Strategy to Liberate Everyone*, 2010), noted that every time I dreamed about the scenario in which my mother (or both of us) died, I was seeing and experiencing events as they happen in parallel universes. And that, she added, is the territory of spiritual intermediaries.

4. https://www.historylink.org/file/21084 [accessed 8/16/21].

5. https://www.critfc.org/salmon-culture/tribal-salmon-culture/first-salmon-feast/ [accessed 5/7/21].

6. These song lyrics were transcribed and translated by Vi Hilbert, renowned elder of the Upper Skagit in Washington State.

7. The Whatcom County Library System hosts a video showing parts of the ceremony. https://www.youtube.com/watch?v=z2LaL337kPs&ab_channel=wclslibraries [accessed 4/22/21].

8. https://www.nationalgeographic.com/animals/fish/facts/taimen [accessed 5/3/21].

9. http://calliidlagadus.org/web/index.php?odas=183&giella1=eng [accessed 5/3/21].

10. I spent three fortunate years studying regularly with Joe Heaney when I was a graduate student at the University of Washington; he was a visiting artist from 1982 to 1984, when he died of complications from emphysema. For each of the many Irish-language songs he taught me, he shared lengthy stories about context and intention.

11. Note that the transcription traps the notes into a fixed meter and completely ignores the breathing rhythm and "feel" of the song (as sung by Julie Fowlis). As with all transcriptions, please recognize that this is simply intended to represent something of the song in all its variation.

12. I have Seumas Gagne, whose years of study in Scotland have connected him with the wisdom of so many people, to thank for this insight.

13. https://www.juliefowlis.com/alterum/?fbclid=IwAR0MqyYV0_29qBNn1ZDocE1KABx RHMyad3zvCPkhhAJRoe72r8J7LMzQ7ew [accessed 4/27/21].

14. To learn more about Indigenous whaling, visit the National Park Service site about Indigenous history connected to whaling in New Bedford, Massachusetts. https://www.nps.gov/nebe/learn/historyculture/indigenous-history.htm

15. Dr. Pauline Yu, a marine scientist at The Evergreen State College, taught me everything I know about salmon and whale biology and sound transmission. The biological insights of this chapter are credited entirely to her, with gratitude.
16. To learn more about the specifics of humpback whale songs, visit this website: https://whaletrust.org/whale-song/
17. https://www.youtube.com/watch?v=VLZTJuiw35w&ab_channel=IndigenousTourismBC [accessed 4/30/21].
18. https://hawaiihumpbackwhale.noaa.gov/heritage/native-culture.html [accessed 5/6/21].
19. Among bird mythologies of the world, I could have focused on Horus (Egypt), the Phoenix (Greece), and Quetzalcoatl (Aztecs), though the last one is a feathered serpent. However, I chose to examine the lore of living birds as counterparts to the salmon, seal, and whale of the first section of the chapter.
20. He also readily acknowledges the worldwide importance of two, four, five, and seven as well (Dundes 1980: 135). This is a handy excuse for me, though, and my use of three examples for both sea and sky in this chapter.
21. One of its ancestors, *Argentavis magnificens*, is said to have had a wingspan of over 26 feet across (Campbell and Tonni 1983: 390).
22. What is now known as the California condor once occupied a range throughout western North America; they were noted along the Columbia River by settler-explorers Lewis and Clark in their journals.
23. From the website of the Alaska Native Knowledge Network: http://www.ankn.uaf.edu/npe/culturalatlases/yupiaq/marshall/raven/WhiteRaventurnsBlack.html [accessed 5/19/21].
24. This track, sung from the perspective of the owl god by Chiri Yukie, can be heard via YouTube: https://www.youtube.com/watch?v=p8NwNlnFN7w&ab_channel=Release-Topic [accessed 6/24/2024].
25. From the 2017 paper titled "Owl Beliefs in Nyungar Culture" by Ken Macintyre and Barb Dobson,   https://anthropologyfromtheshed.com/project/owl-beliefs-in-nyungar-culture/ [accessed 5/18/21].
26. He was declared as such by Pope John Paul II in 1979.
27. Note Seamus Heaney's poem "St. Kevin and the Blackbird" about this event.
28. For example, this *Daily JSTOR* piece by Colleen English from 2018, which sums up numerous poems, statements, and stories: https://daily.jstor.org/telling-the-bees/ [accessed 5/18/2021].

Chapter 3

1. My first experience of this phenomenon of connecting across more than one faith tradition occurred as a comical aspect of my own upbringing in Berkeley, California. My emphatically secular (but culturally Christian) parents raised me to be a secular Buddhist (and, rather vaguely, a Confucianist, as it turned out). Almost all of the art in their home was Japanese; my architect-father's extensive ceramics collection was mostly Chinese and Korean. I knew China's Tang Dynasty from Japan's Edo Period (and knew that the latter started about 700 years after the end of the former) by the time I was ten. We celebrated the American (and Swiss—one of my heritage locations) cultural elements of Christmas (cookies and presents!) and Easter (decorated eggs and candy!), and we listened to the same scratchy LP recording of Japanese *kabuki* every year as we decorated the Christmas tree. We sang the carols as expected, and my brother and I (in elementary school) would also periodically shout out the *kakegoe* (掛け声) from the kabuki recording in the midst of the carols. The video https://www.youtube.com/watch?v=plGfpYinnUg [accessed 07/14/2025] beautifully explains kakegoe with examples along with gorgeous acting. My brother and I weren't actually *blending* the musics or the faiths, however. Nothing about that struck me as odd; it was just home. Decades later, in Indonesia, when I heard devout Sundanese Muslims singing—with longing—about the gods and narratives of their own Hindu past, it seemed exactly right.

2. This is one of the many reasons why I ended up in ethnomusicology rather than in music theory.

3. It is often referred to as "the land of saints and sinners."

4. The Devotional Revolution was a deliberate re-Catholicization of Ireland in the years after the Famine; through a series of coordinated efforts on the part of Church leadership, attendance at Mass soared (from 20 percent before the Famine to over 80 percent afterward). Furthermore, a dramatic increase in the number and variety of rituals led to a higher rate of professed devotion (Larkin 1972: 325–352).

5. I am grateful to Sister M. Danielle Peters of the Marian Library at the University of Dayton for compiling this information. https://udayton.edu/imri/mary/b/bible-quotes-by-mary.php [accessed 1/14/2024].

6. However, the central Shintō shrine at Ise in Mie Prefecture is dedicated to the sun goddess Amaterasu; she is the ancestor of the imperial family.

7. The Allied Forces compelled the emperor to renounce his divinity and end State Shintōism as the official religion at that point.

8. This naming depends on the location; *itako* is used for Aomori Prefecture, *ogamisama* in Miyagi Prefecture, *onnakama* in Yamagata Prefecture, and *waka* in Fukushima Prefecture. I am drawing in this section primarily from the existing research on *itako*.

9. You can hear Itako Kamiyose chanting in this recording; it is from the Hungaroton album *Kagura: Japanese Shintō Ritual Music* (HCD18193). https://www.youtube.com/watch?v= ITWmKluAMYE [accessed 07/13/2025].

10. The link takes you to a recording of shōmyō chant from the UNESCO album *Japan: Shōmyō Buddhist Ritual* (UNES08036, released in 1975). https://www.youtube.com/watch?v=CWkw ZWzhQj4&list=RDCWkwZWzhQj4&start_radio=1 [accessed 07/13/2025].

11. Variants of African sacred practices combine with local variants of Roman Catholicism all over South America and the Caribbean, including Santería in Cuba, Vodou in Haiti and the Dominican Republic, Orisha in Trinidad, Hoodoo in the United States (usually connected to Protestantism), and elsewhere.

12. In my decades of involvement in the *batería* of Samba Olywa (the local samba group of Olympia, WA), our dancers who dress as Baianas to lead our seasonal processions are very much aware of the importance of their position, even in our secular community.

13. Multiple representations of this festival are online; here is one with the hymn and a series of photographs. https://www.youtube.com/watch?v=r-m1raEdyNA&ab_channel=AlmiroVieira [accessed 05/27/21].

14. At least partly as a result of the COVID pandemic, approximately one quarter of the Brazilian population has begun following Pentecostalism (growing more numerous each year), which regards Candomblé as evil.

15. I wish to gratefully acknowledge the skills of Viviane Sukanda-Tessier in her translations of the songs "Ceurik Rahwana" and "Kulu-Kulu Bem," which appear in the liner notes of the compact disc *Tembang Sunda: Sundanese Classical Songs* (Nimbus NI 5378, 1993)

16. Upon hearing the news that I was studying *tembang Sunda*, multiple Sundanese people on separate occasions burst into song, singing the word "Pajajaran," which—not coincidentally—often begins the first song of the evening.

17. The *pélog* mode uses the equivalents of the pitches (bottom to top) F, A, B-flat, C, E, and F. *Sorog* uses the pitches F, A, B-flat, D, E, and F. *Saléndro* uses a relatively equidistant tuning of F, G#, B-flat, C, D#, and F.

18. These two sentences may well serve as the shortest summary of the *Rāmāyana* in print.

19. A video of a live performance of "Ceurik Rahwana" and "Kulu-Kulu Bem" can be found here: https://www.youtube.com/watch?v=xRToULuqNSw&list=RDxRToULuqNSw&start_ra dio=1 [accessed 07/13/2025].

20. A recording of "Hamdan" can be found here: https://www.youtube.com/watch?v=whKK9swl V3M [accessed 07/13/2025].

Chapter 4

1. See, for example, the Southeast Asian goddess figure known in Thailand as Phra Mae Thorani, who wrings water from her hair in order to ensure abundant rain and the growth of rice; an image of her is central to the logo of the Metropolitan Water Authority of Bangkok (https:// www.mwa.co.th/home/, accessed 06/30/2025).

2. There are also mermen in the world, as both a folk archetype and in its mediated incarnation in popular culture; however, they are far less common, and they are not known for their songs. While this chapter has as its focus the eroticism of the feminine in connection with water, the counterparts to this image appear in multiple places in the northern hemisphere. The figure of Triton may be known to people interested in Greek mythology, but the *marmennill* of Old Norse, the Auvekoejak of the Inuit people, and others are locally important. In popular culture of the United States, the character of Aquaman has existed in comic books since the 1950s.

3. https://www.rogerebert.com/reviews/o-brother-where-art-thou-2000# [accessed 2/4/21].

4. Some songs about the winged maiden-harp actually refer to her as a "siren," and she is, in fact, luring men to their deaths; fighting for the nation means dying for Ireland.

5. Sirens—"clear voiced" and bewitching with their "seductive melodies"—were described in the *Argonautica* as bird-women by Apollonius of Rhodes, but that was not until the third century BCE: "But now, half human and half bird in form, they spent their time watching for ships from a height that overlooked their excellent harbour; and many a traveller, reduced by them to skin and bones, had forfeited the hope of reaching home" (Rieu, trans. 1959: 171).

6. Fewer than 1,000 professional geisha exist in Japan, out of a population of 125 million people. Geisha comprise 0.0015 percent of Japanese women.

7. https://www.macalester.edu/russian-studies/about/resources/miscellany/vodka/   [accessed 07/07/2025].

8. The popular image of the rusalki as mermaids—half fish, half woman—appears to have been a literary conceit of the nineteenth century. Its appearance in books and stories then spread as an aspect of "re-folklorization" into areas where it has not previously been recorded (Dynda 2017: 84). Its presence in stories of the rusalki does not make it wrong; it simply adds to what local people believe.

9. See also the Sundanese-focused "Liminalities of Faith" chapter, which goes into the relationship between Hinduism and Islam through the analysis of two local songs.

10. I had to undergo a lengthy ceremony during my fieldwork in West Java that enabled me, a woman, to study the kacapi zither. It was essentially a symbolic sex change, which I wrote about in *The Sound of the Ancestral Ship: Highland Music of West Java* (Williams 2001: 213–217).

11. The song "Mupu Kembang" appears in the second minute of this video: https://www.youtube.com/watch?v=PzejzdEjGTA [accessed 07/13/2025].

12. "The Legend of Iara: Folklore," https://www.todamateria.com.br/lenda-da-iara/ [accessed 04/07/2024]. The writer—Daniela Dana—claims that this is an Indigenous tale, specifically of the Amazon region.

Chapter 5

1. As someone raised in a diverse neighborhood of Berkeley, California, in the 1960s, the kids of recent immigrants at my school were mostly Asian Americans (of Filipino, Chinese, Japanese, and Korean descent); Angel Island in the San Francisco Bay had been a major point of entry for their parents and grandparents until 1940. The Johnson-Reed Act—also known as the Immigration Act—of 1924 had cut off access to the United States from most of Asia except for people from the Philippines.

2. This is a link to The Migration Series online, with accompanying interview with Jacob Lawrence. https://lawrencemigration.phillipscollection.org/the-migration-series [accessed 6/24/21].

3. https://archive.nytimes.com/www.nytimes.com/books/first/m/margolick-fruit.html [accessed 6/24/21].

4. "Strange Fruit" has been listed as one of the "Songs of the Century" and was inducted into the Grammy Hall of Fame in 1978; *Time Magazine* called it the "song of the century." https://blogs.loc.gov/loc/2015/04/the-power-of-a-poem/ [accessed 6/24/21].

5. https://www.today.com/tmrw/black-new-year-s-eve-traditions-covid-19-can-t-t203786 [accessed 6/25/21].

6. "João Gilberto Sang Lullabies to the Future," by Chris Richards. https://www.washingtonpost.com/lifestyle/style/joao-gilberto-sang-lullabies-to-the-future/2019/07/07/1770b426-a0cb-11e9-b732-41a79c2551bf_story.html [accessed 6/1/21]

7. It is also the featured instrument of Annie Proulx's *Accordion Crimes* (1996), which details the travels of a single accordion through multiple immigrant communities in the United States.
8. "When Irish Eyes are Smiling" was written by Chauncey Olcott, George Graff, Jr., and Ernest Ball in 1912. "Mother Machree" was written by Rida Johnson Young, Chauncey Olcott and Ernest Ball in 1910. "My Wild Irish Rose" was written by Chauncey Olcott. Olcott was an Irish-American writer, actor, and singer. "Danny Boy" was written by (Englishman!) Frederic Weatherly in 1913.
9. The soaring line "And I'll be heeeere in sunshine or in shadow" is not for the faint of heart, as it wrings tears from many listeners, to the point that it has been satirized by the Muppets. https://www.youtube.com/watch?v=OCbuRA_D3KU&ab_channel=Blakwulf [accessed 7/5/21].
10. "Danny Boy" has become, to many Irish-Americans (and Irish-American wanna-bes), the Irish-American version of selections from *Fiddler on the Roof*.
11. At one event I played "The Irish Washerwoman" on my fiddle after a request to do so, only to be immediately asked by a different listener to play "The Irish Washerwoman."
12. I'll never forget a sentence from my older brother's high school Spanish textbook: "El burro es un animal muy importante para la economia del Mexico." One needs no fluency in Spanish to understand not just that sentence, but everything that it implies: *all* Mexicans (and by extension, all Spanish speakers) are poor farmers who rely on burros because they can't afford fancy machinery. The book cover featured a young man in a huge sombrero hat, leading a burro. Fortunately, the book appears to be out of print, and the fact that my brother has lived in Spain for over 40 years should clarify that his high school Spanish-speaking skills have progressed far beyond a single sentence.
13. I am so grateful to Dr. Leticia Nieto for talking with me about these issues in connection with her home state of Puebla and the songs, foods, and ideas that are vital to the community.
14. After Los Angeles, which hosts the largest number of Mexican-born immigrants, Chicago is number two with more than half a million.
15. Many people have recorded this song; this version—by Antonio Aguilar—includes strings and horns. https://www.youtube.com/watch?v=EG9jXZEl_Yk&ab_channel=giovanniguzman. For those readers who speak Spanish, the very interesting "Historia de la Canción Mixteca" covers the composer and some of the artists who have covered it. https://www.youtube.com/watch?v=yg0whs5pw_o&ab_channel=lam%C3%BAsicatambi%C3%A9nseve%21 [both sites accessed 7/7/21].
16. The lyrics may be found at the Genius site; this link is to a YouTube clip of the song. https://www.youtube.com/watch?v=5HRvBdWaAY4&ab_channel=%D9%81%D9%8A%D8%B1%D9%88%D8%B2%D8%A7%D9%84%D8%B5%D8%A8%D8%A7%D8%AD [accessed 7/7/21].
17. Its long influence extends far outside of the Balkan peninsula, however; the melody appears all over Central, South, and Southeast Asia, in Russia, in the Caribbean, and anywhere the Balkan and Turkish diasporas have ventured.
18. Seeing the 1937 film *The Lost Horizon* as a teen, I distinctly recall raising an eyebrow over the idea that the main character—"some white guy," as I complained to my parents—would be so convinced that the obviously Central Asian mythical land of Shangri-La was home. "He wasn't even born there and he can't even speak the language." I obviously hadn't yet visited Hawai'i.
19. Full name: Joseph Kekuku'upenakana'iaupuniokamehameha Apuakehau.
20. Touring Hawaiian musicians across the segregated South found places to stay at boarding homes run by African-American families because they were forbidden from staying at whites-only hotels; musical connections were an obvious result. https://www.smithsonianmag.com/smithsonian-institution/how-hawaiian-steel-guitar-changed-american-music-180972028/ [accessed 7/1/21].
21. https://www.youtube.com/watch?v=LrVSUO4zcCs&ab_channel=SURFSTYLEY4 [accessed 6/27/21].
22. The actual statute on the books is quite compelling and explicitly states the obligations; it consigns Hawaiians to a perpetual state of service to others. https://www.hawaii.edu/uhwo/clear/home/lawaloha.html [accessed 6/27/21].
23. In my case, it is the unique scent of redwood, eucalyptus, and the Pacific Ocean that marks the San Francisco Bay Area as home, no matter how many decades have intervened since my upbringing.

Chapter 6

1. As jarring as it feels to me to quote myself, I'm doing it here from my article titled "Poetry Writing as Transgressive Ethnography" (Williams 2022: 366): We know the word "transgression" primarily as a means by which rules are broken, but to transgress in the older, Latinate sense of the word is to literally "step across." In making the break into the experiential world of fieldwork, writing, teaching, and just living as ethnomusicologists, we often have to step across the barrier that separates linearity from cyclic, spiral, and other notions of time and space and move into that region that requires us to be wide open before we can prioritize or make sense of what has happened. This act of transgression is what allows us to see not only what lies before us in our day-to-day existence in the field but also to see and understand the hidden truths of our experiences by opening our eyes a second time and creating.

2. All of this information is available at the Office of Population Affairs and relies on data from 2019, the year before the global pandemic. https://opa.hhs.gov/adolescent-health/adolescent-health-data/americas-diverse-adolescents [accessed 6/19/24].

3. Part of a normal icebreaking exercise in one of my college classes has the students write down the name of a particular song that helped them to survive being thirteen and to discuss the chosen songs in small groups. Within a minute or two, people are laughing excitedly, singing, beating out rhythms, and connecting with each other across boundaries of race, class, gender, and ability. For almost ten years, Green Day's "Boulevard of Broken Dreams" was the song of choice.

4. Taylor Swift, whose philanthropy supports food banks everywhere she tours, is apparently "not a good role model" because she is unmarried and childless. https://www.newsweek.com/taylor-swift-not-good-role-model-opinion-1916799 [accessed 07/03/2024].

5. The English word paraiah has the parai, and the people who play it, at the center of its etymology.

6. *This Is a Music: Reclaiming an Untouchable Drum.* Produced and directed by Zoe Sherinian. DVD. 74 minutes. 2011. The film is available from zsherinian@ou.edu and through Alexander Street Press.

7. Though I have felt like an ethnomusicologist since long before I'd heard the term, as a classical guitar performance major at the University of California (Berkeley), I was also steeped in (and have occasionally still taught) the standard dead-white-elite-European-male undergraduate music curriculum.

8. Monophony and polyphony are elements of musical texture. Monophony is a single melody (as in plainchant or a lullaby); homophony is a main melody with other voices or instruments accompanying in the same rhythm (as in Bach chorales or some musical theater pieces); heterophony is playing or singing the same melody with individual variations (as in bluegrass or Irish music); and polyphony features independent musical lines played simultaneously (as in a fugue).

9. Both of these composers are believed to be what we would now think of as gay. Léonin also wrote homoerotic poetry; his poetic works have now been published in their entirety (Holsinger and Townsend 2000).

10. To listen to the original chant, then Léonin's two-part organum, then Pérotin's multipart organum, visit these links [accessed 7/21/21]:https://www.youtube.com/watch?v=Fi5C Z3lTXP8&ab_channel=BartjeBartmanshttps://www.youtube.com/watch?v=_p9WQlyV PrA&ab_channel=JordanAlexanderKeyhttps://www.youtube.com/watch?v=3oaRM1uD sw8&ab_channel=musicnetmaterials

11. Because of the vagaries of dating manuscript works, even the term "13th-century motet" can be contested; musicologist Mark Everist claims it to be "treacherous" (Everist 2007: 369). In this case, I use several short motet examples to emphasize the societal shift from sacred to secular in that century.

12. A "Mary Garden" features plants associated with the Virgin Mary, such as larkspur ("Mary's foot") or daffodil ("Mary's star"), and usually includes one or more statues of her. They became popular in the medieval era and thrive today as well. https://udayton.edu/marianlibrary/marys gardens/b/background-on-marys-gardens.php [accessed 8/10/21].

13. Sundanese women do play the *kacapi siter*, a flat board zither to accompany local songs, but few local women play the kacapi indung.

14. I ended up writing my dissertation about tembang Sunda and a chapter on jaipongan in an edited volume, though my intention had always been to study kacapi only. Did I surrender to local needs about what I should and shouldn't do? Yes. Did I still ride a motorcycle and break a bunch of other local social rules? Also yes. I had a child many years later and got a divorce more than a decade after that, which placed me in quite average and normal company with hundreds of thousands of other divorced Sundanese mothers.

15. Obviously, I remained white and colonial-looking, though both my body language and my actual skin tone changed. After two years of too much sun for my white skin, my arms were considerably darker than most of my Sundanese friends who carefully guard their skin from the sun. The distinction upended a number of conversations about "white people" and "brown people" and notions of race being equated with skin color, but in the end my blue eyes and odd hair color won out in terms of my being declared *masih berkulit putih* (still white), but *salah lahir* (false born, meaning born in the wrong place).

16. As someone who teaches at a queer-majority institute of higher education—The Evergreen State College, where over 60 percent of the students claim LGBTQ+ status—I can attest that my students and colleagues on the faculty and staff are way ahead of the excruciatingly slow but steady national curve of tolerance >> acceptance >> embrace.

17. I had the great fortune to witness a dazzling performance by the most famous onnagata actor, Bandō Tamasaburō V (b. 1950), in Kyoto in 2002. Men in the audience cheered continuously and shouted "Tamasaburō!" over and over throughout his time onstage. Note also that it is the norm to adopt numerals after one's name in performance practice in Japan, and to change one's stage name and numeration over time.

18. For more information about this woman's extraordinary life and context, Maki Isako's *Onnagata: A Labyrinth of Gendering in Kabuki Theater* (2016) is exceptional.

19. The Meiji Era (1868–1912)—named for the emperor—was a time of enormous upheaval, when Japan adopted and adapted a number of Western ideas, technologies, and cultural elements.

20. All members of the troupe are in the employ of the Hankyu Railway.

21. Sections of some shows have been posted online; a quick perusal will reveal short histories, personal testimonies, and the like. Official videos from the Revue itself feature clips with otokayaku roles at the center. https://www.youtube.com/watch?v=_-u0BiK_70I&ab_channel=%E5%AE %9D%E5%A1%9A%E6%AD%8C%E5%8A%87%E5%85%AC%E5%BC%8F%E3%83%81 %E3%83%A3%E3%83%B3%E3%83%8D%E3%83%ABTakarazukaRevueCompany [accessed 07/06/24].

22. https://kageki.hankyu.co.jp/english/about/about2.html [accessed 07/06/24].

23. https://www.youtube.com/watch?v=kJThaSad32E&ab_channel=LincolnCenter [accessed 07/ 06/24].

24. https://medium.com/@rlggroup2/walking-in-memphis-the-religiosity-of-elvis-and-fans-pil grimage-to-graceland-9c0051e235c8 [accessed 2/16/22].

25. Of the many videos of this song, one to watch is of Nathan Evans singing alone, then others joining in. The BBC noted how the phenomenon—"ShantyTok"—propelled Evans to a new career in just a few weeks. https://www.bbc.com/news/entertainment-arts-55768333 [accessed 7/ 27/21].

26. "Trap" is a word from local Atlanta slang that refers to a place where drug deals are made; its lyrics often focus on the place itself and the actions connected to that place. The word appears in songs by Outkast and Goodie Mob from the mid-1990s. The music of trap has become almost central to much of contemporary hip hop, especially the lightning-fast synthesized triplets on the hi-hat.

27. "Old Town Road" and its controversy as a genre-crossing song is an excellent point of conversation in class (Eaton and Johnson 2020: 64) to explore the limits of genre and personality in American popular music; was Lil Nas X not country enough, not straight enough, or simply not white enough?

28. "Lil Nas X Wants 'Montero' to Help 'Normalize' Same-Sex Lust in Music," by Stephen Daw, quoted in *Billboard.com*, 3/29/21. https://www.billboard.com/articles/news/9547933/lil-nas-x-montero-call-me-by-your-name-lyrics-breakdown/1 [accessed 7/29/21].

29. "Historians Decode the Religious Symbolism and Queer Iconography of Lil Nas X's 'Montero' Video," by Andrew R. Chow, quoted in Time.com, 3/30/21.https://time.com/5951024/lil-nas-x-montero-video-symbolism-explained/ [accessed 7/29/21].

30. https://twitter.com/LilNasX/status/1419314047678357510 [accessed 7/29/21].
31. This video from Austin City Limits TV is a live performance of "Black Myself." https://www.yout ube.com/watch?v=vjd9zlSiHZM [accessed 07/18/2025].
32. "Amythyst Kiah Is Done Hiding: Black Singer-Songwriter of 'Black Myself' Shares Her Journey Toward Her Truth," by Rachel Cholst. https://countryqueer.com/stories/interview/amythyst-kiah-the-making-of-a-grammy-nominee/ [accessed 8/2/21].
33. https://www.npr.org/2021/06/22/1008986901/amythyst-kiahs-latest-album-is-wary-strange [accessed 8/2/21].
34. See NPR interview, above.

Chapter 7

1. The exact wording of the American Indian Religious Freedom Act of 1978 is here: https://www. govinfo.gov/content/pkg/COMPS-5293/pdf/COMPS-5293.pdf [accessed 07/25/2025].
2. The exact wording of Section 35 of the Constitution Act of 1982 is here: https://indigenousfoun dations.arts.ubc.ca/constitution_act_1982_section_35/ [accessed 07/25/2025].
3. Keola Donaghy offers the following story: Around the time of the monarchy overthrow in Hawai'i, there was a very influential Hawaiian politician, Iosepa Nāwahiokalani'opu'u who was a supporter of the queen who lived in Hilo. Supporters of the Hāole arranged for the steamboat that travels from Hilo to Honolulu to leave hours early, stranding him in Hilo and preventing him from doing his legislative duties. His supporters took him to Honolulu by canoe, and he arrived in time for the legislative session (Donaghy 2024: 71).
4. It was created in 2016 as a collaborative effort between Vina Brown and Frank Brown (Heiltsuk) and Hillary Beattie and Ian Mauro (non-Indigenous academics). https://www.glwafilm.com/ [accessed 07/23/2025].
5. From the online article "The Tribal Canoe Journey, an Odyssey to Reclaim Tradition and Territory," in *Canadian Geographic* (2018/2025) by Julian Brave Noisecat. https://canadiangeo graphic.ca/articles/the-tribal-canoe-journey-an-odyssey-to-reclaim-tradition-and-territory/ [accessed 07/23/2025].
6. From the *Peninsula Daily News* in Port Angeles, Washington: https://www.peninsuladailynews. com/news/craft-sessions-set-to-make-gifts-for-canoe-journey/ [accessed 07/25/2025].
7. The Jamestown S'Klallam Tribe's site features information about canoes construction, blessings, protocols, and more. http://www.tribalmuseum.jamestowntribe.org/hsg/exhibits/canoe/proto col.php [accessed 07/23/2025].
8. In *The Tribal Journeys Handbook and Study Guide* (2011), Tulalip Nation member Ray Fryberg discusses his experience of hearing about an orca and trying to connect with it. After several hours of searching, an orca appeared *only* after two young men on the canoe began singing and drumming. It followed them, waited while they introduced themselves in their language, and lifted up the canoe before spraying them "right in the face!" (Fryberg 2016: 14). In 2025, several orcas approached a canoe and swam with them; because the Pacific Northwest is home to orcas, seals, salmon, bald eagles, bears, cougars, and more, paying attention to non-human relations is important.
9. The Snoqualmie Tribe website has links to frequently asked questions and clear instructions about protocols. https://culture.snoqualmietribeweb.us/canoe-journey-information/ [accessed 07/22/2025].
10. Hawai'i News Now hosts a more than four-hour video of the *wa'a* welcoming ceremony of the Festival of Pacific Arts held on the island of O'ahu in 2024. The festival welcomed twenty-five different nations that year. The video includes a transcript and features music, dance, speeches, gestures, protocols, and so much more. https://www.youtube.com/watch?v=ldzc5oAkfmY [accessed 07/17/2025].
11. https://www.spc.int/festival-of-pacific-arts-and-culture [accessed 07/26/2025].
12. A longer discussion of Carolinian canoes appears at the UNESCO Intangible Cultural Heritage site. https://ich.unesco.org/en/USL/carolinian-wayfinding-and-canoe-making-01735 [accessed 07/25/2025].
13. Regional variants of the name exist, including *waka* in Māori (with the w sound) and *va'a* in Tahitian.

14. https://www.festpachawaii.org/ [accessed 07/26/2025].
15. Hawai'i Now Daily has many short videos of interviews at hinowdaily.com.
16. The ESO—European Southern Ocean—blog has a wealth of resources about constellations. https://www.eso.org/public/australia/blog/navigating-the-stars/ [accessed 07/26/2025].
17. It was once a rural area of upper Manhattan, During the American Revolution, the Lenape people had been violently expelled and the land cleared. Dutch immigrants had arrived in the mid-seventeenth century and settled it for farming. It wasn't until the rail lines were extended from lower Manhattan into the region in the 1880s that significant building took place with the expectation that the crowded tenements of lower Manhattan would empty as people would take the opportunity to move north. Overbuilding led to a large number of residences remaining empty; however, the efforts of Black real estate entrepreneur Philip Payton Jr. welcomed Black tenants into the area.
18. Alain Locke was the first Black Rhodes scholar, later receiving the PhD in philosophy from Harvard University in 1918.
19. In this article from *The Guardian*, author Michael Henry Adams offers an interesting discussion from a British perspective of how it appeared. https://www.theguardian.com/us-news/2019/jun/30/gay-harlem-renaissance-1930s-jimmie-daniels-cecil-beaton [accessed 7/13/21].
20. I thank my dear departed teaching colleague Kabby Mitchell III (1957–2017) for this insight; as a Black gay man who danced with the famous Alvin Ailey dance troupe and the Dance Theatre of Harlem, Kabby spent years of his life researching insider views of early gay Harlem, speaking to those who lived it during the time, and teaching about it to his colleagues and students. His life was cut short due to illness before he had the chance to write about what he had learned.
21. The video for "Prayers in a Song" is hosted by PBS Wisconsin Education, and is part of an educational collection titled *The Way*, intended for Wisconsin middle and high schoolers. The notes below the video ask the question of how language and culture are informed by location, and reads the following: "The collection explores connections between traditional ways and those of today and expands and challenges current understanding of Native identity and communities through language and culture stories from First Nations communities around the central Great Lakes."https://www.youtube.com/watch?v=BlQJClNQDBo [accessed 07/28/2025].
22. The video for "Alright" is on YouTube: https://www.youtube.com/watch?v=ep97FZrRSPk [accessed 07/28/2025].
23. "Japan's Indigenous Ainu Community Don't Want a Theme Park: They Want Their Rights," in *Equal Times* December 10, 2020. https://www.equaltimes.org/japan-s-indigenous-ainu-community?lang=en [accessed 07/30/2025].
24. Shigeru Kayano (1926–2006) was an Ainu politician and language activist who campaigned successfully for official legal recognition of the Ainu as a distinct people with a unique culture of their own in 1997.
25. "Ainu People Reclaim Their Rights," in *Cultural Survival* March 3, 2020. https://www.culturalsurvival.org/publications/cultural-survival-quarterly/ainu-people-reclaim-their-rights [accessed 07/30/2025].
26. This video (0824 #81 Ainu's New Identity) features a translated interview with Sakai Mina. http://youtube.com/watch?v=9dgexEvTEjs&t=57s [accessed 07/30/2025].
27. From earlier in the chapter, readers might remember the canoe families of the Pacific Northwest and the *iwi* of Oceania. But for speakers of minority and/or endangered languages, the extended family network is reinforced and generations drawn together through the performance of songs in that language.
28. liberatokani.com [accessed 07/28/2025].
29. Bandmember Móglaí Bap spray-painted the word CEARTA on a bench the night before an Irish-language-rights march in Belfast, and was forced to spend the night in jail because he refused to speak English when he was caught by the police. This act of defiance is widely regarded as part of the resistance to not just the dominance of the English language, but to the English power structure as well. The scene is commemorated in the film *Kneecap*. The lyrics to the song "C.E.A.R.T.A." are fully translated into English at this site, https://lyricstranslate.com/en/cearta-right.html, and the official music video is available here: https://www.youtube.com/watch?v=8Sf0htzbMKk [both websites accessed 07/26/2025].
30. The film also starred Michael Fassbender, whose own Irish-language skills came in handy for his role as a pro-Irish-language father.
31. While their plentiful use of swear words might be startling to an outsider, it is fairly normal to the average Irish person of any age.

Glossary

aloha greeting, hospitality, compassion, and more (Hawai'i)

apsara female spirit in Hinduism (India)

Candomblé blended religious practice (Brazil)

devadasi hereditary female temple courtesan (India)

epistemology theory of knowledge and ways of knowing

fado musical genre known for its references to heartache and grief (Portugal)

gamelan bronze gong and drum ensemble (Indonesia)

geisha artist trained to entertain (Japan)

haole a person who is non-Hawaiian (Hawai'i)

heterophony a single melody played with variations by multiple instruments

homophony melody in one voice with harmony in the others

kabuki stylized dance drama (Japan)

kacapi boat-shaped zither (West Java, Indonesia)

kami Shintō deities (Japan)

kawih basic song type (West Java, Indonesia)

lexical relating to words

liminality state of being at the threshold

melisma multiple notes performed on a single syllable

monophony a single musical line

ontology theory of being

organum multi-voice song based on a line of plainchant

motet sacred choral music

ohanami cherry-blossom viewing, drinking, and singing (Japan)

orixás deities connected to the natural world (Brazil)

plainchant Catholic chant associated with liturgy

polyphony multipart musical lines

rusalka female nature spirit (Russia)

saudade combination of longing, nostalgia, grief, and joy (Portugal/Brazil)

sean-nós old-style singing in Irish-Gaelic (Ireland)

selkie seal/human hybrid (Scotland/Ireland)

tembang Sunda aristocratic sung poetry (West Java, Indonesia)

vibrato rapid variation of pitch

wa'as combination of longing, nostalgia, grief, and joy (West Java, Indonesia)

widadari female nature spirit (West Java, Indonesia)

References

Aarnem, Antti and Stith Thompson. 1961. *The Types of the Folktale: A Classification and Bibliography*. Helsinki: The Finnish Academy of Science and Letters.

Adelaar, Willem F.H. 2004. *The Languages of the Andes*. Cambridge, UK: Cambridge University Press.

Aikau, Hōkūani K. and Hōkūlani K. Aikau. 2015. "Following the Alaloa Kīpapa of Our Ancestors: A Trans-Indigenous Futurity with the State (United States or Otherwise)," *American Quarterly* 67/3: 653–661.

Aitken, Stuart C. 2010. "The Edge of the World: Embattled Leagues of Children and Seals Teeter on the Rim," *Yearbook of the Association of Pacific Coast Geographers* 72: 12–32.

Almqvist, Bo. 1990. "Of Mermaids and Marriages: Seamus Heaney's 'Maighdean Mara' and Nuala Ní Dhomhnaill's 'an Mhaighdean Mhara' in the Light of Folk Tradition," *Béaloideas* 58: 1–74.

Amoss, Pamela T. 1987. "The First Fish God Gave Us: The First Salmon Ceremony Revived," *Arctic Anthropology* 24/1: 56–66.

Anderson, Benedict R.O'G. 1983. *Imagined Communities: Reflections on the Origin and Spread of Nationalism*. New York, NY: Verso.

Anderson, Gordon A. 1971. "Notre Dame Latin Double Motets ca. 1215–1250," *Musica Disciplina* 25: 35–92.

Appadurai, Arjun. 1990. "Disjuncture and Difference in the Global Economy," *Theory, Culture, and Society* 7: 295–310.

Apollonius of Rhodes (E.V. Rieu, trans.). 1959. *The Voyage of Argo: The Argonautica*. New York, NY: Penguin Classics.

Armstrong, Jeannette C. 1998. "Unclean Tides: An Essay on Salmon and Relations," in *First Fish, First People: Salmon Tales of the North Pacific Rim*, Judith Roche and Meg McHutchison, eds. Seattle, WA: One Reel Productions and University of Washington Press, pp. 180–193.

Armstrong, Regis J., J.A. Wayne Hellmoann, William J. Short, eds. 2004. "The Treatise on the Miracle of Saint Francis (1250–1252)," in *The Francis Trilogy of Thomas of Celano*. Hyde Park: New City Press, pp. 329–333.

Asai, Susan. 1997. "Origins of the Musical and Spiritual Syncretism of Nōmai in Northern Japan," *Asian Music* 28/2: 51–71.

Auden, Wystan H. 1968. *Secondary Worlds: Essays*. London: Random House.

Ault, Alicia. 2017. "Medicine Creek, the Treaty that Set the Stage for Standing Rock," *Smithsonian Magazine*, June 9 issue. https://www.smithsonianmag.com/smithsonian-inst itution/standing-rock-there-was-medicine-creek-180963623/ [accessed 7/26/21].

Austern, Linda Phyllis and Inna Naroditskaya, eds. 2006. "Introduction: Singing Each to Each," in *Music of the Sirens*. Bloomington, IN: Indiana University Press, pp. 1–15.

Bacchilega, Christine. 2007. *Legendary Hawai'i and the Politics of Place: Tradition, Translation, and Tourism*. Philadephia, PA: University of Pennsylvania Press.

Baier, Randal E. 1985. "The Angklung Ensemble of West Java: Continuity of an Agricultural Tradition," *Balungan* 2: 8–16.

Bandem, I Madé and Fredrik Eugene DeBoer. 1995. *Balinese Dance in Transition: Kaja and Kelod*. New York, NY: Oxford University Press.

Barber, Sarah B., Gonzalo Sánchez, and Mireya Olvera. 2009. "Sounds of Death and Life in Mesoamerica: The Bone Flutes of Ancient Oaxaca," *Yearbook for Traditional Music* 41: 94–110.

Barría, Narciso García. 1997. *Tesoro Mitológico del Archipiélago de Chiloé: Bosquejo Interpretativo*. Santiago de Chile: Editorial Andres Bello.

Barz, Gregory. 2020. "Queering the Field: An Introduction," in *Queering the Field: Sounding Out Ethnomusicology*, Gregory Barz and William Cheng, eds. New York, NY: Oxford University Press, pp. 7–27.

Beavert-Martin, Virginia R. 1999. "Native Songs Taught by Ellen W. Saluskin (Hoptonix Salyalilx," in *Spirit of the First People: Native American Music Traditions of Washington State*. Willie Smythe and Esmé Ryan, eds. Seattle: University of Washington, pp. 62–71.

Bechtold, Toni A., Lorenz Kilchenmann, Ben Curry, and Maria A.G. Witek. 2023. "Understanding the Relationship Between Catchiness and Groove: A Qualitative Study with Popular Music Creators," *Music Perception* 40/5: 353–372.

Becker, Alton L. 1995. *Beyond Translation: Essays Toward a Modern Philology*. Ann Arbor, MI: University of Michigan Press.

Becker, Howard. 1963. *Outsiders: Studies in the Sociology of Deviance*. New York, NY: Free Press.

Bendix, Regina. 1997. *In Search of Authenticity: The Formation of Folklore Studies*. Madison, WI: University of Wisconsin Press.

Benjamin, Elizabeth. 2016. *Dada and Existentialism: The Authenticity of Ambiguity*. London: Palgrave Macmillan.

Blarney, Stephen A., trans. 2010. *Etymologies of Isidore of Seville*. New York, NY: Cambridge University Press.

Bogoras, Waldemar. 1902. "The Folklore of Northeastern Asia, as Compared with that of Northwestern America," *American Anthropologist* 4/4: 577–683.

Bogoras, Waldemar. 1904–1909. *The Chukchee*. Leiden: Brill; reprint by AMS Press (New York, NY, 1975). [Cited in Keeling 2012: 249.]

Braham, Persephone. 2018. "Songs of the *Sirenas*: Mermaids in Latin America and the Caribbean," in *Scaled for Success: The Internationalisation of the Mermaid*. Philip Hayward, ed. Hertfordshire, UK: John Libbey Publishing Ltd., pp. 149–170.

Brandon, James R., William P. Malm, and Donald H. Shively. 1978. *Studies in Kabuki: Its Acting, Music, and Historical Context*. Honolulu: University of Hawai'i Press.

Breuner, Nancy Frey. 1992. "The Cult of the Virgin Mary in Southern Italy and Spain," *Ethos* 20/1: 66–95.

Brown, Katherine B. [Schofield]. 2007. "The Social Liminality of Musicians: Case Studies from Mughal India and Beyond," *Twentieth-Century Music* 3/1: 13–48.

Burnside, John. 2015. "Apiculture: Telling the Bees," *Nature* 521: 29–30.

Butler, Judith. 1990. *Gender Trouble: Feminism and the Subversion of Identity*. New York, NY: Routledge.

Campbell, Kenneth E., Jr. and Eduardo P. Tonni. 1983. "Size and Locomotion in Teratorns (Aves: Teratornithidae)," *The Auk* 100: 390–403.

Carr, James Revell. 2014. *Hawaiian Music in Motion: Mariners, Missionaries, and Minstrels*. Urbana, IL: University of Illinois Press.

Carr-Gomm, Philip. 2009. *Sacred Places: Sites of Spiritual Pilgrimage from Stonehenge to Santiago de Compostela*. London: Quercus.

Carroll, Michael P. 1981. "Levi-Strauss, Freud, and the Trickster: A New Perspective Upon an Old Problem," *American Ethnologist* 8/2: 301–313.

Chambers, E.K. 1903. *The Mediaeval Stage*, vol. 1. London: Oxford University Press.

Chandler, Kaitlyn, Wendi Field Murray, María Nieves Zedeño, Samrat Clements, and Robert James. 2017. *The Winged: An Upper Missouri River Ethno-ornithology*. Tucson, AZ: University of Arizona Press.

Chenu, M.-D. 1997. *Nature, Man, and Society in the Twelfth Century: Essays on New Theological Perspectives in the Latin West*, edited by J. Taylor and L.K. Little. London: University of Toronto Press.

Child, Francis James, ed. 1882. "10: The Twa Sisters," *The English and Scottish Popular Ballads*, vol. 1. New York, NY: Dover Publications, pp. 118–141.

Christiansen, Reidar T. 1958. *The Migratory Legends*. Helsinki: Academia Scientarum Fennica.

Clarke, Philip A. 2007. "Indigenous Spirit and Ghost Folklore of 'Settled' Australia," *Folklore* 118/2: 141–161.

Cohen, Simona. 2021. "The Indian Hair-Wringing Apsaras and Her Discriminating Goose: Meanings and Migrations," *Religions of South Asia* 15/2: 142–177.

Cotterill., Simon. 2001. "Ainu Success: The Political and Cultural Achievements of Japan's Indigenous Minority," *Asia-Pacific Journal* 9/12: 2.

Crenshaw, Kimberlé. 1989. "Demarginalizing the Intersection of Race and Sex: A Black Feminist Critique of Antidiscrimination Doctrine, Feminist Theory and Antiracist Politics," *University of Chicago Legal Forum* 1/8: 139–167.

Dalby, Liza. 2000. *Little Songs of the Geisha: Traditional Japanese Ko-Uta*. Rutland, VT: Tuttle.

Dalrymple, William. 2008. "Serving the Goddess: The Dangerous Life of a Sacred Sex Worker," *The New Yorker* (August 8, 2008). https://www.newyorker.com/magazine/2008/08/04/serving-the-goddess.

Danasasmita, Saleh and Atja Danasasmita. 1981. *Sanghyang Siksakandang Karesian*. Bandung: Proyek Pengembangan Permuseuman Jawa Barat.

Darwin, Gregory. 2015. "On Mermaids, Meroveus, and Mélusine: Reading the Irish Seal Woman and Mélusine as Origin Legend," *Folklore* 126/2: 123–141.

Davidson, H.R. Ellis. 1988. *Myths and Symbols in Pagan Europe: Early Scandinavian and Celtic Religions*. New York, NY: Syracuse University Press.

Davies, Rachel Lindley. 2013. "Marian Aspects of Montpelier Codex Motets." Unpublished PhD thesis, University of Birmingham, Birmingham, UK.

de Alcantara, Pedro. 2011. *Integrated Practice: Coordination, Rhythm & Sound*. New York, NY: Oxford University Press.

Dennison, W. Traill. 1893. "Orkney Folk-Lore," *The Scottish Antiquary, or, Northern Notes and Queries* 7/28: 171–177.

Diamond, Heather A. 2008. *American Aloha: Cultural Tourism and the Negotiation of Tradition*. Honolulu: University of Hawai'i Press.

Díaz, Juan Diego. 2021. *Africanness in Action: Essentialism and Musical Imagination of Africa in Brazil*. New York, NY: Oxford University Press.

Diettrich, Brian. 2018. "A Sea of Voices: Performance, Relations, and Belonging in Saltwater Places," *Yearbook for Traditional Music* 50: 41–69.

Diettrich, Brian, Jane Freeman Moulin, and Michael Webb. 2011. *Music in Pacific Island Cultures: Experiencing Music, Expressing Culture*. New York, NY: Oxford University Press.

Diner, Hasia R. 2001. *Hungering for America: Italian, Irish, and Jewish Foodways in the Age of Migration*. Cambridge, MA: Harvard University Press.

Donaghy, Joseph Keola. 2024. *Mele on the Mauna: Perpetuating Genealogies of Hawaiian Musical Activism on Maunakea*. Bloomington, IN: Indiana University Press.

Downer, Lesley. 2006. "The City Geisha and Their Role in Modern Japan: Anomaly or Artistes?" in *The Courtesan's Arts: Cross-Cultural Perspectives*, Martha Feldman and Bonnie Gordon, eds. New York, NY: Oxford University Press, pp. 223–252.

Drewal, Henry John, with Charles Gore and Michelle Kisliuk. 2006. "Siren Serenades: Music for Mami Wata and Other Water Spirits in Africa," in *Music of the Sirens*. Linda Phyllis Austern and Inna Naroditskaya, eds. Bloomington, IN: Indiana University Press, pp. 294–316.

Drewal, Henry John, ed. 2008. *Sacred Waters: Arts for Mami Wata and Other Divinities in Africa and the Diaspora*. Bloomington, IN: Indiana University Press.

Dundes, Alan. 1980. *Interpreting Folklore*. Bloomington, IN: Indiana University Press.

Duvan, Nadyezhda. 1998. "The Anga Clan Legend," in *First Fish, First People: Salmon Tales of the North Pacific Rim*, Judith Roche and Meg McHutchison, eds. Seattle, WA: One Reel Productions and University of Washington Press, pp. 94–95.

Dynda, Jiří. 2017. "Rusalki: Anthropology of Time, Death, and Sexuality in Slavic Folklore," *Studia Mythologica Slavica* 20: 83–109.

Eaton, Kalenda and Michael K. Johnson. 2020. "Teaching the Black West," in *Teaching Western American Literature*, Brady Harrison and Randi Lynn Tanglen, eds. Lincoln, NE: University of Nebraska Press, pp. 61–86.

Egonwa, Osa D. 2008. "The Mami-Wata Phenomenon: 'Old Wine in New Skins'," in *Sacred Waters: Arts for Mami Wata and Other Divinities*, Henry John Drewal, ed. Bloomington, IN: Indiana University Press, 217–27.

Ehrenreich, Barbara. 2006. *Dancing in the Streets: A History of Collective Joy*. New York, NY: Holt.

Ellison, Ralph. 1952. *Invisible Man*. New York, NY: Random House.

Episale, Frank. 2012. "Gender, Tradition, and Culture in Translation: Reading the 'Onnagata' in English," *Asian Theatre Journal* 29/1: 89–111.

Erlingsson, Davið. 1999. "Ormur, Marmennill, Nykur: Three Creatures of the Water World," in *Islanders and Water-Dwellers: Proceedings of the Celtic-Nordic-Baltic Folklore Symposium (1996)*, Patricia Lysaght, Séamas Ó Catháin, and Dáithí Ó hÓgáin, eds. Dublin: DBA Publications, pp. 61–80.

Everist, Mark. 2007. "Motets, French Tenors, and the Polyphonic Chanson ca. 1300," *The Journal of Musicology* 24/3: 365–406.

Farraj, Johnny and Sami Abu Shumays. 2019. *Inside Arabic Music: Arabic Maqam Performance and Theory in the 20th Century*. New York, NY: Oxford University Press.

Feldhaus, Anne. 1995. *Water and Womanhood: Religious Meanings of Rivers in Maharashtra*. New York, NY: Oxford University Press.

Feldman, Martha and Bonnie Gordon, eds. 2006. "Introduction," in *The Courtesan's Arts: Cross-Cultural Perspectives*. New York, NY: Oxford University Press.

Fienup-Riordan, Ann. 2017. "How Raven Marked the Land When the Earth Was New," *Études/Inuits/Studies* 41/1–2: 215–241.

Foreman, Kelly M. 2008. *The Gei of Geisha: Music, Identity, and Meaning*. Burlington, VT: Ashgate Publishing, SOAS Musicology Series.

Fryberg, Ray. 2016. "Ray Fryberg's (Tulalip) Killer Whale Story," in *Tribal Journeys Handbook and Study Guide*. American Friends Service Committee Pacific Northwest Regional Indian Program. [https://www.dshs.wa.gov/sites/default/files/ESA/dcs/documents/Tribal/201 6Tribal%20Journeys%20Handbook.pdf].

Fryer, Peter. 2000. *Rhythms of Resistance: African Musical Heritage in Brazil*. Middletown, CT: Wesleyan University Press.

Fukuoka, Madoka. 2014. *Indonesian Cross-Gender Dancer Didik Nini Thowok*. Osaka: Osaka University Press.

Garland, Ellen, Luke Rendell, Luca Lamoni, M. Michael Poole, and Michael J. Noad. 2017. "Song Hybridization Events During Revolutionary Song Change Provide Insights into Cultural Transmission in Humpback Whales," *Proceedings of the National Academy of Sciences* 114/30: 7822–7829.

Gibson, Ian. 1989. *Federico García Lorca: A Life*. New York, NY: Pantheon.

Gidal, Marc. 2016. *Spirit Song: Afro-Brazilian Religious Music and Boundaries*. New York, NY: Oxford University Press.

Gilday, Edmund T. 1993. "Dancing with the Spirit(s): Another View of the Other World in Japan," *History of Religions* 32/3: 273–300.

Goodman, Linda J. and Helma Swan. 1999. "Makah Music: Preserving the Traditions," in *Spirit of the First People: Native American Music Traditions of Washington State*, Willie Smyth and Esmé Ryan, eds. Seattle, WA: University of Washington Press, pp. 81–105.

Goscilo, Helena. 2007. "Watery Maidens: Rusalki as Sirens and Slippery Signs," in *Poetics, Self, Place: Essays in Honor of Anna Lisa Crone*. Bloomington, IN: Slavica, pp. 50–70.

Graham, Kenneth. 1908. *The Wind in the Willows*. London: Methuen and Company.

Griffin, Farah Jasmine. 2008. "On Time, In Time, Through Time: Aaron Douglas, *Fire!!* and the Writers of the Harlem Renaissance," *American Studies* 49/1–2: 45–53.

Gunderson, Frank. 2010. *Sukuma Labor Songs from Western Tanzania: "We Never Sleep, We Dream of Farming."* Leiden and Boston, MA: Brill Publishing.

Haines, Roberta. 1999. "Singers, Dancers, Dreamers, Travelers," in *Spirit of the First People: Native American Music Traditions of Washington State*, Willie Smyth and Esmé Ryan, eds. Seattle, WA: University of Washington Press, pp. 6–24.

Hall, Stuart. 1990. *Cultural Identity and Diaspora*. Durham, NC: Duke University Press.

Hakim, Catherine. 2010. "Erotic Capital," *European Sociological Review* 26/5: 499–518.

Handlin, Oscar. 2002. *The Uprooted: The Epic Story of the Great Migrations that Made the American People*, 2nd edition. Philadelphia, PA: University of Pennsylvania Press.

Hansen, Kathryn. 1999. "Making Women Visible: Gender and Race Cross-Dressing in the Parsi Theatre," *Theatre Journal* 51/2: 127–147.

Harjo, Joy. 2015. *Conflict Resolution for Holy Beings*. New York, NY: W.W. Norton and Co.

Harnish, David D. and Anne K. Rasmussen. 2011. "Introduction: The World of Islam in the Music of Indonesia," in *Divine Inspirations: Music and Islam in Indonesia*, David D. Harnish and Anne K. Rasmussen, eds. New York, NY: Oxford University, pp. 5–41.

Harrison, Regina. 1989. *Signs, Songs, and Memory in the Andes: Translating Quechua Language and Culture*. Austin, TX: University of Texas Press.

Hau'ofa, Epeli. 1993. "Our Sea of Islands," in *A New Oceania: Rediscovering Our Sea of Islands*, Eric Waddell, Vijay Naidu, and Epeli Hau'ofa, eds. University of the South Pacific, School of Social and Economic Development, pp. 2–16.

Hebert, David G. and Sean Williams. 2020. "Ethnomusicology, Music Education, and the Power and Limitations of Social Media," in *The Oxford Handbook of Social Media and Music Learning*, Janice L. Waldron, Stephanie Horsley, and Kari K. Veblen, eds. New York, NY: Oxford University Press, pp. 467–487.

Heins, Ernst. 1977. "Goong Renteng: Aspects of Orchestral Music in a Sundanese Village." Unpublished PhD dissertation, University of Amsterdam.

Hersch, Charles B. 2017. *Jews and Jazz: Improvising Ethnicity*. New York, NY: Routledge.

Hickman, Money L. 1978. "Views of the Floating World," *MFA Bulletin* 76: 4–33.

Higgins, Nathan Irwin. 2007. *Harlem Renaissance*, updated edition. New York, NY: Oxford University Press.

Hilder, Thomas R. 2012. "Repatriation, Revival and Transmission: The Politics of a Sámi Musical Heritage," *Ethnomusicology Forum* 21/2: 161–179.

Hillers, Barbara. 1994. "Music from the Otherworld: Modern Gaelic Legends About Fairy Music," *Proceedings of the Harvard Celtic Colloquium* 14: 58–75.

Holford-Strevens, Leofranc. 2006. "The Sirens in Antiquity and the Middle Ages," in *Music of the Sirens*. Linda Phyllis Austern and Inna Naroditskaya, eds. Bloomington, IN: Indiana University Press, pp. 16–51.

Hooker, Lynn. 2007. "Controlling the Liminal Power of Performance: Hungarian Scholars and Romani Musicians in the Hungarian Folk Revival," *Twentieth-Century Music* 3/1: 51–72.

hooks, bell. 1984. *Feminist Theory: From Margin to Center*. New York, NY: Routledge.

Holsinger, Bruce and David Townsend. 2000. "The Ovidian Verse Epistles of Master Leoninus (ca. 1135–1201)," *The Journal of Medieval Latin* 10: 239–254.

Horne, Lena and Richard Schickel. 1966. *Lena*. London: Andre Deutsch.

Hunn, Eugene S. and Thomas F. Thornton. 2010. "Tlingit Birds: An Annotated List with Statistical Comparative Analysis," in *Ethno-Ornithology: Birds, Indigenous Peoples, Culture and Society*, Sonia C. Tidemann and Andrew Gosler, eds. New York, NY: Earthscan, pp. 181–209.

Isaka, Maki. 2016. *Onnagata: A Labyrinth of Gendering in Kabuki Theater*. Seattle, WA: University of Washington.

Jacobs, John. 1985. *English Fairy Tales*. New York, NY: Grosset and Dunlap.

Jacques-Coper, Andrés, Guillermo Cubillos, and José Tomás Ibarra. 2019. "The Andean Condor as a Bird, Authority, and Devil: An Empirical Assessment of the Biocultural Keystone Species Concept in the High Andes of Chile," *Ecology and Society* 24/2: 35–45.

Jensen, Allan. 1980. "A Structural Approach to the Tsimshian Raven Myths: Levi-Strauss on the Beach," *Anthropologica* 20/2: 159–186.

Jones, Kyle E. 2014. "'Searching and Searching We Have Come to Find': Histories and Circulations of Hip Hop in Peru," *Alternativas* 2: 1–32.

Jones-Bamman, Richard. 1993. "'As Long As We Continue to *Joik*, We'll Remember Who We Are.' Negotiating Identity and the Performance of Culture: The Saami Joik." Unpublished PhD dissertation, University of Washington (Seattle).

Kamusella, Tomasz. 2014. "The Making of Modern Japan," *The Antioch Review* 72/1: 28–43.

Kane, S. 2015. "Bird Names and Folklore from the Emberá (Chocó) in Darién, Panamá," *Ethnobiology Letters* 6: 32–62.

Kawamura, Kunimitsu. 2003. "A Female Shaman's Mind and Body, and Possession," *Asian Folklore Studies* 62/2: 257–289.

Kayano, Shigeru. 1998. "Kamuy Yukar: Song of the Wife of Okikurmi," in *First Fish, First People: Salmon Tales of the North Pacific Rim*, Judith Roche and Meg McHutchison, eds. Seattle, WA: One Reel Productions and University of Washington Press, pp. 29–37.

Keeling, Richard. 2012. "Animal Impersonation Songs as an Ancient Musical System in North America, Northeast Asia, and Arctic Europe," *Ethnomusicology* 56/2: 234–265.

Kisliuk, Michelle. 2008. "The Intersection of Evangelism, AIDS, and Mami Wata in Popular Music in Centrafrique," in *Sacred Waters: Arts for Mami Wata and Other Divinities*, Henry John Drewal, ed. Bloomington, IN: Indiana University Press, 413–420.

Kojima, Kenji, Masuzo Yanagida, and Ichiro Nakayama. 2004. "Variability of Vibrato: A Comparative Study Between Japanese Traditional Singing and Bel Canto," *Proceedings of the International Conference on Speech Prosody*: 151–154. https://www.isca-archive.org/spe echprosody_2004/kojima04_speechprosody.pdf [accessed 1/25/2026].

Kokusho, Kankōkai. 1914. *Tokugawa Bungei Ruijū* [Collection of Literary Material for the Tokugawa Period], vol. 2. Tokyo.

Krupnik, Igor. 2017. "Siberian Yupik Names for Birds: What Can Bird Names Tell Us About Language and Knowledge Transitions?" in *Études/Inuit/Studies* 41/1–2: 179–213.

Lalonde, Amanda. 2015. "The Music of the Living-Dead," *Music and Letters* 96/4: 602–629.

Lancashire, Terrence. 2001. "'Kagura'—A 'Shinto' Dance? Or Perhaps Not," *Asian Music* 33/1: 25–59.

Lane-Kamahele, M. Melia. 2017. "Nānā I Ke Kumu (Look to the Source)," *George Wright Forum* 34/3: 308–314.

Langlois, Krista. 2018. "When Whales and Humans Talk," *Hakai Magazine, Coastal Science and Societies*, April 3. https://hakaimagazine.com/features/when-whales-and-humans-talk/ [accessed 1/25/2026].

Larkin, Emmet. 1972 "The Devotional Revolution in Ireland, 1850–75," *The American Historical Review* 77/3: 625–652.

Laušević, Mirjana. 2007. *Balkan Fascination: Creating an Alternative Culture in America*. New York, NY: Oxford University Press.

Least-Heat Moon, William. 1991. *PrairyErth*. Boston: Mariner Books.

Lee, Alexander. 2019. "A History of Börek," *History Today* 69/9. https://www.historytoday.com/archive/historians-cookbook/history-borek.

Levine, Mark. 2009. "Doing the Devil's Work: Heavy Metal and the Threat to Public Order in the Muslim World," *Social Compass* 56: 564–576.

Levitin, Daniel J. 2006. *This Is Your Brain on Music: The Science of a Human Obsession*. New York, NY: Dutton Publishing.

Levy, Mark. 2000. "Southeastern European (Balkan) Music," in *The Garland Encyclopedia of World Music*, v. 3 (The United States and Canada), Ellen Koskoff, ed. New York, NY: Taylor and Francis, pp. 919–932.

Lewis, David. 1972. *We, the Navigators: The Ancient Art of Landfinding in the Pacific*. Honolulu: University of Hawai'i Press.

Lorde, Audre. 2006. "The Uses of the Erotic: The Erotic as Power," essay reprinted in *Sexualities and Communication in Everyday Life: A Reader*, Karen E. Lovaas and Mercilee M. Jenkins, eds. Thousand Oaks, CA: Sage Publications, pp. 87–91.

Low, Chris. 2011. "Birds and KhoeSān: Linking Spirits and Healing with Day-to-Day Life," *Africa: Journal of the International African Institute* 81/2: 295–313.

Lund, Jens. 2004. *Tour Guide: Interstate 5 North Heritage Tour Seattle to Blaine*. Olympia, WA: Northwest Heritage Resources.

Lysaght, Patricia. 1997. "Caoineadh os Cionn Coirp: The Lament for the Dead in Ireland," *Folklore* 108: 65–82.

Malinowski, Bronisław. 1944. *A Scientific Theory of Culture and Other Essays*. Chapel Hill, NC: University of North Carolina Press.

Malm, William P. 1959. *Japanese Music and Musical Instruments*. Rutland, VT: Charles E. Tuttle.

Marginean, Ruxandra. 2001. "Naturalizing *Nō*: Interpreting the *Waki* as the 'Representative of the Audience'," in *Japanese Theatre and the International Stage*, Samuel L. Leiter, ed. Leiden: Brill, pp. 89–108.

Marglin, Frédérique A. 1990. "Refining the Body: Transformative Emotion in Ritual Dance," in *Divine Passions: The Social Construction of Emotion in India*, Owen Lynch, ed. Berkeley, CA: University of California Press, pp. 212–236.

Margolick, David. 2000. *Strange Fruit: Billie Holiday, Café Society, and an Early Cry for Civil Rights*. Philadephia, PA: Running.

Matossian, Mary K. 1973. "When God Was a Woman," *Journal of Social History* 6/3: 325–343.

Matsue, Jennifer Milioto. 2016. *Focus: Music in Contemporary Japan*. New York, NY: Routledge.

Maultsby, Portia K. 2017. "The Politics of Race Erasure in Defining Black Popular Music Origins," in *Issues in African American Music: Power, Gender, Race, Representation*, Portia K. Maultsby and Mellonee V. Burnim, eds. New York, NY: Routledge, pp. 47–65.

Mayer, Adam and Jeffrey M. Timberlake. 2014. "'The Fist in the Face of God': Heavy Metal Music and Decentralized Cultural Diffusion," *Sociological Perspectives* 57/1: 27–51.

Meintjes, Louise. 1990. "Paul Simon's *Graceland*, South Africa, and the Mediation of Musical Meaning," *Ethnomusicology* 34/1: 37–73.

Merriam, Alan P. 1964. *The Anthropology of Music*. Evanston, IL: Northwestern University Press.

Miller, Bruce-*Subiyay*. 1999. "Seeds of Our Ancestors: Growing Up in the Skokomish Song Tradition," in *Spirit of the First People: Native American Music Traditions of Washington State*, Willie Smyth and Esmé Ryan, eds. Seattle, WA: University of Washington Press, pp. 25–43.

Mingyue, Liang. 1985. *Music of the Billion: An Introduction to Chinese Musical Culture*. New York, NY: Heinrichshofen Edition.

Moriuchi, Emi and Michael Basil. 2019. "The Sustainability of Ohanami Cherry Blossom Festivals as a Cultural Icon," *Sustainability* 11: 1–15.

Moro, Pamela A. 2019. *Violins: Local Meanings, Globalized Sounds*. New York, NY: Routledge Publishing.

Morris, Henry. 1937. "Features Common to Irish, Welsh, and Manx Folklore," *Béaloideas* 7/2: 168–179.

Morrison, Matthew D. 2024. *Blacksound: Making Race and Popular Music in the United States*. Oakland, CA: University of California Press.

Moyle, Natalie Kononenko. 1986. "Mermaids (Rusalki) and Russian Beliefs about Women," in *New Studies in Russian Language and Literature*, Anna Lisa Crone and Catherine V. Chvany, eds. Columbus, OH: Slavica Publishers, pp. 221–238.

Mulk, Inga-Maria and Tim Bayliss-Smith. 2007. "Liminality, Rock Art and the Sami Sacred Landscape," *Journal of Northern Studies* 1–2: 95–122.

Mullally, Una. 2019. "Kneecap: 'Low-Life Scum' of West Belfast Rap Whose Time Has Come," *The Irish Times*, April 12. https://www.irishtimes.com/culture/music/kneecap-low-life-scum-of-west-belfast-rap-whose-day-has-come-1.3854738 [accessed 1/25/2026].

Nagasawa, Sōhei. 2011. "Field Note: The Deity and the Mountain: Ritual Practice and Environment in Japan's Hachine Take 'Kagura'," *Asian Ethnology* 70/1: 105–116.

Naroditskaya, Inna. 2006. "Russian *Rusalkas* and Nationalism: Water, Power, and Women," in *Music of the Sirens*. Linda Phyllis Austern and Inna Naroditskaya, eds. Bloomington, IN: Indiana University Press, pp. 216–249.

Neel, David. 1995. *The Great Canoes: Reviving a Northwest Coast Tradition*. Seattle, WA: University of Washington Press.

Ní Fhlionn, Bairbre. 1999. "Tadgh, Donncha and Some of their Relations: Seals in Irish Oral Tradition," in *Islanders and Water-Dwellers: Proceedings of the Celtic-Nordic-Baltic Folklore Symposium (1996)*, Patricia Lysaght, Séamas Ó Catháin, and Dáithí Ó hÓgáin, eds. Dublin: DBA Publications, pp. 223–245.

Nieto, Leticia. 2010. *Beyond Inclusion, Beyond Empowerment: A Developmental Strategy to Liberate Everyone*. Olympia, WA: Cuetzpalin.

Nugent, B. Pauline. 2008. "The Sounds of Sirens: 'Odyssey' 12.184–91," *College Literature* 35/4: 45–54 [Homer: Analysis and Influence].

O'Brien, Flann [Myles na Gopaleen]. 1975. *The Best of Myles (Myles na Gopaleen)*. New York, NY: Picador.

Ó Ceallaigh, T.J. and Áine Ní Dhonnabháin. 2015. "Reawakening the Irish Language through the Irish Education System: Challenges and Priorities," *The International Electronic Journal of Elementary Education* 8/2: 179–198.

Oda, Ito with Tomo Matsui. 1998. "Traveling by Dugout on the Chitose River and Sending the Salmon Spirits Home: Memoir of an Ainu Woman," in *First Fish, First People: Salmon Tales of the North Pacific Rim*, Judith Roche and Meg McHutchison, eds. Seattle, WA: One Reel Productions and University of Washington Press, pp. 123–130.

Olkowicz, S., M. Kocourek, R.K. Lučan, M. Porteš, W.T. Fitch, S. Herculano-Houzel, and P. Němec. 2016. "Birds Have Primate-Like Numbers of Neurons in the Forebrain," *Proceedings of the National Academy of Sciences* 113: 7255–7260.

Olsen, Loran. 1999. "Native Music of the Pacific Northwest: A Washington State Perspective," in *Spirit of the First People: Native American Music Traditions of Washington State*, Willie Smyth and Esmé Ryan, eds. Seattle, WA: University of Washington Press, pp. 106–116.

Perea, Jessica Bissett. 2021. *Sound Relations: Native Ways of Doing Music History in Alaska*. New York, NY: Oxford University Press.

Philipson, Robert. 2006. "The Harlem Renaissance as Postcolonial Phenomenon," *African American Review* 40/1: 145–160.

Pierotti, Raymond. 2020. "Learning About Extraordinary Beings: Native Stories and Real Birds," *Ethnobiology Letters* 11/2: 44–51.

Pruden, Leo, trans. 1988. *Abhidharmakośa-bhāsya*, 4 volumes. Berkeley, CA: Asian Humanities Press.

Przybylski, Liz. 2018. "Customs and Duty: Indigenous Hip Hop and the US-Canada Border," *Journal of Borderlands Studies* 33/3: 487–506.

Przybylski, Liz. 2023. *Sonic Sovereignty: Hip Hop, Indigeneity, and Shifting Popular Music Mainstreams*. New York, NY: New York University Press.

Pukui, Mary Kawena. 1983. *'Olelo No'eau: Hawaiian Proverbs and Poetical Sayings*. Honolulu, HI: Bishop Museum Press.

Ragland, Cathy. 2009. *Música Norteña: Mexican Migrants Creating a Nation Between Nations*. Philadelphia, PA: Temple University Press.

Rambelli, Fabio. 2002. "The Ritual World of Buddhist 'Shinto': The Reikiki and Initiations on Kami-Related Matters (*Jingi-kanjō*) in Late Medieval and Early-Modern Japan," *Japanese Journal of Religious Studies* 29/3–4: 265–297.

Ramnarine, Tina K. 2009. "Acoustemology, Indigeneity, and Joik in Valkeapää's Symphonic Activism: Views from Europe's Arctic Fringes for Environmental Ethnomusicology," *Ethnomusicology* 53/2: 187–217.

Rasmussen, Anne K. 1997. "The Music of Arab Detroit: A Musical Mecca in the Midwest," in *Musics of Multicultural America: A Study of Twelve Musical Communities*, Kip Lornell and Anne K. Rasmussen, eds. New York, NY: Schirmer Books, pp. 73–100.

Rasmussen, Anne K. 2000. "Middle Eastern Music," in *The Garland Encyclopedia of World Music*, v. 3 (The United States and Canada), Ellen Koskoff, ed. New York, NY: Taylor and Francis, pp. 1028–1041.

Rasmussen, Anne K. 2010. *Women, the Recited Qur'an, and Islamic Music in Indonesia*. Berkeley, CA: University of California.

Rendall, Luke, Mauricio Cantor, Shane Gero, Hal Whitehead, and Janet Mann. 2019. "Causes and Consequences of Female Centrality in Cetacean Societies," in *Philosophical Transactions of the Royal Society B* [Biological Sciences] 374/2018.0066: 1–13.

Rice, Timothy. 2014. "Ethnomusicology in Times of Trouble," *Yearbook for Traditional Music* 46: 191–209.

Ricklefs, M.C. 1993. *A History of Modern Indonesia Since c. 1300*, 2nd edition. Palo Alto, CA: Stanford University Press.

Robertson, Jennifer. 1998. *Takarazuka: Sexual Politics and Popular Culture in Modern Japan*. Berkeley, CA: University of California Press.

Robinson, Dylan. 2020. *Hungry Listening: Resonant Theory for Indigenous Sound Studies*. Minneapolis, MN: University of Minnesota Press.

Roburn, Shirley. 2013. "Sounding a Sea-Change: Acoustic Ecology and Arctic Ocean Governance," in *Thinking with Water*, Cecilia Chen, Janine MacLeod, and Astrida Neimanis, eds. Montreal: McGill[-Queen's University Press, pp. 106–128.

Roca, Roger Sansi. 2005. "Catholic Saints, African Gods, Black Masks and White Heads: Tracing the History of Some Religious Festivals in Bahia," *Portuguese Studies* 2121: 182–200.

Roche, Judith and Meg McHutchison. 1998. "Introduction," in *First Fish, First People: Salmon Tales of the North Pacific Rim*, Judith Roche and Meg McHutchison, eds. Seattle, WA: One Reel Productions and University of Washington Press, pp. 12–13.

Rodger, Gillian M. 2018. *Just One of the Boys: Female-to-Male Cross-Dressing on the American Variety Stage*. Champaign, IL: University of Illinois Press.

Roediger, David R. 1991. *The Wages of Whiteness: Race and the Making of the American Working Class* New York, NY: Verso.

Rosaldo, Renato. 1989. *Culture and Truth: The Remaking of Social Analysis*. Boston, MA: Beacon Press.

Rowell, Charles H. 1991. "An Interview with Henry Louis Gates, Jr.," *Callaloo* 14/2: 444–463.

Roy, Ratna. 2009. *Neo Classical Odissi Dance*. New Delhi: Harman Publishing House.

Sáenz, Sabine Dedenbach-Salazar. 2017. "Deities and Spirits in Andean Belief: Toward a Systematisation," *Anthropos* 112/2: 443–453.

Saldaña-Portillo, María Josefina. 2015. "*Indigenismo* as Nationalism: From the Liberal to the Revolutionary Era," in *Critical Terms in Latin and Caribbean Thought: Historical and Institutional Trajectories*, Marisa Belausteguigoitia, Yolanda Martínez San-Miguel, and Benjamin Sinfuentes Jariategrui, eds. London: Palgrave, pp. 37–44.

Saliba, Therese. 1999. "Resisting Invisibility: Arab Americans in Academia and Activism," in *Arabs in America: Building a New Future*, Michael W. Suleiman, ed. Philadelphia, PA: Temple University Press, pp. 304–319.

Sasamori, Takefusa. 1997. "Therapeutic Rituals Performed by *Itako* (Japanese Blind Female Shamans," *The World of Music* 39/1: 85–96.

Sault, Nicole. 2020. "Bird Stories from Latin America: Lessons on Change and Adaptation," *Ethnobiology Letters* 11/2: 58–68.

Schroeder, Patricia R. 2004. *Robert Johnson: Mythmaking and Contemporary American Culture*. Champaign, IL: University of Illinois Press.

Schultze, Sydney. 1982. "The Tradition of the Drowning Woman in the Background of 'Anna Karenina," *Russian Language Journal* 36/123–124: 75–87.

Schwarz, A.B. Christa. 2003. *Gay Voices of the Harlem Renaissance*. Bloomington, IN: Indiana University Press.

Screech, Timon. 2006. "Going to the Courtesans: Transit to the Pleasure District of Edo Japan," in *The Courtesan's Arts: Cross-Cultural Perspectives*, Martha Feldman and Bonnie Gordon, eds. New York, NY: Oxford University Press, pp. 255–279.

Seale-Collazo, James. 2012. "Charisma, Liminality, and Freedom: Toward a Theory of the Everyday Extraordinary," *Anthropology of Consciousness* 23/2: 175–191.

Shah, Vidya and Jody M. Luna. 2019. "Introduction to Special Issue: Paradoxes and Possibilities of Movement Building from the In-Between," *International Journal of Critical Pedagogy* 10/2: 11–18.

Sheehy, Daniel. 1997. "Mexican Mariachi Music: Made in the U.S.A.," in *Musics of Multicultural America: A Study of Twelve Musical Communities*, Kip Lornell and Anne K. Rasmussen, eds. New York, NY: Schirmer Books, pp. 131–154.

Sheffield, Carrie Louise. 2011. "Native American Hip-Hop and Historical Trauma: Surviving and Healing Trauma on the 'Rez'," *Studies in American Indian Literatures* 23/3: 94–110.

Sherab, Khenchen Palden and Khenpo Tse Wang Dongyal. 2000. *A Modern Commentary on Karma Lingpa's Zhi-Khro: Teachings on the Peaceful and Wrathful Deities*, edited by Padma Shugchang. https://web.archive.org/web/20080229105933/http://www.turtlehill.org/khen/zhikhro.pdf [accessed 03/26/2024].

Sherinian, Zoe C. 2020. "Sounding Out-Ethnomusicology: Theoretical Reflections on Queer Fieldnotes and Performance," in *Queering the Field: Sounding Out Ethnomusicology*, Gregory Barz and William Cheng, eds. New York, NY: Oxford University Press, pp. 31–52.

Shingal, Ankur. 2015. "The Devadasi System: Temple Prostitution in India," *UCLA Journal of Gender and Law* 22/1: 107–123.

Shubin, Neil. 2009. *Your Inner Fish: A Journey into the 3.5-Billion-Year History of the Human Body*. New York, NY: Vintage.

Sijohn, Cliff. 1999. "The Circle of Song," in *Spirit of the First People: Native American Music Traditions of Washington State*, Willie Smyth and Esmé Ryan, eds. Seattle, WA: University of Washington Press, pp. 44–49.

Skurski, Julie. 1994. "The Ambiguity of Authenticity in Latin America: Dóna Bárbara and the Construction of National Identity," *Poetics Today* 15/4: 605–642.

Slobin, Mark. 1993. *Subcultural Sounds: Micromusics of the West*. Middletown, CT: Wesleyan University Press.

Slominski, Tes. 2020. "Fielding the Field: Belonging, Disciplinarity, and Queer Scholarly Lives," in *Queering the Field: Sounding Out Ethnomusicology*. Gregory Barz and William Cheng, eds. New York, NY: Oxford University Press.

Smyth, Willie. 1999. "Preface," in *Spirit of the First People: Native American Music Traditions of Washington State*, Willie Smyth and Esmé Ryan, eds. Seattle, WA: University of Washington Press, pp. ix–xii.

Solomon, Thomas J. 1997. "Mountains of Song: Musical Constructions of Ecology, Place, and Identity in the Bolivian Andes." Unpublished PhD dissertation, University of Texas at Austin.

Soneji, Davesh. 2012. *Unfinished Gestures: Devadasis, Memory, and Modernity in South India (South India Across the Disciplines)*. Chicago, IL: University of Chicago Press.

Spiller, Henry. 2014. "Interdisciplinarity and Musical Exceptionalism," *Ethnomusicology* 58/2: 341–346.

Srinivasan, Doris M. 2006. "Royalty's Courtesans and God's Mortal Wives: Keepers of Culture in Pre-Colonial India," in *The Courtesan's Arts: Cross-Cultural Perspectives*, Martha Feldman and Bonnie Gordon, eds. New York, NY: Oxford University Press, pp. 161–181.

Stanbury, Peter and John Clegg. 1990. *A Field Guide to Aboriginal Rock Engravings, with Special Reference to Those Around Sydney*. Sydney, Australia: Sydney University Press.

Stephens, Randall J. 2016. "'Where Else Did They Copy Their Styles but from Church Groups?': Rock 'n' Roll and Pentecostalism in the 1950s South," *Church History* 85/1: 97–131.

Sterling, Cheryl. 2010. "Women-Space, Power, and the Sacred in Afro-Brazilian Culture," *The Global South* 4/1: 71–93.

Stivers, Richard. 1976. *Hair of the Dog: Irish Drinking and Its American Stereotype*. New York, NY: Continuum.

Stobart, Henry. 2006. "Devils, Daydreams, and Desire: Siren Traditions and Musical Creation in the Southern Andes," in *Music of the Sirens*. Linda Phyllis Austern and Inna Naroditskaya, eds. Bloomington, IN: Indiana University Press, pp. 105–139.

Stobart, Henry. 2008. "'Sounds of Power': Musical Instruments and Gender," *Ethnomusicology Forum* 17/1: 67–94.

Sturman, Janet L. 2016. *The Course of Mexican Music*. New York, NY: Routledge.

Sumarsam. 2024. *The In-Between in Javanese Performing Arts: History and Myth, Interculturalism and Interreligiosity*. Middletown, CT: Wesleyan University Press.

Sunardi, Christina. 2015. *Stunning Males and Powerful Females: Gender and Tradition in East Javanese Dance*. Urbana, IL: University of Illinois Press.

Swartzlander, Susan. 1988. "'On the Verge of Selfabyss': The St. Kevin Section of Finnegan's Wake," *James Joyce Quarterly* 25/4: 475–485.

Tarling, Richard. 1992. *The Cambridge History of Southeast Asia, vol. 1: From Early Times to c. 1800*. Cambridge: Cambridge University Press.

Taylor, Timothy D. 2012. *The Sounds of Capitalism: Advertising, Music, and the Conquest of Culture*. Chicago, IL: University of Chicago Press.

Teves, Stephanie Nohelani. 2015. "Aloha State Apparatuses," *American Quarterly* 67/3: 705–726.

Thomas, Susan. 2020. "Holding the Line: Sonic Interstitiality at the Close of 2020," *Americas: A Hemispheric Music Journal* 29: vii–xii.

Thornton, Thomas F. and Patricia M. Thornton. 2015. "The Mutable, the Mythical, and the Managerial: Raven Narratives and the Anthropocene," *Environment and Society* 6: 66–86.

Tidemann, Sonia C. and Tim Whiteside. 2010. "Aboriginal Stories: The Riches and Colour of Australian Birds," in *Ethno-Ornithology: Birds, Indigenous Peoples, Culture and Society*, Sonia C. Tidemann and Andrew Gosler, eds. New York, NY: Earthscan, pp. 153–180.

Trask, Haunani-Kay. 1999. *From a Native Daughter: Colonialism and Sovereignty in Hawai'i*, 2nd edition. Honolulu: University of Hawai'i Press.

Troutman, John W. 2013. "Steelin' the Slide: Hawai'i and the Birth of the Blues Guitar," *Southern Cultures* 19/1: 26–52.

Turino, Thomas. 1983. "The Charango and the *Sirena*: Music, Magic, and the Power of Love," *Latin American Music Review* 4/1: 81–119.

Turino, Thomas. 1993. *Moving Away from Silence: Music of the Peruvian Altiplano and the Experience of Urban Migration*. Chicago, IL: University of Chicago Press.

Turkewitz, Julie. 2020. "Peru's Queen of Quechua Rap Wants to Rescue Indigenous Culture with Her Music," *The New York Times*, April 28. https://www.nytimes.com/2020/04/28/world/americas/peru-indigenous-rap-renata-flores.html.

Turner, Victor. 1969. *The Ritual Process: Structure and Anti-Structure*. New York, NY: Routledge.

Tuttle, Pauline. 2006. "Canoe Nations of the Pacific Northwest," in *The Ethnomusicologists' Cookbook*, Sean Williams, ed. New York, NY: Routledge, pp. 197–204.

van Gennep, Arnold. 2019 [1909]. *The Rites of Passage*, 2nd edition. Chicago, IL: University of Chicago Press.

Van Zanten, Wim. 1984. "The Poetry of Tembang Sunda," *Bijdragen tot de Taal-, Land-en Volkenkunde* 140/2–3: 289–316.

Van Zanten, Wim. 1989. *Sundanese Music in the Cianjuran Style*. Providence, RI: Foris Publications.

Voeks, Robert. 1990. "Sacred Leaves of Candomblé," *Geographical Review* 80/2: 118–131.

Waite, William G. 1954. *The Rhythm of Twelfth Century Polyphony, Its Theory and Practice*. New Haven, CT: Yale University Press.

Warner, Elizabeth A. 2011. "Russian Peasant Beliefs Concerning the Unclean Dead and Drought, Within the Context of the Agricultural Year," *Folklore* 122/2: 155–175.

Warner, Michael. 1991. "Introduction: Fear of a Queer Planet," *Social Text* 29: 3–17.

Weiss, Sarah. 2017. "Rangda and the Goddess Durga in Bali," *Fieldwork in Religion* 12/1: 50–77.

Welch, Craig. 2021. "Secrets of the Whales," *National Geographic: The Ocean Issue* 5: 40–79.

Wessing, Robert. 1984. "Sundanese," in *Muslim Peoples: A World Ethnographic Survey*, vol. 2, Richard Weekes, ed. Westport, CT: Greenwood Press.

Wessing, Robert. 1986. *The Soul of Ambiguity: The Tiger in Southeast Asia.* DeKalb, IL: Northern Illinois University Center for Southeast Asian Studies.

Wessing, Robert. 1993. "A Change in the Forest: Myth and History in West Java," *Journal of Southeast Asian Studies* 24/1: 1–17.

Wessing, Robert. 1998. "Bamboo, Rice, and Water," in *The Garland Encyclopedia of Music*, vol. 4: *Southeast Asia*, Terry E. Miller and Sean Williams, eds. New York, NY: Taylor and Francis, pp. 47–54.

Wessing, Robert. 1988. "Spirits of the Earth and Spirits of the Water: Chthonic Forces in the Mountains of West Java," *Asian Folklore Studies* 47/1: 43–61.

Wessing, Robert. 2020. "The Maiden in the Forest: Reflections on Some Southeast Asian Tales," *Archipel* 99: 75–105.

White, Mathew, Amanda Smith, Kelly Humphryes, Sabine Pahl, Deborah Snelling, and Michael Depledge. 2010. "Blue Space: The Importance of Water for Preference, Affect, and Restorativeness Ratings of Natural and Built Scenes," *Journal of Environmental Psychology* 30/4: 482–493.

Whitebear, Luhui. 2023. "Pen of Molten Fire: Dr. Haunani-Kay Trask's Writing as Indigenous Resistance," *American Indian Culture and Research Journal* 46/1: 115–128.

Wilkerson, Isabel. 2010. *The Warmth of Other Suns: The Epic Story of America's Great Migration.* New York, NY: Vintage Books.

Williams, Sean. 2001. *The Sound of the Ancestral Ship: Highland Music of West Java.* New York, NY: Oxford University Press.

Williams, Sean. 2006. "Buddhism in Music," in *Sacred Sound: Experiencing Music in World Religions*, Guy Beck, ed. Waterloo, ON: Wilfred Laurier University Press, pp. 169–189.

Williams, Sean. 2015. "Music as the Food of Longing in Ireland and Irish America," in *A Symphony of Flavors: Food and Music in Concert*, Edmundo Murray, ed. Cambridge: Cambridge Scholars, pp. 46–64.

Williams, Sean. 2018. "Sonic Liminalities of Faith in Sundanese Vocal Music," *Yale Journal of Music and Religion* 4/1: 43–59.

Williams, Sean. 2022. *Musics of the World.* New York, NY: Oxford University Press.

Williams, Sean and Lillis Ó Laoire. 2011. *Bright Star of the West: Joe Heaney, Irish Song Man.* New York, NY: Oxford University Press.

Williams, Sean and Lillis Ó Laoire. 2024. "Vernacular Catholicism in Ireland: The Keening Woman," *Religions* 15/879: 1–14. Special issue, Musicology of Religion: Selected Papers on Religion and Music.

Wilson, David. 2021. "European Colonisation, Law, and Indigenous Marine Dispossession: Historical Perspectives on the Construction and Entrenchment of Unequal Marine Governance," *Maritime Studies* 20: 387–407.

Wissler, Clark. 1912. *Social Organization and Ritualistic Ceremonies of the Blackfoot Indians.* New York, NY: American Museum of Natural History.

Wiyatmi, Else Liliani and Esti Swatikasari. 2020. "Female Deities (Bidadari) in Indonesian Folklore: A Feminist Literary Critical Perspective," *Advances in Social Sciences, Education, and Humanities Research* 401: 18–21.

Woody, Elizabeth. 1998a. "Tradition with a Big 'T'," in *First Fish, First People: Salmon Tales of the North Pacific Rim*, Judith Roche and Meg McHutchison, eds. Seattle, WA: One Reel Productions and University of Washington Press, pp. 64–89.

Woody, Elizabeth. 1998b. "Why I Love with Admiration Every Salmon I See," in *Intimate Nature: The Bond Between Women and Animals*, Linda Hogan, Deen Metzger, and Brenda Peterson, eds. New York, NY: Random House, pp. 29–33.

Worobec, Christine D. 1995. "Witchcraft Beliefs and Practices in Prerevolutionary Russian and Ukrainian Villages," *The Russian Review* 54/2: 165–187.

Wright, Richard. 1993 (1945). *Black Boy (American Hunger: A Record of Child and Youth)*. New York, NY: Harper Collins.

Wulff, Hans J. 2015. "Von Opfern, Spassmachern, Heulern und Selkies: Robben und Seehunde im Film," *Kulturpoetik* 15/1: 29–49.

Xiaodun, Wang and Sun Xiaohui. 2004. "*Yuebu* of the Tang Dynasty: Musical Transmission from the Han to the Early Tang Dynasty," *Yearbook for Traditional Music* 36: 50–64.

Yampolsky, Philip. 1989. "Hati Yang Luka, an Indonesian Hit," *Indonesia* 47: 1–17.

Yukie, Chiri. 2015. "The Song the Owl God Himself Sang, 'Silver Droplets Fall Fall All Around': An Ainu Tale," *Review of Japanese Culture and Society* 27: 127–137.

Index

For the benefit of digital users, indexed terms that span two pages (e.g., 52–53) may, on occasion, appear on only one of those pages.

Note: The titles of songs and films mentioned in the text are filed under their respective categories rather than listed individually.